POLITICAL IDEAS

SECOND EDITION for A-level

Liberalism, Socialism, Conservatism, Feminism, Anarchism

Richard Kelly • Maria Egan
Neil McNaughton

SERIES EDITOR:
Eric Magee

HODDER
EDUCATION
AN HACHETTE UK

The Publishers would like to thank the following for permission to reproduce copyright material.

p.9 © Ian Dagnall / Alamy Stock Photo; p.10 © Hum Images / Alamy Stock Photo; p.11 North Wind Picture Archives / Alamy Stock Photo; p.14 IanDagnall Computing / Alamy Stock Photo; p.16 © Philip Scalia / Alamy Stock Photo; p.19 © matteogirelli / Fotolia; p.29 © Jorisvo / Shutterstock.com; p.35 © Frederic REGLAIN / Gamma-Rapho / Getty Images; p.37 © Chris Kleponis / Pool via CNP/Media Punch / Alamy Stock Photo; p.39 © Damien Storan/PA Images / Alamy Stock Photo; p.41 © Photo Researchers/Science History Images/Alamy Stock Photo; p.43 Cavan Images / Alamy Stock Photo; p.48 © The Keasbury-Gordon Photograph Archive / Alamy Stock Photo; p.56 © Mirrorpix / Trinity Mirror / Alamy Stock Photo; p.57 © Shcherbakov Ilya / Shutterstock.com; p.59 © Encyclopedia / Alamy Stock Photo; p.61 © Johan10 / stock.adobe.com; p.65 © Everett Collection / Shutterstock.com; p.66 age fotostock / Alamy Stock Photo; p.67 © Hulton Archive / Stringer / Getty Images; p.68 © Ms Jane Campbell / Shutterstock.com; p.72 Keystone Pictures USA / Alamy Stock Photo; p.75/t © Cineberg / Shutterstock.com; p.75/b Jeff Morgan 12 / Alamy Stock Photo; p.79 © Mirrorpix / Trinity Mirror / Alamy Stock Photo; p.86 © pixs:sell / Fotolia; p. 91 © INTERFOTO / Personalities / Alamy Stock Photo; p.96 © New York Times Co. / Archive Photos / Getty Images; p.104 © dpa picture alliance / Alamy Stock Photo; p.110 © Walker Art Library / Alamy Stock Photo; p.119 © Jose Giribas / Süddeutsche Zeitung Photo / Alamy Stock Photo; p.125 © Alejandro_Munoz / Shutterstock.com; p.128 © Fotosearch/Archive Photos / Getty Images; p.132 © Goodbishop / Shutterstock.com; p.133 © Pictorial Press Ltd / Alamy Stock Photo; p.136 © Barbara Alper / Archive Photos/Getty Images; p.137 © Wirestock Creators / Shutterstock.com; p.139 © I T S / Shutterstock.com; p.142 © Southworks / stock.adobe.com; p.144 © Margaret Thomas / The Washington Post / Getty Images; p.145 © Mike Goldwater / Alamy Stock Photo; p.148 © Geraint Lewis / Alamy Stock Photo; p.154 © WENN Rights Ltd / Alamy Stock Photo; p.156 © Sundry Photography / Shutterstock.com; p.159 © Marco Secchi / Alamy Stock Photo; p.161 © Mark Kerrison / Alamy Stock Photo; p.165 © © Jaden Schaul / Shutterstock.com; p.170 © Juulijs / stock.adobe.com; p.172 © Pictorial Press Ltd / Alamy Stock Photo; p.175 © David Friedman image by Judd Weiss; p.179 © Everett Collection / Shutterstock.com; p.184 © 4.murat / Shutterstock.com; p.190 © A katz / Shutterstock.com

Every effort has been made to trace all copyright holders, but if any have been inadvertently overlooked, the Publishers will be pleased to make the necessary arrangements at the first opportunity.

Although every effort has been made to ensure that website addresses are correct at time of going to press, Hodder Education cannot be held responsible for the content of any website mentioned in this book. It is sometimes possible to find a relocated web page by typing in the address of the home page for a website in the URL window of your browser.

Hachette UK's policy is to use papers that are natural, renewable and recyclable products and made from wood grown in well-managed forests and other controlled sources. The logging and manufacturing processes are expected to conform to the environmental regulations of the country of origin.

Orders: please contact Hachette UK Distribution, Hely Hutchinson Centre, Milton Road, Didcot, Oxfordshire, OX11 7HH. Telephone: +44 (0)1235 827827. Email education@hachette.co.uk Lines are open from 9 a.m. to 5 p.m., Monday to Friday. You can also order through our website: www.hoddereducation.co.uk

ISBN: 978 1 3983 6917 7

© Richard Kelly, Maria Egan and Neil McNaughton 2023

First published in 2023 by

Hodder Education,
An Hachette UK Company
Carmelite House
50 Victoria Embankment
London EC4Y 0DZ

www.hoddereducation.co.uk

Impression number   10 9 8 7 6 5 4 3 2 1

Year   2027 2026 2025 2024 2023

Illustrations by Aptara, Inc.

Typeset in India by Aptara, Inc.

Printed in Italy

A catalogue record for this title is available from the British Library.

Get the most from this book

Further reading
Websites, books and articles that are relevant to the chapter

Exam-style questions
Revision questions at the end of each chapter

Knowledge checks
Putting learning into practice

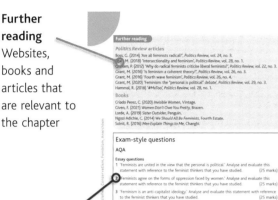

Chapter 5

Anarchism

Learning outcomes
A summary of the learning objectives for each chapter

Key thinker
Feature boxes giving details of the key people covered in the chapter

Key terms
Concise definitions of key terms where they first appear

Contents

Answers to the exam-style questions at the end of each
chapter can be found at www.hoddereducation.co.uk/
political-ideas-feminism

Introduction

This book is aimed at those teaching and studying the 'political ideas' components of A-level Politics specifications. But what, exactly, do we mean by both 'political ideas' and 'political ideologies'? And how do we distinguish them from political *policies*? We are used to discussing specific political policies but these refer largely to short term, pragmatic decisions made by politicians, parties and pressure groups. Policies are developed to deal with particular problems which arise from time to time. Ideas and ideologies, on the other hand, look at longer term issues and consider fundamental solutions to such questions. Furthermore, they are based on strongly held principles, rather than pragmatic responses to short term issues. Two examples can help here.

Let us consider the levels of taxation in a society. A policy to reduce income tax may be a short-term method of pumping more money into the economy, increasing spending and boosting economic growth. It cannot be undertaken permanently but it solves a problem in the meantime. On the other hand, a party or group of politicians might believe that tax levels are generally too high, are a threat to people's economic liberty and individualism, and are a disincentive to work and enterprise; so they should be kept to as low a level as possible in the long term. A low tax society is therefore a political idea.

Political ideologies are a stronger phenomenon altogether. Ideologies are sets of related political ideas which come together to create a vision of some kind of idealised society. Ideologies are based on strongly held, permanent principles and interlocking doctrines. In our example, the idea of a low tax society connects with related doctrines such as opposition to high levels of welfare which may be a disincentive to hard work as much as high taxes, and free, unregulated markets which foster business enterprise. Put these three aims together – low taxation, low welfare and free markets – and we have an ideology, usually known as neo-liberalism.

We can now apply the same analysis to another set of ideas. These concern dealing with poverty and inequality:

- Raising the minimum wage is a short-term **policy** to reduce poverty.
- Reducing the gap in living standards between the rich and poor in the long term is a **political idea**.

■ Creating a more generally equal society with equal rights, empowerment for the working classes, intervention by the state to avoid the 'excesses' of capitalism, and public ownership of major industries to spread the fruits of their production more evenly, are interlocking ideas, forming an **ideology**, which we know as socialism.

This book deals with political ideas and political ideologies, but not with policies. Put another way, policies come and go, while political ideas and ideologies have more permanence.

There are three 'core ideologies' and five 'optional' ideologies. Apart from the fact that students must study all three core ideologies to be able to tackle the examination questions, but only have to study one of the options, there is another distinction to be borne in mind:

The **core ideologies** – liberalism, conservatism and socialism – have dominated Western civilisation for over two hundred years. Political discourse and conflict have therefore largely been based on these three. However, they are predominately based on Western civilisation. Today we must look further afield in our study of political ideas, taking a world view and also considering those ideas that shape the relationships between minorities and the perspectives of alienated sections of society.

The **optional ideologies** – feminism, anarchism, multiculturalism, nationalism and ecologism – have generally shorter histories than the core ideologies but often take their inspiration from different forms of consciousness of the world, ranging from Eastern mysticism to gender awareness to modern scientism. Some aspects of the optional ideas have also challenged the traditional ideas associated with liberalism, conservatism and socialism and, as such, can also be described as post modern.

Five themes

In each chapter, these five themes will enable us to analyse, evaluate and compare political ideas, with a view to helping students prepare for examination questions. As a starting point, these themes should be considered in the following ways:

Human nature. This concerns beliefs about the fundamental nature of mankind's relationship with other people and with the world. In the political ideas presented here we will see that various thinkers have described human nature in enormously varied ways, from egocentric to social, from fundamentally good to fundamentally competitive, from gender obsessed to androgynous (having no gender identity) or from dominant over the natural world (anthropocentric) to claiming to be only an equal part of nature.

State. Nearly all people live under the jurisdiction of one state or another. Political ideas and ideologies, therefore, have adopted principles about the nature of the state, what part (if any) it should play in society, how it should be controlled and whether it is a force for good or evil.

Society. All societies have a particular structure which has either evolved naturally or been imposed by the state and those who govern the state. Most ideologies have, therefore, developed some kind of vision of what their ideal society would look like. Sometimes this is very specific, as is the case with socialism, some forms of multiculturalism and certain types of collectivist anarchism. Sometimes it is more vague, as is the case with conservatism.

Economy. Not all political ideas and ideologies contain a strong economic perspective, but some do and this should be reflected in analysis where it applies. Again, socialism is a clear example, while neo-liberals, as described above, base most of their ideas on economics and economic principles. Even some socialist feminists have been able to link most of their analysis to economic relations between the sexes. Many ecologists also see capitalism as the main culprit in the degradation of the natural environment and so propose to control or even abolish it.

Different types. All of the ideologies covered in this book are somewhat ambiguous, in that they all have various interpretations and prescriptions. For example, socialism is seen as both a revolutionary and non-revolutionary doctrine, while liberalism advocates both a reduction and extension of state activity. Students will thus be made aware of what both unites and *divides* each ideology's key thinkers.

Key thinkers

There are five or six key thinkers identified for each of the political ideologies in the specification. This book describes their main work, beliefs and importance in the development of political ideas. They are not exhaustive, and you may benefit from knowing something of other important writers within the ideology concerned. However, we strongly advise that you refer to each ideology's 5 or 6 key thinkers in your examination answers — as long as such references are relevant and accurate.

As indicated above, each ideology contains different themes and variations. Often, the different thinkers in the text illustrate these variations most effectively. Thus the distinction between, for example, the liberals John Stuart Mill and John Rawls tells us a great deal about how liberalism evolved between the nineteenth and twentieth centuries. Similarly, Marx's revolutionary version of socialism tells us much of how dramatically the ideology has been transformed by more recent, moderate, left-wing thinkers such as Anthony Crosland and Anthony Giddens.

Political Vocabulary

As we have said, accurate and appropriate political vocabulary should be used wherever possible. Fortunately, both this book and the examination specification itself contain key terms with their meanings. You should take time to understand these and practise using them wherever you can. They can also save you time in your writing as they have specific meanings which will reduce the need for lengthy explanations.

You are strongly advised to learn those aspects of vocabulary with which you are not already familiar, while ensuring you are able to use them in the correct context.

Chapter 1

Liberalism

Learning outcomes

This chapter will enable students to:
- understand the core values of liberalism as a political ideology
- understand how liberal thinking has evolved since the seventeenth century
- understand the various strands of liberalism and how they compare.

Key thinkers

This chapter will frequently reference the key liberal thinkers cited in A-level exam specifications:
- John Locke (1632–1704)
- Mary Wollstonecraft (1759–97)
- John Stuart Mill (1806–73)
- Thomas Hill Green (1836–82)
- John Rawls (1921–2002)
- Betty Friedan (1921–2006).

Introduction: an influential ideology

Alexandria Ocasio-Cortez: American liberal or American socialist?

Most commentators agree that liberalism is the most important and influential ideology in the world today. According to a United Nations survey in 2000, almost two-thirds of states around the world could be classed as 'liberal democracies', a seven-fold increase since 1945. The advance of liberal ideas, it seemed, was unstoppable.

This view has since been challenged by developments during the twenty-first century, but liberalism remains an immensely powerful ideology, central to an understanding of modern politics. But what do liberal societies and liberal states embody? How are 'liberals' different from, say, 'moderate' socialists or 'centrist' conservatives? As we shall see, liberalism is not straightforward, and its practitioners are a mixed bunch in terms of their politics.

In the UK and USA, for example, 'liberalism' is usually seen as a 'centre-left' doctrine, challenging the values of conservatism. As a result, self-proclaimed American liberals – such as Joe Biden and Hillary Clinton – find themselves in the same party as self-proclaimed socialists such as Bernie Sanders and Alexandria Ocasio-Cortez, all opposing the supposed conservatism of the Republican Party.

In the states of the southern hemisphere and western Pacific, the term 'liberal' has rather different connotations. In Australia, for example, the Liberal Party is seen as the main opposition to the Labor Party and has a strong appeal to those rejecting leftist or progressive politics.

Clearly, liberalism is both influential and ambiguous. To help us understand this crucial yet complex ideology, it is first necessary to examine how it emerged.

The origins of liberalism and the influence of the Enlightenment

The roots of liberalism lie in the Reformation, a religious movement affecting much of northern Europe in the late fifteenth and sixteenth centuries. Led by religious protestors such as Martin Luther, the founders of 'protestant' Christianity argued that individuals need no longer rely on priests, popes and other intermediaries. Instead, Christianity should assume a more *individualistic* character, with each man and woman undertaking their own *individual* communication with God.

John Locke: Enlightenment icon and classical liberal

However, it was the **Enlightenment** that extended these religious ideas into the political and secular world. The Enlightenment was an intellectual movement that emerged in the mid-1600s, and one that continued to exert a powerful influence during the late seventeenth and eighteenth centuries. It was defined by *reason* rather than religion, *free thinking* rather than blind faith and rational *scrutiny* rather than spirituality. Put literally, it was a movement that aimed to shed 'light' on the assumptions of what some term the Dark Ages (a description sometimes applied to the medieval era) and to replace those assumptions with more tolerant and inquiring attitudes.

Through philosophers such as **John Locke** (Key thinker 1), often seen as the 'father of liberalism', the Enlightenment inspired a range of radical ideas, such as:

- that every individual has an ability to think freely
- that an individual's life should be determined by his or her own judgements
- that the relationship between individuals and governments should be re-examined, in a way that improves the status of the individual.

These ideas are not unusual today, but in the seventeenth century they were revolutionary, with **Locke** considered an incendiary figure in both England and America. Until then, it had been assumed:

- that the natural form of government was autocratic (dominated by a single individual)
- that an autocratic ruler, usually a monarch, had been appointed by God
- that the monarch's wishes should therefore be automatically accepted by his 'subjects' — a doctrine known as 'the divine right of kings'.

Yet the philosophers of the Enlightenment, and **Locke** in particular, disputed such medieval attitudes, arguing that 'ordinary' individuals should create, by themselves and for themselves, a political system based on reason rather than tradition and superstition — a principle which some political scientists now refer to as mechanistic theory.

> **Key term**
>
> **Mechanistic theory** Linked to the writings of **John Locke**, this argues that human beings are rational and can build a state that reflects their needs (e.g. the need for freedom and self-fulfilment). It rejected ideas such as the 'divine right of kings', which argued that a state should reflect God's wishes and that obedience to such a state was a religious duty.

> **Knowledge check**
>
> 1 What was the 'Enlightenment'?
> 2 What was the 'divine right of kings' and why was it at odds with Enlightenment values?

John Locke (1632–1704)

John Locke is usually seen as the father of liberal philosophy, with his book *Two Treatises of Government* (1690) regarded as the cornerstone of liberal thought. He is also seen as the central figure in the original version of liberalism, usually referred to as classical liberalism. Locke's importance to classical liberalism lies in the questions he raised about human nature and the type of state that was therefore appropriate.

■ Locke denied the traditional, medieval principle that the state was part of God's creation. He disputed that the state had been created by a celestial power, involving monarchs who had a 'divine right' to govern. For the same reason, he rejected the notion that ordinary people were 'subjects' of the state, with a quasi-religious obligation to obey the monarch's rulings. He argued that a 'legitimate' state would be one created by mankind to serve mankind's interests and would arise only from the **consent** of those it would govern.

■ Locke asserted that, prior to the state's existence, there was a 'natural' society which served mankind's interests reasonably well. Locke described this natural society as the **state of nature**. However, Locke's state of nature was very different from the 'nasty and brutish' version depicted by conservative thinker **Thomas Hobbes** (see Chapter 3). Owing to Locke's upbeat view of human nature, and his belief that it was guided by rationalism, he also believed the state of nature was underpinned by 'natural rights' (such as the right to property), 'natural laws' and 'natural justice' and was therefore not one that people would desperately wish to leave. The alternative 'state of law' (in other words, the modern state as we know it) was therefore designed to improve upon an essentially tolerable situation, by resolving disputes between individuals more efficiently than was the case under the state of nature.

■ For Locke, the 'state of law' would be legitimate only if it respected natural rights and natural laws, ensuring that individuals living under formal laws were no worse off than in the state of nature. The state's structures must therefore embody the natural rights and natural liberties that preceded it. Similarly, Locke's ideal state would always reflect the principle that its citizens had voluntarily consented to accept the state's rulings, in return for the state improving their situation (a principle which later became known as 'social contract theory').

■ Because of its 'contractual' nature, the state would have to embody the principle of **limited government** – in other words, limited to governing within pre-agreed rules and always requiring the ongoing consent of the governed. The state's limited character would be confirmed by its dispersal of powers. The executive and legislative branches of the state, for example, would therefore be separate, while its lawmakers (i.e. parliamentarians) would be separated from its law enforcers (i.e. the judiciary).

Key terms

State of nature A notion of what life was like before the emergence of a state. It was used by **John Locke** – and, before him, **Thomas Hobbes** – to justify the different types of state they were proposing and why such states would be an improvement upon the state of nature.

Limited government The opposite of arbitrary rule, as practised by medieval monarchs, this relates to **Locke**'s assertion that the state should be 'limited' – in terms of what it can do and how it can do it – by a formal constitution.

The core ideas of liberalism

Knowledge check

3 Summarise the type of state John Locke prescribed.

Key term

Egotistical individualism A term reflecting the liberal belief that human beings are naturally drawn to the advancement of their own, selfish interests. Its defenders claim that, because human beings are rational, egotistical individualism does not necessarily lead to conflict or an insensitivity to the wishes of others.

View of human nature

Egotistical

From **Locke** onwards, liberals have argued that each human being is unique and endowed with certain 'natural' rights: for example, the 'right' to life, liberty and the pursuit of self-fulfilment. They also argue that human beings are fundamentally driven by **egotistical individualism** – in other words, by self-interest. As a result, liberals believe that every individual seeks:

- *self-realisation*: to ensure we discover our 'true' and unique selves, free from the constraints and expectations of others, and unhindered by the conventions of society
- *self-determination*: to ensure we are the masters of our own fate and that the realities of our lives can be attributed to our own efforts and achievements
- *self-fulfilment*: to ensure we have fully utilised our 'natural rights' and made the most of our particular talents (see Figure 1.1).

Liberals argue that when these things are denied, human beings are left demoralised, de-energised and afflicted by the sense of a wasted life. Indeed, this argument was at the heart of complaints articulated in respect of women by liberal feminists like **Mary Wollstonecraft** (Key thinker 2) and **Betty Friedan** (Key thinker 6), both of whom argued that male *and* female individuals shared a desire for self-fulfilment and self-determination.

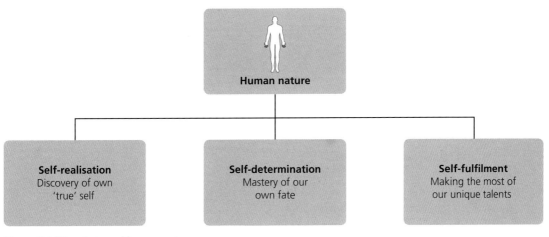

Figure 1.1 Liberal view of human nature

Mary Wollstonecraft

In her acclaimed book *The Feminine Mystique* (1963), **Friedan** protested that huge numbers of female individuals were 'quietly suppressed' by the 'gender expectations' of post-war America, and that such women were subsequently 'de-humanised' by a society that, in this respect, was insufficiently liberal. Specifically referring to women in conventional, suburban environments – 'trapped by an obligation to surrender their own dreams in order that husbands and children can follow theirs' – **Friedan** linked rising levels of female depression and suicide to a 'suffocating sense that the natural urge to feel happy and fulfilled was denied'. Illustrating this point, she depicted a 'fictional but typical' housewife in 1960s, small-town America:

As she made the beds, shopped for groceries and comforted the kids, she was afraid to even ask herself the question '*Is this all?*'

Key thinker 2

Mary Wollstonecraft (1759–97)

While **John Locke** laid the foundations of liberal thought in the seventeenth century, one of those who developed classical liberal ideas in the eighteenth century was Mary Wollstonecraft. Her most important publication, *A Vindication of the Rights of Woman* (1792), remains a classic of political thought and is still strongly linked to feminist ideology. Yet, though gender was crucial to her work, her arguments were rooted in liberal individualism.

- Wollstonecraft's primary claim was that the Enlightenment's optimistic analysis of human nature, and the belief that we are guided by reason, should apply to all human beings, male and female. She went on to argue that, in eighteenth-century England, both society and state implied that women were not rational and thus denied them individual freedom and formal equality. Women, for example, were rarely allowed land ownership or paid employment, and sacrificed what little individualism they had to become wives. Once married, a woman had little legal protection against violence inflicted by her spouse, and no recourse to divorce. Neither could women

vote for those who governed them – a blatant violation, Wollstonecraft pointed out, of 'government by consent'.

- Yet Wollstonecraft was not simply a spokesperson for women's interests. She argued that by fettering female individualism, nations such as England were limiting their stock of intelligence, wisdom and morality. As Wollstonecraft observed, 'such arrangements are not conditions where reason and progress may prosper'.

- Like many upholders of 'classical' liberal ideals, Wollstonecraft welcomed both the American Revolution of 1775 and the French Revolution of 1789. Indeed, her other major work, *A Vindication of the Rights of Men* (1790), attacked **Edmund Burke**'s critique of the French Revolution and his related defence of custom, history and aristocratic rule (see Chapter 3). Wollstonecraft thus stressed her support for republican government, formal equality and a constitution that protected individual rights. But such formal equality, she restated, must be accorded to all individuals, and not just men. For that reason, she applauded the French Revolution's emphasis upon 'citizens' and its apparent indifference to gender differences.

- Wollstonecraft conceded that women themselves were complicit in their subjugation, generally desiring only marriage and motherhood. For this to be corrected, she argued,

formal education should be made available to as many women (and men) as possible. Without such formal tuition, individuals could never develop their rational faculties, never realise their individual potential and never recognise the 'absurdity' of illiberal doctrines like the divine right of kings.

Rational

Critics of liberalism suggest that such egotism makes for selfishness and endless conflict between individuals. Indeed, this gloomy view of egotism is conveyed by the work of key conservative thinker, **Thomas Hobbes** (see chapter 3).

But liberal thinkers dispute this. According to both **Locke** and **John Stuart Mill** (Key thinker 3), we may be egotistical, but our behaviour is also rational and therefore respectful to others; guided usually by reason and logic rather than emotion and impulse. In this way, our rationality allows us to realise that selfishness and disrespect for others can rebound to our disadvantage. Put simply, if we do not respect others, in *their* pursuit of self-realisation, then others might not respect us – with the result that we ourselves could be left frustrated. As a result, liberals see human nature as fundamentally self-centred, but also thoughtful and empathetic, drawn to intelligent compromise and mutual understanding with others.

Progressive

Most liberal thinkers are also keen to argue that human nature is not set in stone. Instead, it is constantly progressing and developing through greater knowledge, an improved understanding of the world around us, and greater education. In short, human beings today are likely to be more rational, intelligent and respectful than they were in the past.

This idea is called developmental individualism and links strongly to the doctrine of 'utility' or 'utilitarianism' – a doctrine advanced by the radical philosopher Jeremy Bentham (1748-1832), and asserting that human beings are guided by the pursuit of pleasure and the avoidance of pain. However, as **Mill** wrote:

> I regard utility as the ultimate appeal on all ethical questions; but it must be utility in the largest sense, grounded on the permanent interests of man as a progressive being ... better to be a human being dissatisfied than a pig satisfied; better to be Socrates dissatisfied than a fool satisfied.

Optimistic

Given their belief in our rationality and improvability, liberals are clearly optimistic about the human condition and reject the idea of Original Sin – the Old Testament doctrine which insists that humanity is innately flawed and inclined to fail. From the writings of **Locke** onwards, liberalism has always challenged this bleak view, offering instead a more positive view of human nature.

Liberalism argues that human nature has the capacity to effect steady progress and increase human happiness. Liberals admit that life is not without difficulty. But they insist that, through rational discussion and informed debate, solutions will normally be found to problems that routinely arise. In this respect, the slogan 'Yes, we can!', underpinning Barack Obama's presidential campaign in 2008, neatly summarised the optimistic outlook of liberal politics.

Liberalism involves optimistic assertions: 'Yes We Can' billboard, erected in Washington, DC, after inauguration of Barack Obama (2009)

Comparing ideas

Human nature

Liberalism's optimistic view of human nature, and its belief in mankind's rationality, are shared by some other ideologies, notably socialism and anarchism. But this is refuted by traditional conservatism, which offers a 'philosophy of imperfection' and a more sceptical view of human potential (see Chapter 3). New Right conservatism shares liberalism's belief that human beings are egotistical, but this notion is rejected by socialist thinkers, who instead stress our 'fraternal' and 'communal' characteristics.

View of society

The 'natural' society

John Rawls (Key thinker 5) defined society as the peaceful, voluntary interaction of multiple individuals. However, liberals from **Locke** onwards have argued that society was not dependent upon the existence of a state. Owing to their belief that human nature is respectful and fundamentally decent, liberals argue that society *predates the state* – hence **Locke**'s reference to the 'natural society' and a mainly peaceful 'state of nature'. Due to mankind's rationality, this natural society was one which facilitated 'natural rights', 'natural laws' and 'natural justice' – see Figure 1.2.

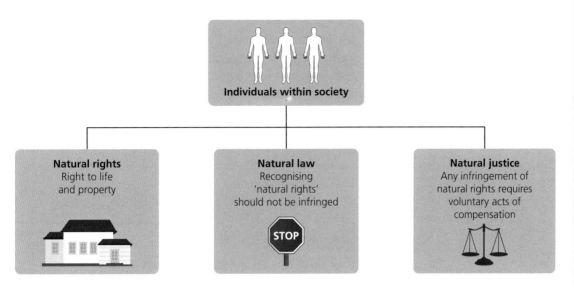

Figure 1.2 The liberal view of a natural society

According to liberalism, life before the state was not 'nasty, brutish and short' (as conservative thinkers like **Hobbes** argued). Instead, liberals argue that pre-state life was agreeable and generally efficient, and not something we would have automatically wished to end.

The individualistic society

Consistent with their 'egotistical' view of human nature, liberals state that a 'legitimate' society must be one where the maximum number of individuals can pursue self-realisation and self-determination (see Box 1.1). As such, it will be one where individuals are free from any barriers stemming from prejudice or discrimination. As **John Stuart Mill** emphasised during the mid-nineteenth century, the main job of liberal politicians was to create the conditions for such an individualistic society.

This notion was also articulated by **Mary Wollstonecraft** in 1790. Claiming that 'natural rights' applied to both men *and* women, she noted that such rights – particularly the right to property – were withheld from the women of eighteenth-century English society. Her demands that society be reformed were later echoed by **Betty Friedan**, who asserted that the patriarchal, male-dominated society conflicted with women's quest for self-determination and was therefore at odds with liberal individualism.

In supporting individualism, liberal thinkers are especially concerned about individuals with *minority* or *underrepresented* characteristics. For example:

- the cause of religious nonconformists in seventeenth-century England was championed by **Locke.**
- women in eighteenth-century England, particularly those aspiring to property and education, were championed by **Wollstonecraft**.
- women seeking professional careers in 1960s America were backed by **Friedan**.
- more recently, those who identify as lesbian, gay, bisexual, transgender, queer and other sexual minorities (LGBTQ+) have been supported by writers like Shon Faye.

In all cases, liberals are keen to protect the individuals concerned against what **Mill** termed 'dull conformity' and 'suffocating convention'.

> ## Knowledge check
>
> 12 What does liberalism mean by 'individualism'?
> 13 Why did Mary Wollstonecraft think that women were being denied 'natural rights'?

> ## Box 1.1: Individualism
>
> Individualism is a vital principle of liberal ideology. It involves:
>
> - maximising the number of individuals achieving self-determination (control of their own lives)
> - maximising the number of individuals achieving self-realisation (discovering their 'true' selves and potential)
> - maximising the number of individuals attaining self-fulfilment (a sense of their 'personal mission' being achieved).

The tolerant society

Liberal support for minorities connects with liberalism's commitment to a more tolerant society, without which universal self-realisation is impossible. As a result, liberals are fond of citing a statement often misattributed to the French philosopher Voltaire (1694–1778): 'I disapprove of what you say, but I will defend to the death your right to say it.' This notion was to be developed in the mid-nineteenth century by **John Stuart Mill**, who insisted that the state should tolerate all actions and opinions unless they were shown to violate the 'harm principle'. This principle states that individuals should be free to do and say anything that does not harm the liberty of other individuals.

> ### Key term
>
> **Tolerance/'harm principle'**
> This refers to the liberal notion, famously expressed by **John Stuart Mill**, that views and actions we dislike should still be tolerated, as long as they do not harm the liberty of others.

Although liberalism has always placed importance on the value of the individual, liberal thinkers came to recognise that individuals do not necessarily seek tolerance in isolation from others. Instead, liberal thinkers like **Thomas Hill Green**

John Stuart Mill

(Key thinker 4) accept that individuals will be drawn to, and rely on, *societies* that tolerate their individualism. Here again, there was a concern for individuals with minority causes and characteristics. However, while tolerance of minorities may seem a straightforward issue for liberalism and individualism, it can raise serious problems. For example, to what extent should a liberal society tolerate minority positions that seem *illiberal*? And how should liberals respond if the agenda of one 'discriminated-against' minority clashes with another?

These have long been tricky issues for liberals; and their usual response has been to argue that greater 'enlightenment' will produce greater, all-round tolerance and consensus. Intolerance and general opposition to liberal ideas are often assumed by liberals to stem from ignorance or misunderstanding. For this reason, **Mill**'s faith in consensus via education remains crucial to the liberal project, providing the means through which the interests of society's minorities can be reconciled – both to society's majority interests and to the interests of other minorities.

Knowledge check

14 Why is 'tolerance' sometimes a problematic issue for liberals?

Key thinker 3

John Stuart Mill (1806–73)

Regarded by many as one of the greatest English philosophers, John Stuart Mill's contribution to liberal thought is immense. The son of utilitarian philosopher James Mill, he was not just an intellectual but also a politician and campaigner who brilliantly developed some of the ideas put forward by **Locke** and **Wollstonecraft**. Mill would also provide a valuable bridge between classical liberalism and modern liberalism, which explains why his political ideas are said to represent 'transitional liberalism' and 'developmental individualism'.

■ Mill's most enduring idea, outlined in his seminal work *On Liberty* (1859), was one which later became known as 'negative freedom'. Put simply, it argued that freedom mainly involved an absence of restraint. This connected to Mill's 'harm principle' – the notion that an individual's actions should always be tolerated, by either the state or other individuals, unless

it could be demonstrated that such actions would harm others.

■ With a view to clarifying tolerance, Mill divided human actions into 'self-regarding' and 'other-regarding'. Self-regarding actions, such as religious worship or the expression of personal views, did not restrict the freedom of others and should therefore be tolerated. Other-regarding actions, such as violent behaviour, clearly harmed the freedom of others and should therefore be forbidden by a liberal state. Toleration of diverse opinions was especially important, Mill argued, as it meant new ideas could emerge while allowing bad ideas to be openly ridiculed.

■ Mill's importance lay in the fact that many of his arguments represented something more sophisticated than early classical liberalism. He saw liberty, for example, not just as a 'natural right' but as the engine of ongoing human development. Mill therefore viewed human nature not so much as a 'finished article' but rather 'a work in progress'.

■ This naturally affected Mill's approach to the core liberal principle of individualism. Mill did not just want to liberate individuals as they were. Instead, he wished to see what individuals could become – a concept he termed 'individuality' and which has since been termed 'developmental individualism'.

■ Mill's distinction between individualism and individuality profoundly affected his view of democracy. He was particularly concerned that the liberal principle of 'government by consent' would be compromised if the interests of some liberal-minded individuals were denied by the votes of most (uneducated) voters. In short, Mill feared that a democratic state could lead to a 'tyranny of the majority'.

Knowledge check

15 Summarise why Mill thought democracy carried dangers, and how he thought those dangers could be countered.

16 What did Mill mean by the 'harm principle'?

Comparing ideas

Society

Like socialists, liberals believe that society is 'natural' and predates the state. However, while socialists believe that society is naturally marked by fraternity, solidarity and communalism, liberals believe it is defined by individuals seeking autonomy. Supporters of conservatism, meanwhile, reject the premise of a natural society, arguing that society is dependent upon order and the existence of a strong state.

Key term

Economic liberalism Otherwise known as capitalism, this reflects liberalism's belief that private property is a natural right and that private enterprise allows individual liberty.

Knowledge check

17 What is meant by a 'natural right'?

18 Why do liberals consider property a vital way of promoting individualism?

View of the economy

Defence of private property

At the heart of economic liberalism lies an unswerving belief in the private ownership of property. Given the liberal view of human nature and society, this should not be surprising. As **John Locke** emphasised, property is a 'natural right' which predates the existence of any state. Later, liberal thinkers like **John Stuart Mill** also argued that property facilitated individualism – incentivising individual enterprise, reflecting each individual's preferences and providing a sense of independence. In short, property is seen by liberals as a crucial vehicle for self-realisation and self-determination. Furthermore, as **Locke** pointed out, when property is owned by a multitude of individuals, this offers further protection against concentrated power and overbearing rulers who threaten natural rights.

Defence of capitalism and inequality

An obvious effect of liberalism's support for private property is its enthusiasm for capitalism. Ever since the original liberal economist, Adam Smith (1723–90), extolled free trade and free markets in the late eighteenth century, liberalism has been strongly associated with private enterprise and private ownership of the economy.

As with its approach to society, liberalism's support for a capitalist economy is strongly linked to its upbeat view of human nature. In making the case for free-market economics, for example, Adam Smith optimistically asserted that, if obstacles to free trade were swept away, and if individuals were allowed to trade freely, the 'invisible hand' of market forces would eventually enrich both individuals and nations.

Although capitalism produces inequality of outcome, liberals defend this on two grounds. First, economic liberals at the UK's Adam Smith Institute, for example, assert that individual wealth, and individual economic success, will eventually 'trickle down' to the majority in society. Secondly, they endorse **Mill**'s view that unequal outcomes are consistent with a 'meritocratic' society – one that encourages individualism, and which rewards those who have *earned* their advantages. However, as **John Rawls** argued, liberals should only defend inequality of outcome if it is accompanied by *equality of opportunity*.

As we shall see when we examine different types of liberalism later in this chapter, liberals disagree about which type of capitalism is best for liberty and prosperity. Liberals in the nineteenth century, such as **Mill**, commended laissez-faire capitalism, whereas liberals in the mid- to late twentieth century, such as **Rawls**, tended to favour Keynesian capitalism. Such differences relate to the nature and objectives of a liberal state.

> **Key term**
>
> **Keynesianism** Based on the work of liberal economist John Maynard Keynes (1883–1946), this is a form of capitalism that involves the state directing and managing market forces to ensure steady growth, full employment and therefore (Keynes believed) greater individual liberty.

> **Knowledge check**
>
> 19 What are the benefits of capitalism from a liberal point of view?

> **Comparing ideas**
>
> ### The economy
>
> Given the resulting inequality, liberalism's support for private property and capitalism is readily shared by conservatives, particularly New Right conservatives. Socialism, with its greater concern for *equality of outcome*, tends to be more critical of economic liberalism, with some socialist thinkers (like **Karl Marx**) demanding the overthrow of both capitalism and private property.

View of the state: foundations

Rejection of anarchism

Liberalism is not the only ideology to promote individualism: the idea is also found among some strands of anarchism, such as anarcho-capitalism, which argue that the state should be abolished in the interests of individual freedom. What makes liberalism distinctive is its belief that self-realisation, self-determination and self-fulfilment are all best served by the *existence of a state*, rather than leaving individuals in a condition of anarchy (where formal laws and authority are absent). However, given **John Locke**'s emphasis on 'natural rights', and the related belief that society predates the state, liberals do not accept that *any* kind of state is preferable to anarchy. Instead, they insist that the state must meet certain conditions so that individuals are not left worse off than they were in the state of nature.

Rejection of 'traditional'/pre-Enlightenment states

Liberals dismiss the kind of states common in the pre-Enlightenment era because liberals believe in consent and social contracts. Medieval states were invariably marked by:

- *Divine right of kings*: the doctrine that the monarch's power had been conferred by God and to question it was effectively blasphemous.
- *Monarchical absolutism*: where power rested almost exclusively with a king or queen.
- *Arbitrary power*: where the monarch exercised power randomly, unrestrained by any clear code of governance.
- *Hereditary power*: where power was exercised by those who happened to inherit it, rather than those who demonstrated their ability to use it rationally.

Early liberals, like **Locke**, argued that such states were both *morally illegitimate*, in that they were unlikely to respect natural rights, and *intellectually illegitimate*, in that they were an affront to mankind's rationality and cognitive potential.

The contractual state

By contrast, liberals support what **Locke** termed 'government by consent' — or, more specifically, the consent of the governed. **Locke** insisted that the state has legitimacy only if those under its jurisdiction *agree* to be under its jurisdiction. This idea has a profound effect on the relationship between politicians and people. Far from being the 'subjects' of the state, as the traditional state asserted, the people under the liberal state become its 'citizens', with ultimate control over those who govern. As **Locke** maintained, 'government should always be the servant, not master, of the people'.

The notion of 'government by consent' is closely linked to that of 'government by contract' — or what **Locke** and other

> **Knowledge check**
>
> 20 What is meant by 'arbitrary power'?

Enlightenment theorists dubbed a social contract. As we have seen, liberals believe that the 'natural society' or 'state of nature' is not necessarily undesirable. Therefore, individuals will only contract *out* of the 'state of nature' and contract *into* a formal state if they are promised advantages in return. Furthermore, if those advantages stop, citizens are entitled to declare the state illegitimate, cancel the 'contract' between the government and governed and return to the 'state of nature'. As the American Declaration of Independence declared in 1776, when a government becomes tyrannical, 'it is the Right of the People to alter or to abolish it'.

View of the state: objectives

Promotion of natural rights

The main objective of a liberal state is to improve upon rights that individuals enjoyed in the state of nature – notably the right to life, liberty, property and the pursuit of self-fulfilment. Again, this was famously embodied by both the US Constitution and the American Declaration of Independence that preceded it:

> ... all men are created equal, that they are endowed by their Creator with certain unalienable Rights, that among these are Life, Liberty and the pursuit of Happiness.

John Rawls therefore endorsed the idea that liberalism is 'state-sponsored individualism', as opposed to the 'stateless individualism' of anarchist thinkers such as **Max Stirner**. Furthermore, if the state is structured in a certain way, it can allow individuals to enjoy their natural rights more easily than in the state of nature. As **Locke** conceded, the state of nature would still involve occasional clashes of self-interest (over entitlement to uncultivated land, for example), with such clashes only being resolved after informal – yet lengthy – quests for compromise. By contrast, the liberal state would offer faster and fairer methods of resolution, such as through impartial courts, allowing individuals more swiftly to resume the exercise of their natural rights.

Equal opportunities, unequal outcomes

Given liberalism's belief that every individual is born equal with equal natural rights, it is logical for the liberal state to ensure that individuals are treated equally. Indeed, one of the chief justifications for a liberal state is its capacity to provide everyone with equal opportunities for self-fulfilment. The liberal

Key term

Equality of opportunity
Liberals believe that all individuals should have an equal chance to develop their potential. Liberals also believe, however, that equality of opportunity usually leads to unequal outcomes, arising from unequal abilities.

Knowledge check

24 Why might liberals defend an unequal society?

25 What sort of intolerance would a liberal state not allow?

26 What did John Stuart Mill and T.H. Green recommend as a way of ensuring greater tolerance in society?

state will not be static in this respect. As **T.H. Green** and **John Rawls** argued, the liberal state must evolve to counter new threats to individual liberty.

It is important to note, however, that liberal states (unlike most socialist states) will be far less concerned about *equality of outcome* – an obvious side-effect of liberalism's support for private property and capitalism. Once again, liberals like **Rawls** argue that, while **equality of opportunity** should be pursued, inequality of *outcome* is the inevitable and desirable consequence of individual diversity. Consequently, the liberal state will strive to enable equal opportunity while allowing a *meritocratic* inequality of outcome, one that rewards individual effort and achievement rather than hereditary advantages.

Promotion of tolerance

As indicated earlier, liberals wish to see a society that values tolerance. Consequently, the liberal state aims to promote tolerance through its laws and institutions – for example, by making illegal blatant forms of *intolerance* regarding freedom of speech and religion. Classical liberals such as **John Stuart Mill** claimed that education was another vital way in which greater tolerance could be encouraged. But it was 'modern' liberals like **T.H. Green** who argued that only the state could ensure the universal education required by a tolerant society. During the twentieth century, liberals such as **Betty Friedan** argued that the state's role in promoting tolerance should be extended further, so as to illegalise racial and sexual discrimination. **Friedan** also believed that a more tolerant society could be 'psychologically embedded' by the state, via bureaucratic agencies with an 'educational' function (such as the UK's Equality and Human Rights Commission). This leads us to the organisation and mechanics of a liberal state.

Comparing ideas

The state

Although socialists share the liberal view that the state should promote liberty, unlike liberals they believe the state should also promote equality of outcome, solidarity and social justice. For conservatives, the primary purpose of the state is to facilitate order and safety, although New Right conservatives share liberalism's view that the state should respect individual freedom.

View of the state: structures and mechanisms

A constitutional ('limited') state

At the heart of the liberal state is a belief that power should not be exercised in an arbitrary and unlimited way. Instead, the state's power should be **limited** by:

- The *preconditions* of government: the terms on which the governed initially give their consent to be governed, as part of the original social contract between the state and its citizens.
- The *procedures and methods* of government, as rationally agreed when the contract between state and citizens is being reached.

These conditions and procedures would be duly enshrined in a *constitution:* in effect, the rule book of a liberal state. This constitution would be constructed after exhaustive rational discussion among its architects (exemplified by the US Founding Fathers at their Philadelphia Convention in 1787) and would define the extent and procedures of state power.

Inherent to this constitution would be a 'formalised' equality, reflecting the liberal belief that human beings are born equal (i.e. they have **foundational equality**). As such, a liberal constitution aims to give the same legal and political rights to all – such as the universal right to petition government – and apply the 'rule of law' so that state rules are applicable to everyone, regardless of class or status.

A fragmented state

John Locke's belief that the state's powers should be 'fragmented and scattered' was a reaction to pre-Enlightenment states, where power was concentrated in the monarchy. Liberals argue that power is more likely to be exercised wisely if it is shared evenly, reflecting the famous view of Lord Acton (1834–1902) that 'power tends to corrupt ... and absolute power corrupts absolutely'.

Dispersed state power also reflects liberalism's optimistic view of human nature. If individuals are generally rational and respectful, and inclined to peaceful self-determination, it seems reasonable to empower as many people as possible. This idea has its most celebrated expression in the Constitution of the United States. Heavily indebted to the philosophy of **Locke**, the Constitution displays a series of 'checks and balances' to prevent

Key term

Foundational equality
The liberal belief that all individuals are born equal and are therefore entitled to equal treatment by the state. It therefore connects to formal equality, involving equality before the law and equal possession of legal rights.

Knowledge check

27 What is a constitution?
28 What advantage do liberals see in a state that disperses its power?

the concentration of power. These have since become common in liberal states across the world and are exemplified in Box 1.2.

Box 1.2: The liberal state – how is power dispersed?

- A formal 'separation of powers' between the executive, legislature and judiciary.
- A separation of powers within the legislature itself, producing a 'bicameral' (two-house) legislature.
- A Bill of Rights, overriding the 'transient' policies of governments.
- A Supreme Court, whose decisions may override those of elected governments.
- A federal state, whereby many of the state's functions are delegated to various regional governments.

Key term

Meritocracy The liberal idea that both society and the state should reward individual effort and achievement, rather than inherited advantage. Society and the state should be led by individuals who have proved their abilities and talents.

A representative state

Consistent with **Locke**'s assertion that the state derives its power from its citizens, rather than the divine right of kings, it is important for a liberal state to be reliably representative of the citizens it serves. For the American colonists of the 1770s, it was the lack of such 'representativeness' that sparked a revolt against the English Crown. This revolt was partly inspired by **Locke**'s theory of 'government by consent' and was encapsulated by the slogan 'no taxation without representation'.

Therefore, the liberal state will always include representative bodies, such as parliaments, that allow rational discussion between representatives of the people, who are *accountable* to the people. As **Betty Friedan** argued, liberals must always reject the conservative idea of a *paternalistic* state, where politicians feel a quasi-parental obligation to 'look after' people. Instead, they must demand legislatures that respect and articulate citizens' interests.

A meritocratic state

Like a liberal society, a liberal state must be meritocratic, governed by those who have *earned* rather than inherited their authority. In this respect, the liberal state again stands in contrast to the pre-Enlightenment state, where the principle of hereditary power usually applied. As Thomas Paine (1737–1809) remarked, when justifying the French Revolution's overthrow of the nobility in 1790, aristocratic rule was 'beyond equity, beyond reason and most certainly beyond wisdom'.

A democratic state?

The question of whether a liberal state should be democratic is complex. At first glance, the 'liberal state' and the 'democratic state' seem complementary. With its claim that people are born equal and generally rational and that government should always involve the 'consent' of the governed, liberalism might be presumed to demand that all adults have an equal vote and that the result of votes should always be respected.

However, the situation is complicated by liberalism's respect for 'natural rights', which liberals regard as non-negotiable. But what if some would-be voters are *not* respectful of such 'rights'? What if those 'rights' prove less than popular at the ballot box?

For liberal thinkers, this dilemma has two consequences. First, classical liberals like **John Locke** and **John Stuart Mill** had reservations about universal adult suffrage, or the idea that all adults should be allowed to vote. **Locke** disapproved of the vote being given to those without property, on the grounds that it would threaten the 'natural rights' of property-owners. **Mill** feared that, if votes were given to the 'uneducated', it could lead to a lack of tolerance towards minority viewpoints, the subsequent erosion of 'individuality', and a society that stifled brilliance and originality.

Although **Betty Friedan** and **John Rawls** endorsed universal suffrage, they and other modern liberals have still been keen to stress *representative* democracy (allowing legislators to seek a liberal consensus) as opposed to *direct* democracy and its use of devices like referendums. Such devices, liberals claim, are inherently geared to majority opinion and may threaten the natural rights of minority interests – a threat which **Mill** termed 'the tyranny of the majority'.

The second consequence of liberalism's ambivalent attitude to democracy is that the liberal state will seek to *constrain the effect of elections*. This leads us to the final aspect of a liberal constitution and a liberal state.

Judicial supremacy

As shown in Box 1.2, the dispersed power of a liberal state usually includes 'supreme' courts and unelected judges – in other words, state officials who may veto the policies of an elected government if they determine that some policies clash with a state's Bill of Rights. The Bill of Rights is a constitutional document which protects certain 'rights', such as the 'right' to free speech, from the actions of politicians. Like so much else in liberalism, this arrangement stems from a belief that 'natural rights' are sacrosanct and cannot be threatened, and that certain policies are unacceptable, regardless of their popularity.

Liberals are also wary of parliamentary sovereignty – a doctrine that places ultimate power in the hands of an elective body – as they fear it could lead to the legitimisation of 'illiberal' ideas (such as the persecution of certain minority groups) that happen to be temporarily popular at recent elections. Consequently, the liberal state seeks to protect itself from 'elective dictatorship' and any 'populist' government which shows scant regard for 'natural rights'.

Knowledge check

31 What is a Bill of Rights?

Debate 1

Liberal democracy – a contradiction in terms?

Yes

- Democracy tends to be guided by majorities. It therefore threatens individuals with minority views and characteristics.
- Classical liberals favoured a limited electorate, to safeguard property rights.
- **John Stuart Mill** thought votes should be given only to those with appropriate education.
- Natural rights theory implies that certain principles are non-negotiable, regardless of election results.
- Liberals thus seek to mitigate democracy's results via constitutional devices such as a Bill of Rights and a Supreme Court.

No

- Liberalism endorses self-determination, and democracy allows individuals to shape their lives at the ballot box.
- Liberalism endorses 'government by consent', which democracy facilitates.
- Liberalism dislikes the concentration of political power, which democracy helps avoid.
- Liberalism believes human nature is rational, so electors should be capable of sensible decisions.
- **Mill** thought democracy would have an 'educative' effect upon voters, and thus aid developmental individualism.

Evaluation check: To what extent does liberalism 'trust the people'?

Different types of liberalism

Classical liberalism

Classical liberalism is the original form of liberal thinking. It comprises key liberal thinkers such as **John Locke**, **Mary Wollstonecraft** and **John Stuart Mill**, as well as Enlightenment philosophers like Voltaire, the US Founding Fathers of the late eighteenth century and economists like Adam Smith. Until

Debate and discussion were central to classical liberalism

the late nineteenth century, classical liberalism was also the pre-eminent form of liberal thinking. Since then, however, it has been seriously challenged in Europe and America by the different methods and perspectives of modern liberalism (see below).

Nonetheless, since the mid-twentieth century, the central beliefs of classical liberalism have been revived and updated by influential 'neo-liberals', such as philosopher Friedrich von Hayek (1899–1992) and think-tanks like the Adam Smith Institute. Historically, classical liberalism is best understood with reference to the following characteristics.

Revolutionary implications

John Locke's belief in government by consent, and his assertion that a state should be the servant not master of the people, may seem mainstream today. Yet, in the context of the seventeenth and eighteenth centuries, such ideas were revolutionary and potentially violent.

By rejecting the twin pillars of the traditional European state – the divine right of kings and monarchical absolutism – **Locke**'s philosophy became associated with the Glorious Revolution of 1688 and the establishment of constitutional government in England. It also helped inspire the American revolt against British rule in 1775, when **Locke**'s belief in natural rights and government by consent were again proclaimed by the rebels.

Support for 'rationalism', and the notion that human nature was guided by reason, was also controversial in the late

Knowledge check

32 Why was liberalism originally seen as a revolutionary doctrine?

Key term

Negative liberty The belief of **John Locke** and **John Stuart Mill** that liberty means individuals are 'free from' interference by both governments and other individuals. It was central to classical liberalism and, from the mid-twentieth century, neo-liberalism.

Knowledge check

33 What did Mill think was necessary to ensure liberty?

Key term

Minimal government A feature of classical liberalism, minimal government reflected the concept of 'negative liberty' by minimising state activities (e.g. legislating and taxing as infrequently as possible).

eighteenth century and proved central to the French Revolution of 1789 (an episode marked, ironically, by mass public executions and accompanying hysteria).

Other key thinkers within classical liberalism, such as **Mary Wollstonecraft**, argued that the prevailing view of women was an affront to both reason and liberty. Although her central thesis, that both male *and* female individuals had natural rights, did not produce the sort of upheaval seen in France, it was still considered dangerous by many in authority. Indeed, Wollstonecraft was an early supporter of the French Revolution.

'Negative' liberty

Negative liberty is a key feature of classical liberalism and closely connected to the seminal text, *On Liberty*, by **John Stuart Mill**. Although the term was not coined until a century after **Mill**'s death (by the philosopher **Isaiah Berlin**), it reflects **Mill**'s view that freedom means individuals being left alone to determine their own destiny. **Mill** argued that, unless it could be shown that a man's exercise of liberty 'harmed' that of others, any interference with his actions infringed his natural right to freedom. In short, for classical liberals like **Mill**, liberty largely meant an absence of interference.

A logical extension of this view was that a man alone on a desert island might be lonely, but he could still exercise a high degree of personal freedom. This concept of liberty reflected the classical liberal view that human beings were naturally autonomous and chimed with **John Locke**'s notion that society was naturally 'atomistic' — that is, defined by a multitude of self-interested and self-sufficient individuals. Yet negative liberty also had consequences for both the size of the state and the emerging 'science' of economics.

Minimal government

Classical liberals endorse the idea of minimal government, which is different from the *minimal state*. The typical liberal state, with its various 'checks and balances', is actually quite extensive (see Box 1.2) and certainly more elaborate than the 'minarchist' state favoured by libertarians (see Chapter 3).

The notion of minimal government therefore relates more to *how much governing* the state should undertake rather than the *structure* of the state. Given that classical liberals saw liberty as the absence of restraint, the belief in minimal government is unsurprising. According to **Locke** and **Mill**, governments should be limited not just in terms of *how* they can act, but in terms of *whether* they act. Consistent with 'negative liberty', the limited constitutional state should therefore co-exist with minimal government activity.

The case for the minimal state was perhaps best summarised by the idea that 'the government which governs best is that which governs least'. Or, as Thomas Jefferson noted, 'when government grows, our liberty withers'. Minimal government is not guaranteed by a limited, constitutional state. But it is certainly less likely in a state that allows concentrated and arbitrary power.

Laissez-faire capitalism

For classical liberals, their belief in minimal government also informed their view of economics. More specifically, it shaped their view of how the state should respond to capitalism. The most famous expression of classical liberal economics came from Adam Smith's *The Wealth of Nations* (1776), which was later commended strongly by **John Stuart Mill**.

Smith argued that capitalism had a limitless capacity to enrich individuals and society — as long as state intervention in the economy was severely restricted. Reflecting the notion of negative liberty, the state's role was to adopt a mainly **laissez-faire** ('leave alone') approach to the workings of a market economy, so that market forces could operate and flourish 'naturally'. Smith advocated the end of tariffs, duties and other forms of economic protectionism, and the spread of free trade between nation-states and their commercial classes. These ideas were radical in 1776 but become orthodox in Britain and the USA during the nineteenth century.

Comparing ideas

Liberty

The classical liberal faith in negative liberty and laissez-faire capitalism was later revived by neo-liberals such as Friedrich von Hayek and New Right conservatives including **Ayn Rand**. But it is refuted both by socialists like **Karl Marx**, who were highly critical of the aggressive capitalism it unleashed, and traditional conservatives like **Michael Oakeshott** who were more sceptical about human behaviour.

Ambivalent about democracy

As indicated earlier, liberalism and democracy have never been easy bedfellows; and democracy posed particular problems for classical liberalism. Both **John Locke** and the US Founding Fathers thought that universal adult suffrage, which empowered the majority, threatened the 'natural' property rights of a minority. As a result, most classical liberals believed that the right to vote should be confined to property owners. This largely explains the allegation of early socialists, such as **Karl Marx**, that classical liberalism was just a philosophical cover for 'bourgeois' class interests.

Later classical liberals like **John Stuart Mill** and Jeremy Bentham, however, were more resigned to the inevitability of democracy. Indeed, **Mill** argued that it would eventually complement the 'developmental' aspect of human nature. Mass engagement with election debates, **Mill** argued, along with the process of 'rationally' deciding whom to support, was a form of political education that would enhance everyone's capacity for reason. As a result, **Mill** argued, democracy could fortify, rather than threaten, liberal society. He was therefore prepared, eventually, to champion votes for women.

But **Mill** was still hesitant. By the mid-nineteenth century, most adults had no formal education and were therefore ill-equipped (in **Mill**'s view) to make rational choices. Consequently, **Mill** argued that universal adult suffrage must be preceded by universal education. He was confident that mass education would establish a liberal consensus within society and then ensure liberal outcomes in elections. As a result, the traditional liberal fear about democracy – that it would lead to rule by an illiberal majority – would recede.

Although **Mill**'s views about democracy were expressed in the mid-nineteenth century, they still find echoes in liberal circles today. For example, the assumption that those who disagree with liberal views are simply those who 'do not understand', probably on account of 'limited' education, was especially noticeable after the Brexit referendum of 2016. Many Remainers, who regarded themselves as liberal, observed that just a small minority of university graduates had voted 'Leave' and that Brexit was therefore a result of voters who were 'ignorant'. **Mill** might well have agreed. In fact, he argued that individuals with a university education (such as **Mill** himself) were particularly 'rational' and therefore deserved more than one vote in elections.

Knowledge check

37 What did Mill see as the precondition of democracy?
38 Why did Locke and other classical liberals want the suffrage to be restricted to property owners?

Modern liberalism

Modern liberalism emerged in the late nineteenth century and has remained the most powerful form of liberalism in Europe and the USA. Its key thinkers include **T.H. Green**, **Betty Friedan** and **John Rawls**, but it is also linked to British prime ministers such as David Lloyd George (1863–1945), US presidents like F.D. Roosevelt (1882–1945), economists like John Maynard Keynes and vital government inquiries like the Beveridge Report of 1942 (see Box 1.3). Modern liberalism remains central to the thinking of parties like the Democrats in the USA, the Liberal Democrats in the UK and the 'Alliance of Liberals and Democrats for Europe' in the European Parliament (see Boxes 1.4–1.6).

Modern liberalism was a response to the social and economic changes that had occurred since the era of **John Locke**, especially those arising from the Industrial Revolution of the eighteenth and nineteenth centuries. These changes made many aspects of classical liberalism – like the notion of 'autonomous' individuals seeking self-fulfilment in rural, 'atomised' societies – seem quaint, if not absurd. With the mass of individuals now dependent on heavy industry for work, and on urban landlords for homes, most individuals were now at the mercy of forces beyond their control. As such, it was harder to sustain **Locke**'s claim that, to be 'free', individuals merely required laissez-faire governments and a constitution that enshrined natural rights.

In response to this threat, philosophers such as **T.H. Green** made a crucial acknowledgement: that having conquered the original enemies of liberty – monarchical absolutism and arbitrary power – liberals now faced new enemies that were *social* and *economic*. This, in turn, led **Green** and others to reappraise the philosophical basis of 'liberty' and the scope of a liberal state.

Box 1.3: Modern liberalism in the twentieth century

- *Liberal government 1906–10*: In the UK, it was a Liberal government, led by Herbert Asquith (1852–1928) and his chancellor David Lloyd George, that provided one of the earliest instances of modern liberalism in action. The most important illustration of this was the 'People's Budget' of 1908, which introduced a state pension, designed to liberate people from the financial problems of old age and funded by increased taxation of property owners.
- *Keynesian economics*: In his key work, *The General Theory of Employment, Interest, and Money* (1936), John Maynard Keynes argued that the state must constantly 'steer' the economy towards maximum employment. Keynes' brand of *dirigisme*, or state-directed capitalism, influenced a series of western governments in the mid-twentieth century, shaping President F.D. Roosevelt's New Deal in the USA in the 1930s and the economic strategy of UK governments between 1945 and 1979.

- *Beveridge Report*: William Beveridge (1879–1963) was a liberal social scientist whose 1942 report, 'Social Insurance and Allied Services', provided the bedrock of Britain's post-war 'welfare state'. Beveridge predicted that individuals in the post-war world would face 'five giants' threatening their freedom: poverty, unemployment, poor education, poor housing and poor health care. In a powerful statement of modern liberal thinking, Beveridge argued these threats could only be overcome by a 'welfare state' that would 'enable' individuals 'from cradle to grave'.

Key thinker 4

Thomas Hill Green (1836–82)

- Along with a number of other late Victorian philosophers (such as L.T. Hobhouse), T.H. Green may be described as one of the founding fathers of modern liberalism and is closely linked to a revised concept of freedom known as 'positive liberty' – one which challenged the 'negative' version associated with **Mill**.
- Green rejected the classical liberal view that society was composed of egotistical individuals driven only by self-interest, claiming that human beings were also motivated by a desire to promote the common good.
- Green therefore argued that personal happiness derived not just from self-indulgence or self-gratification, but from attending to the happiness of others.
- Green argued that the state should promote the widest possible degree of choice and opportunity for everyone and was confident this view would be shared by most of those living in a liberal society.
- Although neo-liberals, such as Friedrich von Hayek, claimed that Green's views amounted to socialism, Green argued that the state should still prioritise individual liberty and believed individuals should still be encouraged to pursue self-interest. He merely maintained that liberty and happiness had a social dimension, and that individuals were not oblivious to the happiness of others.
- Green's views would later provide a philosophical justification for Liberal politicians like David Lloyd George (UK prime minister, 1916–22) who wished to expand and enlarge the state's responsibilities.

Knowledge check

39 Summarise how T.H. Green's version of liberty differed from that of classical liberals.

40 How did Green's version of liberty echo that of other modern liberals?

41 When was the Beveridge Report and how did it seek to advance individual freedom?

Positive liberty

Taking issue with **Mill**'s concept of 'negative' liberty, **Green** argued that freedom should not be seen merely as the absence of restraint and 'freedom from' oppressive rulers. Instead, it should be regarded as something more altruistic – a concept that involved individuals 'enabling' other individuals, thus allowing them the freedom to pursue individual fulfilment.

According to **Green**, this approach was not to be confused with the state-led collectivism of socialists such as **Beatrice Webb**, or the aristocratic paternalism of conservatives like **Edmund Burke** (see Chapters 2 and 3). Instead, it was about empowering individuals to help themselves, thereby enabling them to control their lives in a way that would have been

John Rawls

impossible had they been left alone. This concept eventually became known as 'positive liberty' and had profound effects upon how modern liberals regard the state.

The enabling state

Whereas classical liberalism endorsed negative liberty, and therefore minimal government, modern liberals demand a much larger state to facilitate positive liberty. In other words, they believe that only *more* government will 'enable' individuals to overcome socioeconomic threats to freedom.

For this reason, modern liberals such as **John Rawls** argue that individual liberty generally requires more laws, more state spending and more taxation. As a result, this brand of liberalism has become strongly linked to the UK's post-war welfare state and various other 'big government' initiatives (such as the 1930s 'New Deal' in the USA – see Box 1.3).

Having backed an **enabling state**, modern liberals faced criticism from so-called neo-liberals, who sought to rescue the classical liberal principle of minimal government. According to Friedrich von Hayek, for example, positive liberty was merely 'socialism in disguise' and therefore 'the road to serfdom' (or long-term dependence on others), creating a situation where liberty and enterprise were stifled by state welfare. **Rawls** naturally resisted such a suggestion, arguing that only an enlarged state could create the equality of opportunity necessary for individual freedom.

Rawls also claimed that, although an enabling state would require some people to sacrifice more in the form of taxation, they could still be rationally persuaded that this was consistent with their self-interest (see Key Thinker 5). As a result, **Rawls** argued that the enabling state was compatible with the perennial liberal principle of government by consent.

John Rawls (1921–2002)

An American philosopher, Rawls is thought to be the most important exponent of modern liberalism in the twentieth century. His major work, *A Theory of Justice* (1971), remains a key reference for students of liberal thinking and has two principal objectives:

- First, to restate the idea that 'foundational equality' meant not just formal equality under the law and constitution but also greater social and economic equality. This was necessary, Rawls argued, to ensure a just society, where all lives could be fulfilled. Yet this could only be provided, Rawls stated, by a significant redistribution of wealth via an 'enabling' state, extensive public spending and progressive taxation.
- Secondly, Rawls set out to show that such a redistribution of wealth was consistent with liberal principles. To do this, he set up a philosophical experiment with two key conditions:
  - In the first condition, Rawls envisaged individuals constructing, from scratch, a society they felt would be superior to their current one. Rawls called this exercise 'the original position'.
  - The second condition was one Rawls termed the 'veil of ignorance', whereby individuals would not know the sort of people they themselves might be in this new society. They might, for example, be white or from an ethnic minority; rich or poor; exceptional or average.
- Rawls argued that, when faced with such conditions, rational human beings would choose a society where the poorest members fared significantly better than in present society. From a liberal angle, Rawls argued that the key point here was that this 'fairer' society, where inequalities were reduced via higher state spending and taxation, was one which most individuals would endorse. It was therefore consistent with liberalism's historic stress on government by consent.
- Rawls denied this was simply a fresh justification for socialism and egalitarianism. He noted that, while most individuals would choose to improve the lot of the poorest, they would still want a society where the talented and enterprising were rewarded. As a result, Rawls argued that while the conditions of the poor should be improved by the state, the gap between poorest and richest would not necessarily be narrowed – thus ensuring that this brand of liberalism remained distinct from socialism.

Knowledge check

46 Summarise how Rawls reconciled liberal principles to the growth of state intervention.

Box 1.4: The 'enabling state' in action – President Biden's health-care reforms

Introduced by a presidential executive order of January 2021, Joe Biden's reforms to US health care built upon President Obama's Affordable Care Act 2010 ('Obamacare'). They were an example of modern liberalism, for several reasons:

- They involved an 'enabling state', extending the reach and influence of governments in US society.
- They stemmed from a belief that individual liberty can be obstructed by economic factors, such as the inability to afford adequate health care.
- They involved greater public spending and potentially more taxation.

Biden's reforms involved the federal government:

- guaranteeing health-care provision for anyone unable to meet increased premiums levied by private health-care providers.
- empowering voters to purchase alternative, state-sponsored health care (Medicare).
- capping any premium increases by health-care providers.
- lowering the age of eligibility for state-sponsored health care (Medicare).

Enabling health care: President Joe Biden, 2021

Box 1.5: 'Tolerance' in action – the Liberal Democrat manifesto, 2019

The Liberal Democrat manifesto for the 2019 general election called for 'a more tolerant Britain' and promised to 'wage war on discrimination'. Its specific proposals included:

- funding for protective security measures at venues where minority communities gather.
- reform of the Gender Recognition Act 2018, removing the requirement for medical reports on individuals who 're-assign'.
- compulsory gender-neutral school uniform for state schools.
- greater wheelchair access in public transport stations.
- new property and inheritance rights for co-habiting couples who have not married or entered civil partnerships.

Keynesian capitalism

Reflecting its rejection of negative liberty and minimal government, modern liberalism is less prepared to endorse laissez-faire capitalism and more willing to back *dirigiste* capitalism, involving greater state intervention in a market economy. Of crucial influence here was the economist John Maynard Keynes, who argued that minimal state intervention led periodically to mass unemployment, a resulting loss of freedom for millions of individuals, and the grave prospect of fascism and communism. Keynes therefore argued that self-fulfilment and liberty were seriously endangered by joblessness and resulting poverty.

As a liberal, Keynes was naturally keen to protect capitalism. But as a *modern* liberal he believed that the best way to do this was through state 'management' of capitalism, thereby ensuring economic stability and a workforce 'enabled' to be 'free' by full employment (see Box 1.3).

For more recent modern liberal thinkers, such as **John Rawls**, Keynesian economics was crucial. The expansion of state spending that **Rawls** and others prescribed, to overcome the 'five giants' cited by the Beveridge Report (see Box 1.3), needed to be financed by taxation. **Rawls** believed that a sufficient tax yield could only be assured by the steady economic growth promised by Keynesianism, in contrast to the 'boom and bust' cycles associated with laissez-faire capitalism. However, as shown by the UK economy in the 1970s, **Rawls** and others were naïve to assume that Keynesianism would prevent the return of recession.

Liberal democracy

As we saw earlier, classical liberals were wary of democracy, fearing that it endangered natural rights and tolerance. However, once modern liberals began championing the extension of the state, the extension of democracy became harder to resist. As **T.H. Green** admitted, 'if the state is to do more for its people, then the state must do more to secure their consent'. In other words, positive liberty and an enabling state required the embrace of universal adult suffrage.

It was a modern liberal prime minister (David Lloyd George) who oversaw the start of enfranchisement for women in 1918. More recently, Liberal parties in the UK have championed a reduced voting age, first to 18 and now to 16, while calling for the 'democratisation' of Parliament (via an elective House of Lords) and elected devolved government in the nations of the UK.

Knowledge check

47 How is Keynesian economics meant to promote individual freedom?

48 Which economic problems were Keynesianism economics supposed to cure?

Knowledge check

49 Why did increased state intervention make liberals more sympathetic to democracy?

50 How have recent liberal politicians championed greater democracy?

51 How have recent liberal politicians tried to restrain the possible effects of democracy?

Yet modern liberalism's support for democracy is not unreserved. It has shown little interest, for example, in direct democracy and referendums. It has even been willing to limit representative democracy through its backing of the UK Human Rights Act (which transferred powers from elective representatives to unelected judges) and its firm support for the European Union (despite the undemocratic nature of key EU institutions, such as the European Commission). Like classical liberals, modern liberals seem inclined to excuse democratic shortcomings in return for ensuring 'liberal' outcomes, such as the EU's guarantee of free movement for its individual citizens. Modern liberals were also inclined to see the Brexit referendum as a shocking example of **Mill**'s 'tyranny of the majority' and a vindication of his view that big decisions are best left to liberal-minded parliaments.

Box 1.6: Liberal democracy in action – mission statement of the 'Alliance of Liberals and Democrats for Europe' (ALDE), 2021

Founded in 2004, ALDE is a group that brings together liberal-minded politicians in the EU and European Parliament. It aims to promote values that are 'both liberal and democratic', and calls upon the EU to:

- develop in as decentralised a way as possible
- develop stronger democratic links to EU citizens
- develop higher standards of accountability and transparency in its dealings with EU citizens
- respect and promote personal freedom and self-fulfilment for all EU citizens.
- promote the protection of minorities, regardless of ethnic background, gender, sexual orientation, faith or age.

European liberalism: ALDE politicians, 2021

Debate 2

Has modern liberalism abandoned the principles of classical liberalism?

Yes

- Classical liberalism defined liberty as individuals being left alone (negative freedom). Modern liberals think individuals are not free unless they are actively 'enabled' via interference from others (positive freedom).
- Classical liberalism championed a minimal state. Modern liberals champion an enlarged state.
- Classical liberalism often saw taxation as 'theft' and sought to restrict it. Modern liberals see increased taxation as the means to increased public spending.
- Classical liberalism favoured laissez-faire capitalism from which the state is detached. Modern liberals favour Keynesian capitalism, where the state seeks to 'manage' market forces.
- Classical liberalism had an ambivalent view of democracy, prioritising the interests of property owners. Modern liberalism has championed representative democracy.

No

- Both classical and modern liberalism have an optimistic view of human potential.
- Both classical and modern liberalism believe in rationalism and the tolerance of minorities.
- Both classical and modern liberalism see individualism as the 'end goal' of politics and society.
- Both classical and modern liberalism believe in capitalism and criticise state ownership.
- Both classical and modern liberalism believe in a constitutional ('limited') state and 'government by consent'.

Evaluation check: To what extent are classical and modern liberalism distinct ideologies?

Social liberalism

Key term

Social liberalism
Reflecting the work of **Betty Friedan**, this updates liberalism's historic belief in tolerance. It calls for legislation which illegalises discrimination against individuals on grounds of race, gender, sexual orientation, disability and gender identification.

Modern liberalism is also defined by efforts to update the classical liberal stress on tolerance — especially tolerance of minorities. This approach has become widely known as **social liberalism**.

From the mid-twentieth century onwards, modern liberalism became strongly linked with calls for greater racial and sexual toleration. Key thinkers such as **Betty Friedan** protested that too many individuals in modern society were denied equality of opportunity on account of 'essentialist' factors like ethnicity, gender and sexual orientation. Given their acceptance of positive liberty and an enabling state, modern liberals like **Friedan** argued that solving such problems required fresh legislation and various forms of 'affirmative action' — that is, discrimination favouring groups that had, historically, been discriminated against (often referred to as 'positive discrimination'). From the

Betty Friedan

1960s onwards, modern liberalism thus became associated with both affirmative action and other initiatives, such as:

- the USA's Equal Employment Opportunity Commission, established in 1964, which required 'affirmative action' or 'positive discrimination' in respect of hiring employees from racial minorities
- the US Supreme Court's *Roe* v *Wade* decision of 1973, protecting a woman's right to abortion
- the UK's Race Relations Acts of 1965, 1968 and 1976, banning various forms of racial discrimination
- the UK's Marriage Act 2013, legalising same-sex marriages.

As **Friedan** explained, such 'corrective' legislation was perfectly consistent with the original aim of the liberal state: namely, the promotion of tolerance and equal opportunity. However, social liberalism has most recently been linked to individuals affected by 'gender dysphoria', or a mismatch between someone's biological sex and their gender identity. Indeed, many regard the campaigns for transgender rights as the latest liberal challenge for those championing tolerance. As transgender activist Shon Faye wrote, 'We are symbols of hope for non-trans people too, who see in us the possibility of living more fully and freely'. However, among modern liberals this remains a polarising debate, with many liberal feminists seeing transgenderism as a threat to the individual rights of cisgender women.

Knowledge check

52 What new threats to individualism were identified by Betty Friedan?
53 Explain why Friedan's feminist views were consistent with liberalism in general and modern liberalism specifically.

Key thinker 6

Betty Friedan (1921–2006)

Betty Friedan is linked mainly to the development of feminist ideology, through her acclaimed work *The Feminine Mystique* (1963). Yet her ideas also broadened liberal interest in equality of opportunity.

- As with all liberals, a concern for individualism lay at the heart of Friedan's philosophy. She insisted that all individuals should seek self-determination and the realisation of their potential. Yet, like **Mary Wollstonecraft** two centuries earlier, Friedan identified gender as a serious hindrance to women.
- Friedan argued that it was illiberal attitudes in society, rather than human nature, that condemned most women to underachievement. She maintained that these

attitudes were nurtured and transmitted via society's various 'cultural channels', such as schools, organised religion, the media and mainstream literature, theatre and cinema. These channels of 'cultural conditioning' left many women convinced that their lot in life was determined by 'iron laws' rather than their own rationality and enterprise. Friedan sought to challenge this 'irrational' assumption.

- Friedan's reputation as a liberal as well as a feminist thinker was underlined by the fact that she disdained violence or illegality as a means of pursuing change, arguing that significant progress was possible via the procedures of a liberal state. She thus acknowledged her country's Lockean constitution and believed in its capacity to improve individual lives. Consequently, she rejected the Marxist-feminist argument that the state was dominated by 'patriarchal' corporations. Instead, Friedan favoured liberal constitutionalism.

Debate 3

Do liberals have a consistent view of the state?

Yes

- Liberals consistently believe in a constitutional state, drawn up after rational discussion.
- Liberals consistently believe in 'government by consent' and the notion that the state is a 'contract' between government and governed.
- Liberals consistently believe in 'limited government', with politicians restrained by a constitution.
- Liberals consistently reject any state where power is concentrated.

No

- The liberal state has not consistently upheld foundational equality: it was slow to adopt the principles of democracy, sexual equality and universal adult suffrage.
- The liberal state has not consistently upheld 'government by consent': it allows the wishes of a majority to be defied sometimes via assorted 'checks and balances'.
- The liberal state is not consistently minimal in scope: modern liberals advocate a major extension of state intervention in the name of 'positive liberty'.

Evaluation check: To what extent are liberals wary of the state?

Conclusion: liberalism today

Knowledge check

54 What is meant by 'affirmative action' or 'positive discrimination'?
55 How does the campaign for transgender rights relate to the liberal belief in individualism?

During the late twentieth and early twenty-first centuries, liberals had several reasons to be cheerful. The collapse of Soviet communism in 1989, the emergence of new capitalist states in eastern Europe and the phenomenon of 'globalisation' all strengthened the assumption that capitalism and liberal democracy were somehow 'normal' and irresistible.

Meanwhile, in established liberal democracies, such as the UK and the USA, liberal values seemed reinforced by new trends in politics and society. Parties such as New Labour embraced economic liberalism (as shown by its defence of privatisation); Conservative leaders such as David Cameron embraced social liberalism (as shown by his government's legalisation of same-sex marriage); and individualism was advanced further by the spread of mobile phones and personal computers, and the growing ease with which citizens could express themselves.

Yet there were also developments which seriously challenged liberal assumptions. On 11 September 2001, the atrocities witnessed in the USA marked a new and dramatic stage in Islamist terrorism – an uncompromising, quasi-theocratic phenomenon, and a startling challenge to basic liberal values like rational debate and human rights. Following the collapse of the Soviet Union, Professor Francis Fukuyama had claimed that liberalism marked 'the end of history'. Yet, within a decade, it seemed more credible to argue that the new century would see what Professor Samuel Huntington called 'a clash of civilisations,' between western states upholding liberal norms and certain non-western states that favoured rule by dogmatic religious principles.

Post 9/11, liberal democracies were thus obliged to respond to the new and alarming threats posed by terrorism – for example, through increased state security, heightened state surveillance of suspected individuals and fresh state restrictions on immigration. Such responses seemed to further threaten individualism, while stoking illiberal sentiments such as xenophobia and suspicion of minority religions.

There were other reasons why liberalism faced fresh scrutiny in the twenty-first century. The financial crash of 2008, and the economic crises affecting Eurozone countries like Greece after 2013, revived the socialist critique of economic liberalism. The emergence of Jeremy Corbyn as the UK's Leader of the Opposition in 2015, and the popularity of US politicians such as Bernie Sanders and Alexandria Ocasio-Cortez, all indicated that 'consent' for capitalism was not so widespread.

On the other hand, concern for minority rights remains a crucial aspect of liberalism and, in recent years, has played a prominent part in political discussion. Following the shocking murder of George Floyd in 2020, the issue of justice and freedom for racial minorities resurfaced powerfully in the USA with the Black Lives Matter campaign – an issue which quickly spread to the UK. Likewise, the campaign for transgender rights, and debate concerning the reform of the Gender Recognition Act, attracted increased attention in UK politics and was a source of intense debate at the 2021 Labour Party conference.

Yet this may simply have created fresh problems for liberalism by exposing 'intersectional' clashes between different groups of 'oppressed' individuals. Louder support for transgender rights, for example, has led to criticism from some feminists (and vice versa), while campaigns for gay rights arguably 'harm' the sensibilities of those attached to certain minority-religion communities. It is still unclear if these 'post-modern' disputes can be resolved in a way that ensures tolerance for all.

In recent years, liberalism's critics have also linked modern liberal causes to a 'tyranny of the minority'. Among such critics, there has been a tendency to see 'political correctness' and 'cancel culture' as modern examples of liberalism's historic readiness to constrain illiberal opinion – exemplified by **Mill's**

Black Lives Matter march, January 2022

argument that votes should only be granted to the 'enlightened'. Yet, in an era of growing distrust towards mainstream politicians and authority figures generally, the liberal notion of 'enlightening' public opinion seems hard to sustain. Brexit and other manifestations of political 'populism' (such as the presidency of Donald Trump) clearly highlight the difficulty of ensuring a liberal consensus.

For liberals, the problem was compounded from early 2020 by the onset of the Covid-19 pandemic. In liberal democracies across the world, states responded with a huge extension of their powers and a corresponding reduction of basic individual liberties and, perhaps, natural rights – such as the right of people to leave their home and meet freely with others. Equally as striking, though, was the high level of public support for such restrictions. The conclusion many drew was that people were more inclined to give their 'consent' to a state that prioritised their safety and security than one that prioritised liberty and individualism. Climate change was another grave challenge to liberal assumptions: averting environmental catastrophe is likely to require co-ordinated, collective efforts that require significant restrictions on individual consumption, individual travel and individual choices generally.

Contemporary problems like terrorism, pandemics and climate change might prompt us to revisit the very roots of liberalism. **John Locke**'s political philosophy presupposed a 'state of nature' marked by peace, reason, liberty and ample resources. However, in a world that appears scarred by war, scarcity and tension, **Locke**'s analysis seems increasingly fanciful. Whether this diminishes the political and electoral appeal of liberalism remains to be seen.

Summary: key themes and key thinkers

	Human nature	The state	Society	The economy
John Locke	Human beings are rational, guided by the pursuit of self-interest, but mindful of others' concerns.	The state must be representative, based on the consent of the governed.	Society predates the state: there were 'natural' societies with natural laws and natural rights.	State policy should respect the 'natural right' to private property and arbitrate effectively between individuals competing for trade and resources.
Mary Wollstonecraft	Rationalism defines both genders: intellectually, men and women are not very different.	The monarchical state should be replaced by a republic which enshrines women's rights.	Existing society 'infantilises' women and thus stifles female individualism.	A free-market economy would be energised by the enterprise of liberated women.

	Human nature	The state	Society	The economy
John Stuart Mill	Though rational, human nature is not fixed: it is for ever progressing to a higher level.	The state should proceed cautiously towards representative democracy, mindful of minority rights.	The best society is one where 'individuality' co-exists with tolerance and self-betterment.	Laissez-faire capitalism is vital to progress, individual enterprise and individual initiative.
John Rawls	Mankind is selfish yet empathetic, valuing both individual liberty and the plight of others.	The state should enable less fortunate individuals to advance, via public spending and public services.	The society most individuals would choose is one which allows unequal outcomes, but where the condition of the poorest improves.	Free-market capitalism should be tempered by the state's obligation to advance its poorest citizens.
Thomas Hill Green	Human beings are guided mainly by reason, but their reason is increasingly affected by social and economic circumstances.	The state should actively eliminate social and economic obstacles to individual liberty.	Society was fundamentally altered by industrialisation, which in turn requires a reappraisal of 'freedom'.	A free market economy is the most conducive to individualism, but it can threaten equality of opportunity.
Betty Friedan	Human nature has evolved in a way that discourages self-advancement among women.	The state should legislate to prevent continued discrimination against women.	Society remains chauvinistic towards women, though women are complicit in their repression.	Free-market capitalism could be an ally of female emancipation, if allied to legislation precluding sexual discrimination.

Tensions within liberalism

- **Human nature:** all liberals believe that individuals are generally rational, intelligent, keen to advance their individual happiness and respectful of other individuals' wish to do likewise. However, early classical liberals such as **John Locke** believe that individuals are innately blessed with such qualities, while **John Stuart Mill** and modern liberals like **John Rawls** tend to think such qualities are *potential* features of human nature, to be developed by enlightened liberal authorities.

- **The state:** all liberals believe the state should function according to prearranged rules and procedures, leaving power fragmented and authority subject to the consent of the governed. However, liberals vary on the extent of state activity. Classical liberals such as **Mill**, in accordance with 'negative' liberty, believe state intervention should be minimal and individuals left unchecked (unless they hamper the freedom of others). Modern liberals such as **Betty Friedan**, in accordance with 'positive' liberty, believe state intervention should be more extensive, thus 'enabling' us to reach our potential. Liberals also disagree over how democratic the state should be. Modern liberals like **Rawls** are satisfied that representative democracy enhances constitutional government, whereas classical liberals like **Locke** saw universal suffrage as a threat to property rights.

- **Society:** all liberals believe society predates the state and that certain 'rights' are 'natural'. However, classical liberals like **Locke** see society as a collection of potentially autonomous individuals, seeking various forms of self-determination, while modern liberals such as **Rawls** think industrialised societies leave individuals less autonomous and therefore in need of greater state support.
- **The economy:** following **Locke**'s assertion that property is a 'natural right', all liberals believe the economy should be based on private enterprise. However, while classical liberals support Adam Smith's laissez-faire capitalism (involving minimal state intervention), modern liberals like **Rawls** have more sympathy for Keynesian capitalism (involving extensive state 'management' of market forces).

Further reading

Politics Review articles

Egan, M. (2020) 'Liberalism and freedom', *Politics Review*, vol. 30, no. 1.
Hardy, J. (2019) 'Liberalism and natural rights', *Politics Review*, vol. 29, no. 1.
Tuck, D., and Egan, M. (2021) 'Do liberals believe in state intervention?', *Politics Review*, vol. 30, no. 4.

Books

Faye, S. (2021) *The Transgender Issue: An Argument for Justice*, Allen Lane.
Freeden, M. (2015) *Liberalism: A Very Short Introduction*, Oxford University Press.

Exam-style questions

AQA

Short-answer questions

1 Explain and analyse three reasons why liberalism takes a positive view of human nature. (9 marks)

2 Explain and analyse three ways in which liberalism promotes individual liberty. (9 marks)

Extract question

3 Read the extracts below and answer the question that follows.

Extract 1

The sole end for which mankind is warranted, individually or collectively, in interfering with the liberty of action of any of their number is self-protection. The only purpose for which power can be rightfully exercised over a member of a civilized society, against his will, is to prevent harm to others. His own good, either physical or moral, is not a sufficient warrant. He cannot rightfully be compelled to do or forbear because it will be 'better' for him to do so, or because it will make him happier, or because in the opinion of others it would be wise or even right.

John Stuart Mill, *On Liberty* (1859)

Extract 2

To my mind, there are three things above all that every citizen of this country needs as conditions of a happy and useful life ... He needs freedom from want and fear of want, freedom from idleness and fear of idleness from unemployment, freedom from war and fear of war.

William Beveridge, *Why I Am a Liberal* (1945)

Analyse, evaluate and compare the arguments being made in the above extracts as to the significance of liberty within liberalism. In your answer, you should refer to the thinkers you have studied. (25 marks)

Edexcel

Essay questions

4 To what extent do modern and classical liberals agree over the nature of the state? You must use appropriate thinkers you have studied to support your answer and consider differing views in a balanced way. (24 marks)

5 To what extent does liberalism have a consistent view of liberty? You must use appropriate thinkers you have studied to support your answer and consider differing views in a balanced way. (24 marks)

6 To what extent are liberalism and democracy in conflict? You must use appropriate thinkers you have studied to support your answer and consider differing views in a balanced way. (24 marks)

Chapter 2

Socialism

Learning outcomes

This chapter will enable students to:

- understand the core values of socialism
- understand how socialism has evolved since the nineteenth century
- understand the various strands of socialism
- understand the continuing relevance of socialism today.

Key thinkers

This chapter will frequently reference the key socialist thinkers cited in A-level exam specifications:

- Karl Marx (1818–83)
- Friedrich Engels (1820–95)
- Rosa Luxemburg (1871–1919)
- Beatrice Webb (1858–1943)
- Anthony Crosland (1918–77)
- Anthony Giddens (1938–).

Introduction: a controversial ideology

Like liberalism, socialism is a diverse ideology, embracing followers with a range of competing views. Indeed, even the most basic knowledge of political history shows that socialism attracts a huge variety of advocates: **Karl Marx**, Clement Attlee, Joseph Stalin, Harold Wilson, Mao Zedong, Gordon Brown, Fidel Castro, Ed Miliband, Leon Trotsky, Keir Starmer… these are just some of the people who, at various points, have described themselves as 'socialist'. The issue of what, if anything, unites such a mixed bunch will be an important focus of this chapter.

With such diverse advocates, it is unsurprising that socialism has had such diverse outcomes. In some places, it has been tied to what **Beatrice Webb** (Key thinker 3) termed 'the finest aspects of the human condition … fraternity, comradeship, selflessness and a concern for the underdog'. Yet in other places, such as Russia, China and Cambodia, 'socialist' reform has led to oppression, brutality and genocide – often in the name of **Karl Marx** (Key thinker 1), arguably the most important socialist thinker of all.

Of course, most political ideologies have internal tensions and varied interpretations. Yet those of socialism seem especially stark. Consequently, it is important to understand the core principles of socialism and how they have been applied in such markedly different ways.

The origins of socialism

Like liberalism, socialism is an ideology that grew out of the Enlightenment. Indeed, socialism and liberalism have much in common. For example:

- Both take an optimistic view of human nature.
- Both support 'reason' over faith and superstition.
- Both endorse 'progressive' politics and a challenge to the status quo.
- Both wish to promote 'liberty'.
- Both uphold the idea of 'foundational equality' – that men and women are born equal and deserve equal opportunities in life.

Despite these overlaps, the issue of *private property* is a serious difference between liberals and many socialists, and helps to explain the emergence of socialism as a distinctive ideology. As explained in Chapter 1, support for private property is crucial for key liberal thinkers – indeed, they consider it a 'natural right'. Yet, as early as the eighteenth century, some Enlightenment thinkers were unsure if private property could be reconciled to an improved society. **Jean-Jacques Rousseau** (1712–78), for example, suggested that 'many crimes, wars and murders … many horrors

Knowledge check

1 When and what was the Industrial Revolution?

Key terms

Capitalism Sometimes referred to as economic liberalism, capitalism is an economic system based on private property, private enterprise and competition between individuals and private organisations. Most socialists are concerned about its tendency to produce unequal outcomes.

Common ownership This represents an alternative to both private property and a capitalist economy, and is seen by many socialists as essential to equality and fraternity. It is synonymous with state ownership and public ownership.

and misfortunes arise from disputes concerning private property', and that its abolition should be seriously considered.

However, it was with the onset of the Industrial Revolution, mainly in Germany and Britain during the 18th and 19th centuries, that criticism of private property became more widespread, which in turn led to wider use of the term 'socialism'. Early socialists, particularly 'utopian socialists' such as Robert Owen (1771–1858), offered both a vision of a perfect society and a practical response to the problems supposedly besetting capitalism and industry; one that involved common ownership and 'co-operative' communities. However, as the pace of industrialisation quickened, and as more people came to live and work in towns centred on mines, mills and factories, socialist ideas became more urgent and sophisticated. For many radicals and progressives, notably **Karl Marx** and **Friedrich Engels** (Key Thinkers 1), liberalism was proving a grossly inadequate response to the changes brought about by capitalism. Indeed, given its staunch support for private property and laissez-faire capitalism, classical liberalism was thought to be partly the *cause* of such problems.

As a result, early socialists argued for a new approach that would link the effects of industrialisation to the principles of the Enlightenment, while adopting a more critical view of capitalism and private property. In this respect, socialists were not entirely dissimilar to 'modern liberals' like **T.H. Green** (see Chapter 1). However, **Green**'s ideas – especially in relation to capitalism – were to prove much less radical than the 'evolutionary' socialism of his contemporary, **Beatrice Webb**, and looked extremely tame alongside the revolutionary socialism of **Marx**, **Engels** and **Rosa Luxemburg** (Key thinkers 1 and 2).

The core ideas of socialism

View of human nature

Optimistic

As indicated earlier, socialism grew out of the Enlightenment and therefore takes an optimistic view of human nature and the human condition. Likewise, socialists dismiss any notion that human beings should meekly accept their fate or be fearful of the future. Instead, socialists are confident that human beings are destined for a vastly improved world, both individually and generally. As **Beatrice Webb** noted in 1890:

> There is no excuse for depressive inaction. There is no cause for listless despondency. A better tomorrow is conceivable, achievable and probable.

Key terms

Utopian socialism Linked to philanthropists like Robert Owen, this refers to the earliest form of socialism, one based on a vision of the perfect human existence. For **Karl Marx**, however, its 'utopian' character denoted the absence of any clear method for bringing 'socialism' to fruition.

Fraternity and co-operation These terms represent socialism's belief that the relationship between human beings should be generous and harmonious, and that we should regard our fellow human beings as friends rather than rivals.

Knowledge check

2 What do you understand by the term 'public spending'?

3 Why do socialists view human nature favourably?

As previously indicated, some of the earliest socialists were depicted as utopian socialists, whose 'model' communities reflected their own vision of an ideal society. Although later socialists like **Karl Marx** would sneer at such 'utopianism', **Marx** himself predicted that communism would be a secular paradise, where serious problems were banished, and where human beings were wise, virtuous and happy.

Fraternal

Although liberalism and socialism take a positive view of human nature, they have different reasons for doing so. Whereas liberals see human nature as egotistical and driven by respectful self-interest, socialists see it as fraternal (brotherly) and comradely, naturally inclined towards generosity and concern for others.

Similarly, whereas liberals see humans as naturally competitive, socialists think we are naturally co-operative and collaborative, regarding each other as quasi-siblings rather than fierce rivals. As **Rosa Luxemburg** argued, in her critique of capitalism:

> Our instinct is not to win but to share … and should we be fortunate enough to be on the winning side, our ultimate instinct is to share the fruits of victory with others.

Although he did not share **Luxemburg**'s contempt for capitalism, later socialists like **Anthony Giddens** (Key thinker 5) would make a similar point about our 'co-operative' instincts. According to **Giddens**, even high earners in a capitalist economy could be rationally persuaded that their own success should finance greater help for the less fortunate, rather than just greater rewards for themselves – for example, by paying more in taxation to the state, so that the state could then afford greater public spending on areas (such as welfare payments) that benefit the less fortunate.

Rational

Like liberals, socialists believe human beings are naturally logical and rational. However, on account of our being supposedly fraternal, socialists believe we can act both reasonably *and* collaboratively, thus making 'sensible' decisions more likely.

For both **Beatrice Webb** and later socialist thinkers like **Anthony Crosland** (Key thinker 4), the crucial advantage enjoyed by human beings was their capacity to collectively *plan* progress in a methodical manner. For **Webb**, this pointed to 'the great flaw' in classical liberalism: namely, its laissez-faire (or leave-alone) approach to economic and social activity. As **Webb** asserted, liberals 'generally *hope* for a bright future, instead

Knowledge check

4 With reference to your study of liberalism, what is meant by a 'laissez-faire' approach to politics and economics?

of resolving to *plan* one'. **Webb** accordingly believed that an 'enlightened' state bureaucracy – driven by highly educated people with socialist leanings – could 'gradually but inevitably' guide us to an ever-improving life.

Communal

Given their belief that human nature is fraternal, it is unsurprising that socialists also think it communal. Socialists therefore argue that we naturally seek to be part of a community – such as a club, school or trade union – rather than relentlessly seeking 'autonomy' and individual independence. As **Beatrice Webb** insisted, 'we are not lone wolves … we forever seek out the company of the pack'. This relates to another key term in the socialist vocabulary – that of *solidarity*, or the notion of 'standing together' with those of similar interests. For **Rosa Luxemburg**, this created a sense of virtue and well-being and was also an engine of historic social change; the catalyst that would produce a 'spontaneous' revolution and a new socialist order.

The notion that we are naturally communal, rather than individualistic, is powerfully echoed by the predictions of **Karl Marx**, who argued that the final stage in human development – communism – involved voluntary communities, where everyone would be accommodated according to their 'needs' rather than their individual 'abilities'. As **Marx** indicated, such communities would frequently involve individuals relegating their own selfish interests so as serve the more urgent interests of others. **Marx** insisted, however, that such selflessness would not be regarded as a sacrifice. Once capitalism was destroyed, **Marx** argued, individuals would eventually realise that selfishness was a symptom of 'false consciousness' and that service to a community was the true source of individual pleasure.

Malleable

Karl Marx's claim that human nature would be gradually 'restored' (following the fall of capitalism) touches upon the final aspect of socialism's attitude to human nature: namely, its 'plasticity'. Unlike liberalism, socialism sees human nature as malleable (changeable), rather than permanently fixed at birth. This has enabled certain socialist thinkers to excuse many of humanity's current defects. As **Marx** and **Engels** claimed in their *Communist Manifesto*, human nature had been 'contaminated' by forces beyond the control of most individuals (see View of Society).

More recently, there were faint echoes of this idea in **Anthony Giddens**' analysis of crime and juvenile delinquency. For **Giddens**, and his political protégé Tony Blair, governments

Knowledge check

5 Why do socialists reject the notion that human beings are individualistic?

Human nature

Like liberalism, and unlike conservatism, socialism takes a positive, upbeat view of human nature. However, the reasons for doing so differ from liberalism. Whereas liberals believe human beings have a capacity for dynamic self-determination and self-reliance, socialists emphasise our desire for co-operation and solidarity with others.

6 What do socialists mean when they describe human nature as 'plastic'?

7 Why might socialists argue that human beings are 'social animals'?

8 What do socialists mean by 'collectivism'?

should be not just 'tough on crime' but 'tough on the causes of crime', implying that crime was not simply attributable to wicked individuals (an idea **Giddens** developed in his influential book, *Beyond Left and Right*). As human nature is malleable, socialists believe it is thus repairable – even *perfectible* – through bold socialist reform. This analysis, however, means socialists must answer two key questions: *what* 'contaminates' human nature, and *how* can human nature be improved? This leads on to socialism's view of society.

View of society

Existential

For socialists, the nature of society is crucial: without a proper appreciation of society, they argue, any understanding of human nature is impossible. Society, in other words, is thought to be *existentially* significant to the human condition. This touches upon the origins of the very word '*social*ism': one that highlights the importance of our social environment. As **Anthony Crosland** explained:

> We cannot separate who we are from the sort of society we have. Our perspectives, our prospects, our very personalities, are affected by the society we are born into.

In short, socialists believe that traditional societies often damage both the potential and attitude of their individual members. However, given its 'malleable' view of human nature, socialism also argues that, if society can somehow be improved, the condition and prospects of its individuals will be improved as well. So the next question for socialists is: *how* can society be improved?

Collectivist

Socialists believe society is at its best when it stresses collectivism: the idea that an individual's efforts are practically and morally superior when tied to the efforts and interests of others. Unlike liberals, socialists think that individuals are at their most effective when they act as a unit. A socialist society will therefore be one that encourages the concept of being stronger when working together, while promoting the view that individual interests must always be secondary to the interests of society collectively.

Comparing ideas

Society

Whereas liberals and some conservatives tend to see society as the sum of autonomous individuals, socialists see things the other way round. For socialists, individuals are just the product of the society they inhabit, with individual efforts constrained by that society. Unlike liberals, socialists are also likely to see society as a collection of classes.

Knowledge check

9 What do you understand by the term 'working class'?

Class-focused

To improve society, socialists also believe we must acknowledge the importance of social class. Many socialists highlight a class division between manual and non-manual workers, which supposedly reflects a split between those who are well paid and those who are not. This division also reflects those who 'own' their working lives (determining the extent, timing and focus of their labours) and those whose working lives are determined by others. For **Marx** and **Engels**, this was the essential difference between what they termed the 'bourgeoisie' and the 'proletariat', although many socialists have since preferred less esoteric terms: 'middle class' and 'working class', 'white collar' and 'blue collar', and 'haves' and 'have-nots' are among the best-known examples.

Traditionally, socialists associated the 'working class' with manual (or blue-collar) employment, often in factories and industries like coal and steel. More recently, though, socialists have extended the term to many of those in non-manual (or white-collar) employment – for example, low- or modestly paid office workers with little job security.

Socialists are not alone in acknowledging different social classes. Indeed, this has even applied to traditional conservatism (see Chapter 3). What makes socialism distinct is its frequent assumption that society is shaped and defined by *class differences* and often *class conflict*. Rejecting the classical liberal view that individuals are largely autonomous, socialists argue that many individuals are limited by the social class into which they are born. As a result, socialists highlight grievous inequalities of opportunity between the different social classes, which then create broader inequalities in society. In its quest for a fairer society, it is this supposed problem that socialism seeks to correct.

Egalitarian

You should recall from Chapter 1 that a core belief of liberalism was *foundational equality*: the idea that all men are born equal and of equal value. This, in turn, relates to liberalism's belief in equality of opportunity: that everyone should be treated equally within a 'constitutional' state, so everyone has chance to fulfil their potential.

However, socialists insist such 'formal' equality is meaningless if accompanied by a society that has huge inequalities of wealth and power. Socialists therefore claim that, for society to have *real* equality of opportunity, it must also have greater *equality of outcome*, where differences of wealth and power are reduced and where the gap between society's richest and poorest members narrowed. In short, socialists advocate a society that is *egalitarian.*

This takes socialists back to the issue of class. Socialists argue that, irrespective of character and ability, someone born into a 'lower'-class background will have fewer opportunities than someone born into a 'higher'-class background. In other words, *legal* justice is insufficient; it must be accompanied by social justice. As **Anthony Crosland** repeatedly asserted, the main aim of socialism was to 'narrow the gap between society's weaker and stronger classes'. Or, as **Beatrice Webb** observed, 'The humble should be made mightier and the mighty made humbler.' The issue of *how* leads us to socialism's view of economics.

View of the economy

Fundamental

As an ideology, socialism attaches huge importance to economics. **Karl Marx**, often seen as the 'father of socialism', was also one of the first to highlight clear and unbreakable connections between politics, philosophy and economics. **Marx** argued that it was impossible to understand political argument, or the workings of the state, without first acquiring a proper appreciation of how a state's economy functions. According to **Marx,** for any historic change to occur, radical *political* change must always be accompanied by radical *economic* reform.

Later socialists were not quite so radical in their analyses. **Anthony Giddens**, for example, thought it was perfectly possible to create a better kind of society, with greater social justice, without overhauling the existing capitalist economy. Nevertheless, all socialists – including **Giddens** – believe that economic policy is central to the socialist project of a fairer, more equal society.

Redistributive

Socialists insist that the creation of an egalitarian society must involve the redistribution of wealth and resources, the aim being to narrow the gap between the richest and poorest classes. This principle was reflected in the Labour Party manifesto of 1974 (endorsed by **Anthony Crosland**, then a senior Labour MP), which promised: 'a fundamental and irreversible shift of wealth and power ... in favour of working people and their families'. However, among socialists, there

Harold Wilson, Labour Party leader 1963-1976

are crucial disputes about the broader economic framework in which such 'redistribution' might occur.

Ambivalent about capitalism

Within socialism, the chief economic argument concerns the desirability of capitalism. In other words, can any 'fundamental and irreversible shift of wealth and power' really take place in an economy based on private property? Or does it require a post-capitalist economy based on common ownership? Socialist thinkers have reached different conclusions.

For **orthodox socialists** (or 'fundamentalist' socialists), such as **Karl Marx**, **Rosa Luxemburg** and **Beatrice Webb**, capitalism is wholly *incompatible* with socialist economics, as capitalism always generates huge disparities of wealth. Yet, among *revisionist* socialists, like **Anthony Crosland** and **Anthony Giddens**, effective capitalism is the *precondition* of an effective socialist economic policy, creating the wealth which socialist governments can then redistribute equitably. As **Crosland** once remarked:

> It is difficult to redistribute wealth if there is no wealth to redistribute ... and to ensure wealth we need the engine of private enterprise.

Such varied views about capitalism have caused crippling divisions inside many socialist parties.

Interventionist

Socialists do agree, however, that there should be greater government intervention in the economy. In this respect, all socialists reject a purely laissez-faire, or libertarian, form of capitalism, where 'minimalist' governments allow capitalism and

Comparing ideas

The economy

Whereas liberals and some conservatives desire an economy that liberates the maximum number of individuals, socialists wish for an economy where wealth is redistributed to produce greater equality between classes. Whereas liberals and conservatives endorse capitalism, many socialists are hostile to an economy based on private property.

market forces to operate freely. Given their aim of creating a more equal society, socialists in government have usually adopted a more 'hands-on' approach to the economy than conservative or liberal opponents. Most socialists would have supported, for example, the Equal Pay Act 1970 (introduced by a Labour government that included **Anthony Crosland**), which ensured equal pay for men and women doing similar work. Likewise, few socialists would have disagreed with the minimum wage legislation of 1998 or the Employment Relations Act 1999 (introduced by a Labour government influenced by **Anthony Giddens**), which enhanced the status of both lower-paid and part-time employees.

View of the state

Rejection of anarchism

Remember that the core socialist values discussed so far, particularly equality and collectivism, are not exclusive to socialists: they are also shared by various forms of collectivist anarchism – for example, the anarcho-communism of **Peter Kropotkin** (1842–1921), which argued for the complete and immediate abolition of the state and all types of private property. What makes socialism distinctive from anarchism is its belief that equality, and progress generally, are impossible without a strong state. For this reason, socialism may be described, and even defined, as *state-sponsored egalitarianism*.

Some socialists – notably **Karl Marx** – argued that, eventually, the state will 'wither away' and lead to a utopian anarchist society known as 'communism'. However, even **Marx** accepted that, for the foreseeable future, a strong state is essential. Although socialists disagree about what kind of state is required, there is general agreement about what sort of state should be avoided.

Monument to Peter Kropotkin in Dmitrov, Russia

Rejection of 'medieval' states

Socialists agree that the pre-Enlightenment state is incompatible with the egalitarian society they envisage. Consequently, they reject the monarchical state (based on the absolute authority of one person), the theocratic state (based on religious principles) and the aristocratic state (based on a hereditary ruling class). Instead, socialists advocate a state where political power, as well as economic power, has been redistributed and where decision making reflects the principles of equality and fraternity.

An enlarged state

Socialists also agree that the modern state should be extensive and pervasive. As such, they unanimously reject the kind of 'libertarian' states advocated by modern conservative thinkers such as **Robert Nozick** (1938–2002), which do little more than oversee free-market capitalism. Socialists believe this kind of state will simply allow further selfish individualism, further exploitation of the less fortunate and, ultimately, further inequality.

Although there is disagreement between orthodox socialists like **Beatrice Webb** and revisionist socialists such as **Anthony Crosland** over whether the state should *own* the economy (and, if so, how much), socialists still agree that the state should enlarge and expand its involvement. In this respect, socialists are generally keen to extend *state-sponsored collectivism*.

As demonstrated by anarchists like **Kropotkin**, socialists are not alone in wanting a more collectivist society, where (in the words of **Anthony Giddens**) 'a sense of "we/us" trumps a sense of "me/I"'. Yet, for socialists, the only *effective* form of collectivism is that embodied by the state. Such statist collectivism will include:

- Progressive taxation, where the state finances the cost of a collectivist society, but in a way that ensures the richer classes pay more than the poorer classes.
- Greater public spending, where the state uses its tax yield to improve the condition of society's less fortunate and potentially vulnerable — for example, the state will finance social security payments to the unemployed or disabled, or finance pensions for older citizens no longer in employment.
- Universal public services, where the state uses its tax yield to guarantee public services accessible to all — as with a national health service or a state pension scheme.

Comparing ideas

The state

While liberals believe the state's main duty is the protection of natural, individual rights, and while conservatives prioritise the state's promotion of order and security, socialists believe the state's main role is the promotion of equality and social justice.

Knowledge check

15 What is anarchism and how does it differ from socialism?

16 What is meant by public spending?

Different types of socialism

Having outlined socialism's core themes – relating to human nature, society, the economy and the state – it is important to note that socialists have diverse views about how those themes can be pursued. It is possible, however, to divide these views into two broad categories.

First, there is *revolutionary* socialism, as advocated by **Karl Marx**, **Friedrich Engels** and **Rosa Luxemburg**. This argues that, for socialism to be achieved, both the current political and economic systems must be quickly and entirely dismantled. Secondly, there is the *reformist* or *evolutionary* socialism commended by **Beatrice Webb**, **Anthony Crosland** and **Anthony Giddens**. This claims socialism is best achieved gradually, peacefully and within the structures of an existing state, which can itself be reformed gradually if required.

Revolutionary socialism

Marxism

Critique of capitalism

Unsurprisingly, Marxism is based on the writings of **Karl Marx** – although we should not forget that **Friedrich Engels** was **Marx**'s co-author of the 1848 *Communist Manifesto*. Marxist ideology is chiefly distinguished by its fierce criticism of capitalism, the economic system that emerged via the Industrial Revolution of the eighteenth and nineteenth centuries. **Marx** and **Engels** were not the first writers to evaluate capitalism. However, they were the first to denounce capitalism in a detailed and methodical fashion, using language that effectively reshaped the vocabulary of politics and economics.

Karl Marx

> ### Key term
>
> **Marxism and communism** Marxism refers to the writings of **Karl Marx** in the mid-nineteenth century. **Marx** believed that the destruction of capitalism was both desirable and inevitable, and that it would ultimately lead to communism – a society based on communal living, the common ownership of economic resources and the principle of 'each according to his needs'. **Marx** believed communism was the 'ultimate' society and could not be improved upon.

Karl Marx (1818–83) and Friedrich Engels (1820–95)

No socialist thinker has had more impact upon both socialism and world history than Karl Marx. Aided by his lifelong collaborator Friedrich Engels, Marx proposed a series of revolutionary ideas that would have a seismic effect on political debate. Indeed, works like *The Communist Manifesto* (1848) and *Das Kapital* (1867) remain essential reading for any serious student of political science.

- Born in Germany, Marx and Engels were the first socialist thinkers to offer a detailed analysis of how humans were *social and economic beings*. Specifically, they argued that human nature had been contaminated by the prevailing economic system – capitalism – which encouraged selfishness, ruthlessness and greed. They argued further that capitalism had instilled in mankind a 'false consciousness' far removed from mankind's original nature – one that had been cooperative, selfless and fraternal. The task, they argued, was to create a new, non-capitalist economic system that would revive such noble characteristics.
- Marx and Engels were the first socialist thinkers to explain the centrality of social class. They argued that capitalism created two conflicted economic classes: the bourgeoisie (in effect, the ruling class, which owned and managed the economy) and the proletariat (in effect, the working class, which sold its labour to the bourgeoisie in return for wages). However, they also argued that class differences were toxic, involving harsh inequalities of wealth and power, and the exploitation of the proletariat. Yet, for this same reason, capitalist societies were also unstable and would, eventually, be overthrown by an 'historically inevitable' proletarian revolution.
- Rejecting the liberal view that capitalism promotes prosperity and individual liberty for all, Marx and Engels explained how capitalism usually sought to be competitive by creating 'surplus value', whereby employers paid employees minimum wages, so as to allow most profits to be used for refining the means of production. Yet surplus value would also, they asserted, implant in capitalism 'the seeds of its own destruction' by nurturing resentful class consciousness among workers, who would eventually overthrow capitalism via revolution.
- Marx and Engels were also among the first to challenge the liberal notion that the state was politically neutral. Instead, they argued that the state would always serve the interests of whichever class controlled the economy. Consequently, the liberal state was 'merely a committee' for the ruling capitalist class and could never provide an evolutionary road to socialism. This argument would inspire later revolutionary socialists, such as Ralph Miliband (1924–94) and Tariq Ali (1943–), who ridiculed the 'parliamentary socialism' championed by organisations like the Labour Party.
- Marx and Engels became the first socialists to explain why revolution was not just inevitable but essential, and to describe what should happen once revolution had occurred. They asserted that, in the wake of revolution, an entirely new state should arise that would govern in the interests of the new, economically dominant class – they called this state 'the dictatorship of the proletariat'. Once this alternative state had cemented socialist values, it would 'wither away' and be replaced by communism: a stateless society involving common ownership and the principle of 'from each according to his ability, to each according to his needs'. Such a scenario has never been realised, yet Marx and Engels' idea of a dictatorship of the proletariat proved hugely significant, justifying oppressive political systems in post-revolutionary societies such as the Soviet Union and Mao's China.

Friedrich Engels

The **Marx–Engels** critique had several key features:
- It noted that capitalism gave rise to two conspicuous classes: what **Marx** and **Engels** termed the *bourgeoisie* and *proletariat*. Within a capitalist society, the bourgeoisie comprised a small minority of individuals, while the proletariat comprised the vast majority of the population. There was, however, a profound inequality between the two classes, which duly produced *class conflict* – a tension that would eventually destroy capitalist society.
- Despite being numerically tiny, the bourgeoisie owned and controlled both property and the *mode* (method) *of production* in a capitalist economy. This led to the bourgeoisie having huge advantages in terms of wealth and power, which enabled them to inflict *exploitation* and *oppression* upon the proletariat – for example, by paying low wages or by charging tenants extortionate rents for the most basic accommodation.
- For **Marx and Engels** – both products of a bourgeois upbringing themselves – the bourgeois class was not innately evil or amoral. But the capitalist system, with its relentless quest for profit, compelled the bourgeoisie to act in an amoral way. The chief example of this was the concept of surplus value, which encouraged the bourgeoisie to pay workers less than the 'real' value of their labour. This meant there was little or no correlation between the time and effort expended by proletarian workers and what their employers paid them in return. **Marx** therefore concluded that, under capitalism, the workers suffered *alienation* from the *fruits of their labour* and were *dehumanised* by this particular mode of economic production.
- This alienation was just one example of what was termed false consciousness. Although they believed human nature was originally fraternal, **Marx** argued that both the bourgeoisie and the proletariat were *corrupted by capitalism*, which had fostered envy, greed, resentment, distrust and the pitiless pursuit of self-interest.
- For **Marx** and **Engels**, the ultimate flaw in capitalism was that it was an *inefficient* mode of production; it consistently failed to provide sufficient material resources for the majority. Worse still, it had a *cyclical* tendency to stagnate, leading to unemployment, wage cuts and further misery for the beleaguered proletariat.

Knowledge check

17 According to Marx, what is the difference between the bourgeoisie and proletariat?

18 How did Marx believe capitalism leads to 'exploitation' and 'alienation'?

Key terms

Class consciousness Cited by **Marx** and **Engels**, this was said to be a by-product of capitalism that would eventually develop among the downtrodden working class (proletariat). It would be the engine of revolution and capitalism's destruction.

Dialectic Linked to the philosopher Hegel, this refers to the clash of ideas and interests that supposedly takes place within each 'stage' of history.

Historical materialism Building on the philosophy of Hegel, this refers to the view of **Marx** and **Engels** that the history of human development can be divided into various economic 'episodes'. Each episode was defined by a certain method (or 'mode') of economic production and was brought to a close by a clash between those who defended and those who challenged the existing mode of production.

'Inevitability' of revolution

Although they were clearly contemptuous of capitalism, **Marx** and **Engels** were convinced it would not last for ever. Indeed, they believed its demise was inevitable – for three reasons:

■ First, they believed capitalism 'sowed the seeds of its own destruction'. **Marx** predicted that each of the economic crises produced by capitalism would be worse than the last, and that the plight of the proletariat would steadily worsen. As capitalism moved into its advanced stages, the proletariat would become larger, angrier and more **class conscious** until, eventually, workers realised they had 'nothing to lose but their chains', igniting a revolution that smashed both capitalism and the existing state. In short, capitalism would ultimately be destroyed by the class it created.

■ Secondly, **Marx** and **Engels** dismissed any notion that capitalism could be reformed and improved by the existing state. They argued that any state simply served the interests of its *dominant economic class* – that is, those who owned and controlled the state's material resources. Consequently, the 'liberal' state in capitalist society was merely 'a committee ... managing the everyday affairs of the bourgeoisie'. States in advanced industrial societies could therefore not be expected to reform capitalism or pose any serious challenge to the bourgeoisie.

■ Finally, **Marx** and **Engels** argued that revolution was *historically inevitable*. In this respect, they drew heavily upon the 'historicism' of philosopher Friedrich Hegel (1770–1831), who argued that history was 'episodic': a series of stages, each involving a clash of philosophical ideas, which Hegel described as **dialectic**. In a crucial adjustment, **Marx** and **Engels** stated that each historical stage was in fact a clash of *economic* ideas and economic interests – or, more precisely, a clash between the existing mode of production and a compelling challenge to it that would eventually prevail. They described this process as 'dialectical' or **historical materialism**, illustrated in Figure 2.1.

Primitive society Random economic organisation
⬇
Slave-based economy Unpaid workers form the 'mode of production'
⬇
Feudal economy Rural land owned by aristocrats is leased to tenants
⬇
Capitalist economy Industrialised mode of production, owned and overseen by a new class (bourgeoisie)
⬇
Proletariat and class consciousness
⬇
Revolution and destruction of capitalism
⬇
Dictatorship of the proletariat Socialism and state ownership of the economy
⬇
Communism Arises after socialist state has withered away
⬇
'End of history'

Figure 2.1 Historical/ dialectical materialism (according to Marx and Engels)

From socialism to communism

Following the revolution, **Marx** and **Engels** predicted that a new socialist state – the *dictatorship of the proletariat* – would emerge. Its function would be to oversee the replacement of private ownership by common ownership, and the emergence of a new culture stressing co-operation, fraternity and solidarity.

Once this had been completed, they argued, the socialist state would be redundant, 'wither away' and eventually replaced by a stateless, utopian society known as *communism*. This society, based on the principle of 'from each according to his ability, to each according to his needs', could not possibly be bettered, **Marx** and **Engels** argued. Consequently, they thought communism would be the final stage of economic evolution and the *end of history*.

Marxism–Leninism (orthodox communism)

No account of revolutionary socialism would be complete without reference to Vladimir Ilyich Lenin (1870–1924), leader of Russia's Bolshevik Party prior to the Russian Revolution of 1917 and a key figure during the revolution itself. His methods were both influential and controversial, earning both praise and criticism from Polish contemporary, **Rosa Luxemburg**.

Pre-emptive revolution

Lenin upheld **Marx**'s critique of capitalism and the belief that revolution, socialism and eventually communism were inevitable. However, Lenin was concerned by **Marx**'s insistence that revolution could only occur in societies where capitalism was advanced – a concern shared by **Luxemburg**. For both Lenin and **Luxemburg**, the disturbing implication of Marxism was that less economically developed nations (like Russia in the early twentieth century) would have to endure decades of oppressive rule before the salvation of a socialist revolution.

Lenin therefore argued that pre-industrial societies should use revolution to pre-empt the development of capitalism, so that industrialisation took place under a socialist, not bourgeois, state. His own key work, *What Is to Be Done?* (1902), set out to explain how this might be achieved, and effectively became a crucial modification of *The Communist Manifesto* – in short, Marxism–Leninism.

Knowledge check

19 Why did Marx and Engels believe that capitalism would 'sow the seed of its own destruction'?

20 Why did Marx and Engels believe the 'liberal' state was not neutral in its attitude to society?

21 What is meant by 'dialectical materialism'?

22 What function is served by the 'dictatorship of the proletariat'?

23 What eventually happens to the 'dictatorship of the proletariat'?

24 According to Marx, what is the difference between socialism and communism?

25 How did Lenin's views depart from Marxism?

26 In terms of revolutionary socialism, what is the 'vanguard'?

27 What do you understand by the term 'totalitarian'?

Vanguardism

At the heart of Lenin's prescription was a revolutionary party – or 'vanguard' – which would perform four crucial tasks:

- It would plan and incite the revolutionary overthrow of the existing state (such as the Tsarist regime, in the case of early twentieth-century Russia).
- Prior to and during the revolution, it would offset 'false consciousness' by 're-educating' the masses into the basic virtues of socialism.
- Immediately after the revolution, the vanguard would form a new organisation – the Communist Party. This would embody **Marx**'s 'dictatorship of the proletariat' and duly govern the new, post-revolutionary society. In the process, it would oversee industrialisation, continue the 're-education' of the masses, further dispel 'false consciousness' within society, and prepare the ground for communism and the 'end of history'.
- While governing, the Communist Party would embody Lenin's concept of *democratic centralism*. This would involve a one-party state, with debate and disagreement only occurring within the Communist Party. According to Lenin, the party's eventual decision would represent the settled will of the masses, making any further debate counter-revolutionary and therefore undesirable.

During the twentieth century, Marxism–Leninism would shape not just the Soviet Union but many other countries that underwent 'socialist' revolution without being economically mature – such as Mao's China after 1949, and later Cuba, North Korea, North Vietnam and Cambodia. Often, the outcomes were shocking, leading to totalitarianism (the concentration of political power and elimination of all political opposition), state-led brutality and genocide. For this reason, **Rosa Luxemburg**'s critique of Marxism–Leninism has attracted significant interest, particularly among socialists keen to salvage the notion of revolutionary action.

Key thinker 2

Rosa Luxemburg (1871–1919)

One of those who sought to uphold and develop the ideas of **Karl Marx** was Rosa Luxemburg. Through her membership of the German Social Democratic Party (SPD), Polish-born Luxemburg made a distinctive contribution to the development of Marxist socialism.

- In one of her earliest publications, *Reform or Revolution* (1900), Luxemburg accepted **Marx**'s argument that capitalism promoted exploitation and conflicted with humanity's natural, fraternal instincts. She also agreed that evolutionary socialism was impossible: only revolution could create real change. Like Lenin, she had little sympathy for **Marx**'s 'historicism' and his view that, for revolution to occur, capitalism would have to reach an advanced stage. However, Luxemburg's analysis of how the revolution should come about distinguished her from both **Marx** and Lenin.

■ Luxemburg rejected Lenin's claim that revolution could occur only through the planning and leadership of a vanguard elite. Instead, she envisaged revolution arising 'spontaneously', after class consciousness had gradually been brought about through the proletariat's ongoing battle for progress in the workplace. Mass strike action would develop spontaneously from this and eventually ignite a much wider revolutionary movement that would overthrow the capitalist state. Yet Luxemburg rejected the Marxist–Leninist idea of revolution leading to a dictatorship of the proletariat. Instead, she advocated the immediate construction of a new democracy, underpinned by common ownership, open debate and elections.

■ Luxemburg believed that the political party she helped found in 1918 – the German Communist Party – should contest elections and engage with the existing political system. Leninists were appalled by this 'betrayal' of revolutionary socialism. However, Luxemburg argued that such engagement would make it easier for communist parties to convey a revolutionary message to the masses. This argument was adopted by 'neo-Marxists' half a century later and remains popular among European communist parties today.

Portrait of Rosa Luxemburg

The Luxemburg version

Born in 1871, **Rosa Luxemburg** did not become active in socialist politics until twenty years after **Marx**'s death in 1873. She shared **Marx**'s contempt for capitalism and his belief in the 'inevitability' of revolution. Like Lenin (who was born within a year of **Luxemburg**), she rejected **Marx**'s view that socialism could only occur after capitalism reached an advanced stage. Like Lenin, she was, in her words, 'impatient with injustice, impatient for socialism'. Nevertheless, **Luxemburg** offered a distinctive analysis by challenging Marxism–Leninism in three areas:

■ First, she rejected Lenin's 'vanguard' approach to revolution, which she saw as a new form of elitism and hierarchy. Instead, **Luxemburg** advocated a revolution that erupted 'spontaneously', and which was driven by the masses themselves – for instance, through their trade unions. The revolution would thus be more attuned to socialist principles of fraternity and equality.

■ Secondly, while she shared **Marx** and Lenin's belief in revolution, **Luxemburg** did not accept that engagement with the existing state was pointless. Instead, she saw the existing state's election campaigns as another opportunity to nurture class consciousness, which would hasten the 'spontaneous' revolution she favoured. According to **Luxemburg**, parties like the German Communist Party, which she helped form,

Rosa Luxemburg

could then use their own campaigns to explain the case for revolution, and use any seats they won as a further platform for revolutionary propaganda.

- Thirdly, after the revolution, **Luxemburg** wanted a new, socialist state that would be neither a 'dictatorship of the proletariat' (as prescribed by **Marx)** nor a one-party state (as prescribed by Lenin). Instead, she advocated a new democratic state, underpinned by state ownership of the economy, yet allowing fair elections and genuine party competition.

Like many others who questioned Marxism–Leninism, **Luxemburg** was eventually murdered by 'socialist' opponents. Yet her ideas lingered and were to have a significant influence upon the *neo-Marxist* ideas of later intellectuals like Antonio Gramsci (1891–1937). Her views were also endorsed by various revolutionary socialists in the late twentieth and early twenty-first centuries, including Ralph Miliband and Tariq Ali.

Box 2.1 gives a recent example of a revolutionary socialist statement from a UK political party.

Box 2.1: Revolutionary socialism now – statement from the Socialist Workers Party (UK), 2021

'We are a revolutionary socialist party. We fight against oppression, exploitation and environmental destruction. We think the problems of society stem from a capitalist system that prioritizes profit above all else. Drawing upon the work of Marx, Lenin, Trotsky and Luxemburg, we want to see a revolution where the majority of people take control in society and transform the world …'.

Source: *International Socialism: A Quarterly Review of Socialist Theory* (2021)

Key term

Evolutionary socialism Linked to both the democratic socialism of **Beatrice Webb** and the 'revisionist' socialism of **Anthony Crosland** and **Anthony Giddens**, this rejects the revolutionary politics of **Karl Marx**, Lenin and **Rosa Luxemburg** and instead believes socialism can be achieved within the existing political system. It is also referred to as 'reformist socialism' or 'parliamentary socialism'.

Evolutionary socialism

Democratic socialism

Towards the end of the nineteenth century, socialists such as **Beatrice Webb**, and socialist groups like the Fabian Society, began to challenge one of the central tenets of Marxism: namely, that socialism, and the displacement of capitalism, must be preceded by revolution. These thinkers became known as democratic socialists, advocating a reformist or **evolutionary** brand of socialism within the structures of existing society. During the twentieth century, this became one of the most influential forms of socialist politics, largely owing to the post-war 1945–51 Labour governments led by Clement Attlee and the later writings of Labour MP Tony Benn (1925–2014).

Key thinker 3

Beatrice Webb (1858–1943)

Beatrice Webb made a significant contribution to the development of early democratic socialism and its belief in the 'inevitability of gradualism' (see Box 2.2). Webb's socialism was defined by four principles:

1 Capitalism was the principal cause of 'crippling poverty and demeaning inequality' in society and was a 'corrupting force' for humanity, fostering 'unnatural' levels of greed and acquisitiveness among men and women.
2 Neither conservative paternalism (see Chapter 3) nor philanthropy was a sustainable solution to the problems of poverty and inequality.
3 Poverty and inequality were most likely to be eliminated through vigorous trade unionism and extensive state intervention.
4 Effective reform tends to be gradual rather than revolutionary.

■ Along with her husband, Sidney, Webb became active in the Fabian Society, an organisation committed to evolutionary socialism via reforms made at Westminster. She was instrumental in the Fabians' decision to align with the emerging Labour Party and was involved in drafting Clause IV of Labour's 1918 constitution. Although this committed Labour to 'common ownership' of the British economy, Webb helped ensure that Labour would pursue this goal via the existing political system.

■ In 1909 Webb was the lead author of the Minority Report of the Royal Commission on the Poor Laws, an outcome of a royal commission that examined the state's approach to poverty. Her celebrated report argued that the state should guarantee 'a sufficient nourishment and training when young, a living wage when able-bodied, treatment when sick, and modest but secure livelihood when disabled or aged'. Much of this anticipated the Beveridge Report of 1942, the subsequent 'welfare state' and the record of democratic socialist governments between 1945 and 1951.

Beatrice Webb

Capitalism: a renewed critique

By the end of the nineteenth century, members of the Fabian Society, such as **Webb**, recognised that capitalism had not brought the ever-increasing misery forecast by **Marx**. Instead, they noted that the economic condition of Britain's working class had actually improved significantly since the mid-nineteenth century.

But they still rejected capitalism as a long-term economic system. **Webb** insisted that an economy based on private ownership was inherently 'unpredictable', 'unstable' and 'at odds with the equitable distribution of wealth'. For this reason, democratic socialists like **Webb** commended 'a more orderly economy', where 'economic development could be planned logically' and where clashes of economic interests could be 'resolved constructively by elected governments'.

For **Webb** and other democratic socialists, in order for this to happen, a post-capitalist economy was needed, supervised by an economically expert bureaucracy. This belief was restated in Clause IV of the Labour Party's 1918 constitution (written

Knowledge check

30 Why did the original Clause IV of its constitution seemingly commit the Labour Party to the abolition of capitalism?

31 Why did Beatrice Webb believe that socialism could be achieved within the existing state?

32 Why did democratic socialists think that Marx's predictions had been disproved?

Key term

Fabianism Linked to the ideas of the Fabian Society, an organisation formed during the late nineteenth century by self-styled intellectuals like **Beatrice Webb**. It argues that socialism will be achieved slowly but steadily within the existing state, through democratically elected socialist governments.

Jeremy Corbyn: modern democratic socialist

largely by **Webb**'s husband, Sidney), which stated that Labour aimed to:

> secure for the producers by hand and by brain the full fruits of their industry and the most equitable distribution thereof … upon the basis of the common ownership of the means of production.

However, the term 'common ownership' is misleading. As later democratic socialists explained, Clause IV was in fact commending *state* ownership of the economy, brought about after the state had *nationalised* 'the means of production'. This connected to a fresh view of the state in capitalist society.

The existing state: a critique of Marx

The main distinction between **Webb** and **Marx** concerns their attitude to revolution. While **Marx** judged revolutions inevitable, **Webb** argued they were intrinsically 'chaotic', 'unmanageable' and therefore 'counterproductive'. In other words, democratic socialists argued that revolutions replicated many of the problems they associated with capitalism. As **Webb** explained, 'upheavals marred by mayhem, violence and bloodshed' were not the best starting points for a supposedly superior socialist society.

This view was reinforced by **Webb**'s belief that the state in capitalist society was more versatile and responsive than **Marx** envisaged. In the UK, for example, the franchise had been significantly extended since 1867 so that voting was no longer the preserve of the propertied bourgeoisie; by 1900, roughly half of the UK's adult male population was part of the electorate. This, in turn, seemed to encourage legislation which improved the condition of society's less fortunate – for example, the Factory Act 1874 and the Housing of the Working Classes Act 1890, curbing the power of factory owners and landlords respectively.

Given that such measures were often passed by Conservative governments, **Webb** concluded that democratic socialist governments could use the same methods to bring about more radical, socialist change – a prospect she thought even more likely with the prospect of universal adult suffrage and a predominantly working-class electorate that would 'inevitably' vote for socialism.

Gradualism

According to **Fabians** like **Webb**, democratic socialist governments could use the existing state to promote a *slow but steady* movement to public ownership and socialism – a process Fabians dubbed 'the inevitability of gradualism' (see Box 2.2).

Box 2.2: Democratic socialism and 'the inevitability of gradualism'

According to **Beatrice Webb**, slow but steady progress towards a socialist society would be 'inevitably but gradually' achieved through the democratic process, in the following way:

- Democratic socialist parties campaign peacefully and *gradually* win the attention and trust of voters.
- The majority of voters (the working class) *gradually* and *inevitably* realise they have no vested interest in capitalism.
- Voters *inevitably* elect socialist governments.
- Democratic socialist governments oversee the *gradual* replacement of private ownership with state ownership.
- Voters *inevitably* recognise the progress *gradually* made and *inevitably* re-elect socialist governments.
- A socialist society *gradually* and *inevitably* emerges.
- The benefits of a socialist society are *inevitably* clear, making any reversal of socialism unlikely.

Knowledge check

33 Why was the case for evolutionary socialism strengthened by Attlee's Labour governments?

34 Why was the term 'Fabians' used by some who supported evolutionary socialism?

Indeed, the Fabian Society took its name from Roman general Quintin Fabius, who put patient, piecemeal progress at the heart of his military strategy.

Many see the UK's post-war Labour government as a prime illustration of 'gradualist' democratic socialism in action. Two-thirds of the Labour MPs elected in 1945 had Fabian Society connections, including the new prime minister, Clement Attlee (1883–1967). His government steadily implemented a series of measures that had been carefully planned beforehand, including the nationalisation of industries like coal, iron and steel. In the decades that followed, democratic socialists such as Tony Benn argued that this gradual shift should continue with further nationalisation and further public ownership – an argument updated in the 2017 and 2019 general elections by Labour leader Jeremy Corbyn and his shadow chancellor, John McDonnell (see Box 2.3).

Debate 1

Does socialism require revolutionary change?

Yes

... according to early orthodox socialists:

- **Karl Marx** and **Friedrich Engels** argued that the pre-socialist state reflected the interests of the dominant economic class and would therefore not allow the promotion of socialist values. **Marx** and **Engels** also believed revolution was historically inevitable.
- Lenin believed revolution was necessary to pre-empt and prevent the horrors of capitalist development and 'false consciousness' among the masses.

No

... according to later orthodox socialists:

- Democratic socialists (such as **Beatrice Webb**) believed in the 'inevitability of gradualism' – involving slow, steady change within the existing political system.
- Later democratic socialists like Tony Benn believed the existing state required reform rather than abolition – for example, by reforming the structure of parliament.

- **Rosa Luxemburg** believed revolution would inevitably and 'spontaneously' develop from trade union agitation.

... according to 'revisionist' socialists:

- Social democrats such as **Anthony Crosland** and Third Way revisionists like **Anthony Giddens** believed that, with the advent of a welfare state and mixed economy, the existing political system could ensure steady increases in public spending and, therefore, steady progress towards a fairer society.
- **Giddens** also believed the existing state's structures could be reformed (e.g. via devolution), so as to produce greater political equality.

Evaluation check: Is there a route to socialism using the existing political system (what **Crosland** called a 'parliamentary road to socialism')?

Box 2.3: Democratic socialism now – extracts from the Labour Party manifesto, 2019

Labour's manifesto promised a society based on 'democratic socialist principles' that would 'serve the many not the few'. This would involve a Labour government extending state power in various ways. For example, the party pledged to:

- take 'rail, mail, water and energy services into public ownership'
- provide 'full-fibre broadband to every home through a new public service'
- create 'a new National Education Service … including free university tuition and free lifelong learning'
- provide 'greater funding for the NHS, an end to privatisation and free prescriptions for all'.

Source: *It's Time for Real Change:* The Labour Party manifesto, 2019

Key term

Revisionist socialism A form of evolutionary socialism which assumes that equality can be achieved without the destruction of capitalism. Dating from the late nineteenth century, this view has been associated with the social democracy of **Anthony Crosland** and the Third Way of **Anthony Giddens**.

Social democracy

Like democratic socialism, social democracy rejects revolution and believes the existing state could promote a socialist agenda. However, unlike democratic socialists such as **Beatrice Webb**, social democrats like **Anthony Crosland** do not support the ultimate disappearance of capitalism. Indeed, as revisionist socialists, social democrats see capitalism as the indispensable ally of socialist governments.

Bernstein's legacy

The earliest form of revisionist socialism came from German socialist Eduard Bernstein (1850–1932). Bernstein noted that, by the end of the nineteenth century, there had been a 'steady advance of the working class' under capitalism, especially in those states where capitalism was well developed: a direct contradiction of what **Karl Marx** had predicted half a century earlier. This led Bernstein to argue that, if overseen by socialist governments, capitalist economies could provide an even bigger improvement to workers' conditions – especially if the workers formed the bulk of voters. By the mid-1950s, **Crosland** felt able to argue that Bernstein's view had been powerfully vindicated by changes to society, the economy and the state.

Knowledge check

35 What is the key similarity between democratic socialism and social democracy?

36 What is meant by 'revisionist socialism'?

37 What is the key distinction between democratic socialism and social democracy?

38 Why is Eduard Bernstein seen as the 'father' of revisionist socialism?

Key thinker 4

Anthony Crosland (1918–77)

Anthony Crosland was an English academic who went on to become a senior Labour Party politician, serving as a Cabinet minister during the Labour governments of the 1960s and 1970s. His book *The Future of Socialism* (1956) made a vital contribution to the development of social democracy in Britain.

- Crosland contested that public or common ownership had gone far enough, arguing that public ownership had never been the aim of socialism, merely a method of achieving it. The true objective, Crosland insisted, was equality, which could now be achieved within a managed capitalist economy.
- Crosland asserted that capitalism had been changed as a result of the economist John Maynard Keynes, whose belief in state-managed capitalism became orthodox in western Europe after 1945. Thanks to Keynesian principles, Crosland argued, advanced societies could now afford permanent economic growth and full employment, without requiring any serious extension of public ownership. Thanks to constant growth, these societies could then enjoy a steady expansion of the welfare state which, in turn, would diminish inequality and advance socialism.
- Crosland also noted an important change in society. He argued that owing to economic change, society was less polarised between

employers and employees, and 'infinitely more complex than Marx could ever have imagined'. In particular, Crosland cited 'new classes', such as 'managers' and 'technocrats', whose perspectives were likely to be different from those of traditional workers.

- Crosland argued that socialism now required a 'mixed' economy. This would mainly comprise private enterprise and private ownership, alongside key services and a small number of industries owned by the state. Crosland argued that such a mixed economy had been created by the 1945–51 Labour governments, and that the future of socialism meant more public spending and better public services rather than more public ownership.
- In his later books, *The Conservative Enemy* (1962) and *Socialism Now* (1974), Crosland focused on other issues driving inequality – including education. He argued for a new form of state education, known as comprehensive education, which would create new 'one-size-fits-all' schools catering for all abilities. Crosland believed these schools would break down class divisions far more effectively than any extension of public ownership, as well as ensuring equality of opportunity for all pupils. Crosland pursued this idea while secretary of state for education between 1965 and 1967, initiating a process that made comprehensive education the norm by the time of his death.

Anthony Crosland

Class revisited

Crosland's defence of post-war capitalism owed much to his reappraisal of social class. He argued that the binary 'us and them' society, as outlined by traditional socialism, was now redundant. For **Crosland**, this was mainly connected to a vital *new* grouping that had emerged within modern capitalism: a growing 'managerial' class, comprising supervisors, technocrats, sectional heads and assorted 'experts'. This new class was said by **Crosland** to be 'managing' and directing the post-war economy, but without *owning* it. In other words, **Marx**'s link between *control* and *ownership* of production had been broken. According to **Crosland**, members of this new class were neither 'exploited' proletarians, nor part of an 'exploiting' bourgeoisie. Instead, they made the class system more complicated and made Marxist analysis and revolutionary socialism far less relevant.

The mixed economy

Crosland's views were also shaped by the legacy of the 1945– 1951 Labour governments. Although they did not dismantle capitalism, Attlee's governments had still 'nationalised' significant sections of the economy. The outcome was that the UK now had a *mixed economy* – one that was still largely capitalist, but with the state now owning parts of society where capitalism proved problematic, such as public health and public transport. **Crosland** argued that this 'pragmatic blend of public and private ownership' made further nationalisation unnecessary and unpopular with voters. As a Labour MP, he therefore argued that Clause IV of the party's constitution was obsolete and should be repealed on both electoral and ideological grounds: an idea Labour rejected at its special party conference of 1959.

Keynesianism

Crosland's support for a mixed economy also relates to his belief that the problematic tendencies of capitalism had been eliminated. This belief came from the widespread acceptance after 1945 of Keynesian economics. Keynesianism is sometimes referred to as 'managerial capitalism', in that it allows governments to 'manage' or 'steer' a capitalist economy via adjustable tax rates, interest rates, public spending projects and other forms of state intervention. According to **Crosland**, this new approach guaranteed steady growth, full employment and the removal of one of socialism's traditional objections to capitalism: namely, that it was 'cyclical' and prone to devastating recessions.

Knowledge check

39 What is a 'mixed economy'?

40 What is meant by 'nationalisation' and 'public ownership'?

Key term

Keynesianism Linked to economist John Maynard Keynes, this is a form of capitalism where governments plan and manage the economy to ensure full employment and steady growth.

Knowledge check

41 What is the basic difference between Keynesian capitalism and laissez-faire capitalism?

Public spending not public ownership

For **Crosland**, the main case for Keynesianism – its capacity to ensure constant economic growth – had profound implications for socialism. Constant economic growth allowed a constant growth in tax revenue; enlarged tax revenue allowed a steady growth of public spending; enlarged public spending allowed an expansion of public services; and the expansion of public services allowed a redistribution of wealth, benefiting the poorer classes. In short, public spending, not public ownership, was the new road to equality and socialism.

Welfarism

Knowledge check

42 How does greater public spending serve the cause of socialism?
43 What is meant by the 'welfare state'?
44 Why was the case for social democracy weakened during the 1970s?

In this respect, **Crosland**'s case was again bolstered by the 1945–51 Labour governments. Attlee's ministers had established what is now termed the 'welfare state' – a network of public services and state benefits, which served to mitigate poverty and inequality. These services included a National Health Service, a universal system of state education and an array of social security payments for the needy. For social democrats, the task was now to build upon this welfare state, using the revenues generated by a stable Keynesian economy.

Social democracy proved the guiding ideology of Labour governments in the 1960s and 1970s, with **Crosland** serving

Debate 2

Must socialism involve the abolition of private property and capitalism?

Yes

… according to orthodox socialists:

- Socialism's core values include equality. Private property generates inequality.
- Socialism's core values include fraternity and cooperation. Private property promotes individualism and competition.
- **Karl Marx**, **Friedrich Engels** and disciples like **Rosa Luxemburg** believed that private property (capitalism) led to exploitation and oppression of working people. **Marx** and **Engels** also believed that an economic system based on capitalism was 'historically doomed' to collapse.
- Early democratic socialists like **Beatrice Webb** believed public ownership to be more rational and efficient than private ownership.

No

… according to revisionist socialists:

- As **Anthony Crosland** insisted, the debate about private/public ownership merely concerns the *means* of socialism, not the *ends* – the true 'ends' being equality and fraternity.
- Early revisionists such as Bernstein noted that working-class conditions had improved under capitalism. In other words, **Marx** had misread capitalism's trajectory. This was even more likely to happen, argued Bernstein, with the advent of universal adult suffrage and the likelihood of democratically elected socialist governments.
- Social democratic revisionists, like **Crosland**, stated that increased public spending, not public ownership, was the key to more socialism. Increases in public spending were

- Later democratic socialists, such as Tony Benn, believed that social democracy – an attempt to achieve socialism without curtailing private ownership of the economy – had failed.

perfectly possible, Crosland argued, as long as capitalist economies were allowed to grow steadily – which was supposedly guaranteed by the application of Keynesian economic policies.

- Third Way revisionists, like **Anthony Giddens**, argued that a thriving neo-liberal capitalist economy would provide the state with a growing tax yield. This, in turn, would finance the extra public spending socialism required.
- According to **Giddens**, the globalisation of capitalism and the spread of home ownership in the UK and other countries obliged socialists to accept the idea of private property.

Evaluation check: Can capitalism ever be an ally of socialism?

Key term

Stagflation An economic phenomenon of the 1970s, involving a combination of rising unemployment and rising inflation – a combination which Keynesianism did not envisage.

as a minister in both. However, the onset of recession in the 1970s suggested **Crosland**'s faith in Keynesian economics was misplaced. The **stagflation** that engulfed the UK economy was largely unforeseen by most social democrats and undermined the intellectual case for Keynesianism. This economic setback played a major part in the rise of 'Thatcherism' and New Right conservatism (see Chapter 3). But it also revived interest in earlier forms of socialism, particularly the democratic socialism associated with **Crosland**'s former Cabinet colleague, Tony Benn.

Box 2.4 gives a recent example of revisionist socialist ideas in the electoral programme of a German political party.

Box 2.4: Revisionist socialism now – German Social Democratic Party policies, 2021

Ahead of Germany's federal elections in September 2021, the German Social Democratic Party (SPD) declared its support for the following principles:

- A 'social market economy … ensuring affluence for the entire population'. This would finance …
- 'Extended and superior welfare provision for our citizens … protecting their economic and social well-being and allowing them to avail themselves of a good life'. However, the SPD also stressed …
- 'Responsible and sustainable fiscal policy … National debt must be contained so as not to place a burden on future generations.'
- 'Civil and political rights in an open society … democracy and toleration must be safeguarded.'
- Foreign policy was to focus on 'global peace and European integration … a common European economic and security policy remains an urgent and realistic goal'.

Source: *Die Welt*, 2 September 2021

SDP: Germany's main social democratic party

The Third Way
Neo-revisionism

Developed in the late 1990s by philosopher **Anthony Giddens**, Third Way socialism is an updated version of the revisionism advanced by social democrats in the 1950s. Indeed, the full title of **Giddens**' 1998 book was *The Third Way: The Renewal of Social Democracy*. **Giddens**' work was to have a major influence upon both the 'New Labour' governments of Tony Blair and Gordon Brown (1997–2010) and Gerhard Schröder's Social Democratic government in Germany (1998–2005).

There were several important overlaps between the Third Way of **Giddens** and the social democracy of **Anthony Crosland**:
- Both advocated a form of non-revolutionary socialism.
- Both sought to harness capitalism to the quest for greater equality.
- Both agreed that the future of socialism involved more public spending rather than more public ownership.
- Both believed that Clause IV of Labour's 1918 constitution (committing the party to common ownership) was obsolete. Indeed, one of the defining moments of New Labour came in 1995, when Blair persuaded his party to formally abandon Clause IV – thus succeeding where **Crosland** had failed 36 years earlier.

However, there were also key differences between social democracy and the Third Way, owing to changes in the political climate during the late twentieth century. Such changes included:
- The collapse of the Soviet Union: western capitalism was no longer threatened by communism.
- The resulting spread of market forces and a new economic phenomenon – *globalisation*, where capitalist economies are both more numerous and interconnected. This made it harder for national governments to 'manage' their economies in the manner prescribed by Keynes.
- The lasting impact of 'New Right' governments in the 1980s – notably those of Margaret Thatcher and Ronald Reagan (see Chapter 3). During the same period, parties such as Labour suffered repeated electoral defeats, raising doubts about socialism's relevance to modern democratic politics.
- The decline of the traditional, blue-collar working class. Society was said to be increasingly defined by an enlarged yet diverse white-collar electorate – a process **Giddens** termed *embourgeoisement*. As he noted: 'By 1995, more people in the UK had mortgage accounts than trade union membership cards.'

Knowledge check
45 Why are social democracy and the Third Way thought to be similar?
46 How is the Third Way different from social democracy?

Anthony Giddens

Anthony Giddens (1938–)

Anthony Giddens is known mainly as an important English sociologist. Yet his work on political theory helped create a new strain of thinking within revisionist socialism: the Third Way.

- In *Beyond Left and Right* (1994), Giddens first established his credentials as a socialist sympathiser, highlighting the 'corrosive' effects of capitalism and individualism upon community and fraternity. Yet he also stressed that capitalism and individualism were irreversible and that any future project towards greater equality would have to take account of this.

- Giddens developed this theme in his next book, *The Third Way: The Renewal of Social Democracy,* written at the time of the 1997 general election and published during the first year of the UK's New Labour government. He argued that the survival of social democracy required a recognition that free-market capitalism had an unmatched capacity to empower individuals. However, he also argued that capitalism functioned best when there was a strong sense of social cohesion, which neo-liberalism seemed to overlook. Consequently, a 'triangulation' – reconciling neo-liberalism's view of economics to social democracy's view of society – was required to make centre-left politics relevant in the twenty-first century.

- Giddens claimed this 'triangulation' was especially important given the emergence of 'post-industrial' capitalist societies. Until the late twentieth century, capitalism had involved huge industrial units of mass production, which had spawned tightly-knit urban communities, based on uniform income and employment. These communities, Giddens explained, had complemented human nature's yearning for solidarity and fellowship by giving their members a strong sense of support and identity, which might then encourage them to challenge both economic and cultural elites. Yet, according to Giddens, the post-industrial capitalism of the late twentieth and early twenty-first centuries – involving the decline of heavy industry – had fragmented such communities, 'atomised' the modern workforce and left individuals feeling alienated.

- Giddens accepted that, in many respects, post-industrial capitalism was liberating for individuals – they were now freer than ever to 'self-actualise' and carve out individual identities. Yet those individuals would also find it harder to develop, precisely because society was becoming increasingly amorphous and ill defined. Stripped of the communities that once gave them identity and confidence, individuals were likely to be less sure-footed and more influenced by both economic and cultural elites. So, for Giddens, the great irony was that 'the individualisation of society might result in less individualism'. It was the task of the Third Way to offset this consequence of neo-liberal capitalism.

- Giddens thus proved a key revisionist socialist in that he revitalised the case for further state action in an era of globalised capitalism. In doing so, he suggested that conventional Keynesian economics was obsolete and that socialism needed to accept a more free-market brand of capitalism. He argued that if the free market were to generate the sort of wealth needed to fund modern public services, greater inequality of incomes might be inevitable. These ideas had a deep and controversial influence upon the New Labour governments of 1997–2010.

Triangulation

According to **Giddens**, these changes necessitated a new form of revisionist socialism – one that would 'triangulate' what he deemed the two main ideologies of the 1980s: namely, social democracy and New Right conservatism. This would combine the social values of social democracy with the neo-liberal economics of the New Right. This synthesis would duly produce a new ideology – the Third Way – which offered a new route to both social justice and economic efficiency.

The remixed economy

As we have seen, 'managed' or Keynesian capitalism was of central importance to social democrats like **Anthony Crosland**. However, Keynes had assumed national governments were indeed *able* to 'manage' their economies – an assumption seriously challenged by the globalisation of the 1990s. Echoing the free-market principles of **neo-liberalism**, **Giddens** therefore argued that the Third Way should distinguish itself from social democracy by *extending capitalism* and by exploiting the new opportunities for economic growth provided by globalisation.

This embrace of neo-liberalism might involve deregulating financial services or enlarging the role of the private sector via 'public–private partnerships' in health care and education (as later pursued by New Labour governments after 1997). Far from simply upholding the sort of 'mixed economy' favoured by **Crosland**, the Third Way would thus endorse a 'remixed economy', with a growing role for the (capitalist) private sector. For **Giddens**, this was likely to produce 'higher profits, higher earnings and higher tax yields for higher public spending'. As Peter Mandelson, a prominent New Labour minister, famously informed a group of Silicon Valley executives in 1999: 'We are intensely relaxed about people getting filthy rich … as long as they pay their taxes'.

Cultural equality

Economic policy was not the only distinction between social democratic and Third Way revisionism. The Third Way also placed more emphasis upon cultural equality, reflecting **Giddens**' observation that modern society was 'more diverse, multi-racial and cosmopolitan' than in the 1950s. Consequently, New Labour introduced various laws promoting racial, gender and sexual equality – such as allowing same-sex couples to adopt children – which were eventually underlined by the Equality Act 2010. It is important to note here that New Labour did not necessarily endorse *multiculturalism* (an ideology which

Knowledge check

50 How did the Third Way encourage greater cultural diversity?

Knowledge check

51 How did Giddens' support for racial equality differ from that of modern liberals?

Knowledge check

52 How did Giddens propose to relocate political power?

involves the state actively promoting minority cultures). But New Labour certainly enthused about a *multicultural society*, where minority cultures were recognised and respected.

Communitarianism

For **Giddens**, such measures were intended not simply to promote 'tolerance' of individuals with 'minority' status. Consistent with earlier forms of socialism, their main aim was to repair divisions within *society* and to ensure that *society* was not damaged by racial and cultural tensions. Similarly, while it was important to protect individuals from, say, racism, it was also important to validate ethnic minority *communities*. In this respect, **Giddens**, like earlier socialist thinkers, sought to distinguish himself from modern liberals by stressing the importance of *social cohesion* and *communal solidarity*. Individual freedom was vital, stated **Giddens**, but it was impossible without a stable, harmonious society.

Redistribution of political power

Social democrats and democratic socialists were generally content with an increasingly centralised state: it would ensure, they assumed, a uniform provision of services across society. However, with its stress on 'diversity' and 'inclusion', and its readiness to consider co-operation between various centre-left parties, Third Way socialism was more willing to countenance the 'sharing' of political power. New Labour therefore promoted reforms like devolution for Scotland and Wales, regional governance in England and elective city mayors. Through the idea of elections for the House of Lords, and a reformed electoral system for the House of Commons, **Giddens** was also keen to spread power within the UK Parliament.

However, for socialist critics like Jeremy Corbyn and John McDonnell, this dispersal of power only made it harder for socialist policies to be implemented uniformly by socialist governments at Westminster.

Socialism or liberalism?

Though controversial, **Giddens** insisted that the Third Way's embrace of neo-liberal capitalism was attuned to socialist principles: the Blair–Brown governments, he noted, were able to finance an 8 per cent rise in public spending, introduce new collectivist ideas like 'Sure Start' (for economically disadvantaged families) and generally promote what Blair termed 'renewed equality of opportunity'. However, democratic socialists like John McDonnell argued that Third Way economics also produced a widening inequality of wealth between the richest and poorest sections of society. And, as explained earlier, socialists have historically argued that equality of opportunity is fictional without greater equality of outcome.

This point seemed to be implicitly conceded by Blair and other Third Way politicians, who eventually became cautious about invoking the mantra of 'equal opportunities', instead preferring terms like 'better opportunities for all' and 'opportunities for everyone'. Even **Giddens** suggested that if 'better opportunities for all' were to be financed by extra tax revenue, it might be necessary for the higher paid to acquire even higher earnings, thus increasing inequality of outcome. For this reason, democratic socialists like McDonnell were inclined to regard the Third Way as a branch of liberalism rather than a form of socialism. Indeed, the word 'socialism' did not even appear in New Labour's 1997 election manifesto.

> ### Comparing ideas
>
> #### The Third Way and modern liberalism
>
> There are clear similarities between the socialism of **Anthony Giddens** and the liberalism of **John Rawls**: both endorse capitalism, high public spending and a more tolerant society. One of the main differences concerns *communities:* **Rawls** believes they can restrict individualism, while **Giddens** believe they are essential to human security and fulfilment.

Labour Party launch manifesto for 1997 election

Conclusion: socialism today

At the end of the twentieth century, many commentators believed socialism was a redundant ideology: not so much an 'ism' as a 'was-m'. The collapse of the Soviet Union marked the end of a 70-year experiment in 'socialist' government, while the economic system that socialism historically challenged – capitalism – seemed to be entering a new age of global supremacy.

However, during the first two decades of the twenty-first century, the case for capitalism seemed less secure than some had imagined. The economic crash of 2007–08 forced governments, including Gordon Brown's in the UK, to increase state regulation of the economy and even extend public ownership. Problems in the Eurozone after 2012 – plunging countries like Greece into levels of austerity not seen for 60 years – again shook faith in the efficiency of both market economics and 'managed' capitalism.

In view of these traumas, it was unsurprising that socialist ideas began to re-enter mainstream debate. Policies once confined to socialism's more extreme elements, such as the nationalisation of banks, were implemented by Gordon Brown's government after 2007, while socialist parties such as Syriza in Greece and Podemos in Spain gained substantial public support with strong anti-capitalist messages.

When Jeremy Corbyn became leader of the UK's official opposition party in 2015, he too brought the concept of socialism – and, indeed, anti-capitalism – back into the language of front-line politics. Among voters, this did not prove as misguided as many first assumed. At the general election of 2017, Corbyn's Labour Party achieved 40 per cent of the votes cast while, at both the 2017 and 2019 general elections, Corbyn's Labour was the most popular party among voters aged 18–40. This partly arose from Labour's nuanced opposition to Brexit. But there was also evidence that Corbyn's attacks on economic inequality chimed loudly with younger voters – particularly if they were part of 'Generation Rent', for whom ownership of private property seemed unlikely.

Even in the USA, where socialism had long been off-limits to 'respectable' politicians, socialist ideas became more freely cited in the twenty-first century. Riding a tide of public hostility to 'big business' and 'corporations', socialist politicians were elected to office in states such as Washington and Vermont, while socialist senator Bernie Sanders made a plausible bid for the Democratic nomination in both the 2016 and 2020 presidential elections. Although he was unsuccessful, the high profile of younger socialists in Congress, such as Alexandria Ocasio-Cortez, seemed to ensure that Sanders' brand of socialism would remain part of US politics beyond the Trump–Biden era.

Yet, as the history of 'revisionist' socialism shows, socialism has never been just about opposition to capitalism. Of even greater importance has been its argument that we are deeply affected by our societies – and that the best societies are those promoting fraternity, co-operation and solidarity. During the late twentieth century, liberal thinkers like Francis Fukuyama argued that such values were in retreat, eclipsed by a new era of 'self' and individualism. But recent developments suggest otherwise.

The growing importance of climate change as a political issue seemed to marginalise notions like 'self-fulfilment' and 'self-determination', while highlighting the need for *collective* action and resolve – themes perfectly attuned to socialism's core values. The onset of the Covid-19 pandemic in 2020 also seemed to strengthen socialism's saliency, for three reasons. First, it led to a new stress on the needs of *society*, rather than the specific wishes of individuals. Secondly, the huge extension of state power required to tackle Covid-19 seemed in tune with socialism's big-state instincts. Thirdly, evidence that Covid-19 affected some sections of society more than others, with the poorest suffering most, sparked new and high-profile debates about poverty and inequality, which socialists naturally welcomed.

As the 2020s progressed, it therefore seemed as if socialism's core beliefs had enduring relevance. Yet serious problems still exist for those pursuing a socialist agenda. As we have seen, socialist thinkers have always stressed the importance of social class and working-class solidarity. However, recent elections in Europe and the USA showed that working-class support for socialism – never as great as socialists would have wished, anyhow – was further obstructed by deepening *cultural* divisions in society.

These divisions seemed to place many blue-collar voters on the side of cultural conservatism. Such voters were suspicious, for example, of further immigration or campaigns for certain minority interests, and were increasingly hostile to the 'woke' values of socialism's white-collar exponents – particularly those with university degrees. This 'cultural realignment' among voters played no small part in the result of the Brexit referendum, the election of President Trump in 2016, and the victory of Boris Johnson's Conservatives at the 2019 general election. In that election, Labour – fighting on an explicitly 'socialist' manifesto – had a clear lead among university graduates. Yet, for the first time since 1945, the Conservatives were the most popular party

Key terms

Woke Originating in the USA, this refers to those who are 'awake' to and support causes like racial and sexual equality, transgender rights and anti-colonialism. Common usage of the word later moved away from its original meaning and became increasingly used as a pejorative term.

Blue Labour Involving philosophers like Maurice Glasman and commentators like David Goodhart, this loosely organised movement seeks to make parties like Labour more supportive of socially conservative themes like patriotism, local tradition and family values.

among working-class voters. Modern socialists, it seemed, were increasingly distant from the people they purported to represent.

Among socialists, attempts to resolve this dilemma have since been made by movements such as **Blue Labour**, which seeks 'to harness the case for greater economic equality and greater public ownership ... with the case for patriotism, local pride and family values'. With voters increasingly anxious about the future – particularly in relation to the economy, the environment and public health – the success of such 'leftist-conservative' movements may prove crucial to the future of socialism.

Summary: key themes and key thinkers

	Human nature	The state	Society	The economy
Karl Marx and Friedrich Engels	Human nature, originally fraternal and altruistic, has been contaminated by capitalism, instilling the 'false consciousness' of bourgeois values. Revolutionary socialism, however, will repair this.	The existing liberal-bourgeois state is a tool of the dominant capitalist class; it must be destroyed by revolution and replaced by a new socialist state: the dictatorship of the proletariat.	Capitalist society is sickeningly, yet fatally, defined by class interests and class conflict. A communist society will be the perfect 'end of history'.	Capitalism is corrupt, inefficient and ultimately self-destructive. It should – and will – be replaced by an economy based on collective ownership.
Rosa Luxemburg	Human nature has not been damaged to the extent **Marx** alleged. Fraternity and altruism still flourish in working-class communities punished by capitalist economics.	The existing capitalist state must be destroyed by revolution, but one arising from strike action. The replacement state should be a genuine democracy, complete with free speech and free elections.	Capitalist society is class-ridden and morally indefensible, yet alternative societies, or sub-cultures, exist within downtrodden proletarian communities.	Capitalism is more resilient than **Marx** allowed. Its necessary destruction, and replacement by an economy based on workers' control, will require determination and solidarity among the proletariat.
Beatrice Webb	The damage inflicted by capitalism upon the human psyche will only be made worse by violent revolution. Humanity needs to be guided back, gradually, to its original, cooperative condition.	If harnessed to universal suffrage, the existing state could be used for a gradual transition to socialism.	The poverty and inequalities of a capitalist society continue to depress human potential while fostering regressive competition.	A chaotic capitalist economy will gradually be replaced by one which gives workers the full fruits of their labour, based upon common ownership of the means of production.

	Human nature	The state	Society	The economy
Anthony Crosland	Human nature has a powerful sense of 'fairness' and an innate objection to huge inequalities of outcome.	Democratic socialist governments (for example, Labour 1945–51) prove that the existing state can be used to effect radical, socialist change.	Society is increasingly complicated, altered by the emergence of new social groups comprising 'meritocratic' managers and 'classless' technocrats.	A mixed economy, underpinned by limited public ownership and Keynesian capitalism, will finance the greater public spending necessary to secure equality.
Anthony Giddens	Human nature has been shaped by changing socio-economic conditions. The pro-fairness instinct is still present, but it now competes with a sharpened sense of individual aspiration.	The existing liberal state should be improved, redistributing and decentralising political power while encouraging greater political participation.	Society has undergone embourgeoisement – egalitarians must harness, rather than deny, these forces.	A neo-liberal economy, propelled by privatisation and deregulation, will provide huge tax yields. This will finance huge increases in public spending, which will secure greater equality of opportunity.

Tensions within socialism

- **Human nature:** all socialists believe human nature is malleable and improvable, 'plastic' not permanent. Yet some socialists, such as **Karl Marx**, believe human nature is susceptible to whichever economic system it lives under. Therefore, people are likely to suffer a 'false consciousness' that can be cured only by revolution and the overthrow of capitalism. Other socialists, including revisionists like **Anthony Giddens**, argue that human nature can prosper under capitalism, yet still appreciate the importance of core socialist beliefs such as co-operation, fraternity and collectivism.

- **Society:** all socialists see our social environment (i.e. society) as the crucial determinant of our personalities. Socialists disagree about whether society can be improved gradually. Revolutionary socialists such as **Marx** see existing society as so contrary to socialist values that only a revolution can ensure progress. Evolutionary socialists, like **Beatrice Webb**, believe society can be 'gradually' improved and socialist values established by a series of reforms that 'gradually' curtail private ownership. Revisionists such as **Anthony Crosland** and **Giddens** also argue that society can be steadily improved and believe that such improvements can occur alongside private property and capitalism.

- **The state:** unlike collectivist anarchists, socialists believe a state is vital to the promotion of core socialist values. But they differ dramatically in their views of what kind of state is needed. **Marx** and **Rosa Luxemburg** believed the existing capitalist state would have to be destroyed by revolution and that its replacement would eventually 'wither away' to produce stateless communism. However, **Marx** stated that the replacement would be a 'dictatorship of the proletariat', whereas **Luxemburg** wanted a 'democratic' state that allowed free elections and party competition. Meanwhile, both evolutionary socialists like **Webb**, and revisionists like **Crosland** and

Giddens, believed the existing state can be used to steer society towards socialist values, and that the state in capitalist society requires constitutional reform rather than abolition.

- **The economy:** revolutionary socialists like **Marx** and **Luxemburg** and evolutionary socialists such as **Webb** believe socialism is incompatible with a capitalist economy and private property. Marxists and orthodox communists believe a new non-capitalist economy should be created quickly, via revolution, while democratic socialists like **Webb** believe a non-capitalist economy will be created gradually, via a series of elected socialist governments. Revisionists believe socialism is possible within a capitalist economy. Social democrat revisionists such as **Crosland** believe the economy should be 'mixed' (both private and public ownership) and run along Keynesian lines by governments. Third Way revisionists like **Giddens** believe the economy should be re-mixed in a way that leaves it more privatised and neo-liberal, claiming this will produce a greater tax yield and thus enable more public spending.

Further reading

Politics Review articles

Kavanagh, M. (2021) 'Social democracy and the Third Way', *Politics Review*, vol. 30, no. 4.
Kavanagh, M. (2021) 'Karl Marx's theory of history', *Politics Review*, vol. 31, no. 1.
Tuck, D. (2020) 'Socialism and the economy', *Politics Review*, vol. 29, no. 4.

Books

Gilbert, J. (2020) *Twenty First Century Socialism*, Polity Press.
Newman, M. (2005) *Socialism: A Very Short Introduction*, Oxford University Press.

Exam-style questions

AQA

Short-answer questions

1 Explain and analyse three ways in which socialist thinkers promote equality. (9 marks)

2 Explain and analyse three ways in which socialist thinkers view the state. (9 marks)

Extract question

3 Read the extracts below and answer the question that follows.

Extract 1

In the higher phase of communist society, when the enslaving subordination of the individual has vanished; when labour is no longer merely a means of life but life's principal need; when the productive forces have also increased with the all-round development of the individual, and all the springs of co-operative wealth flow more abundantly … only then will society be able to inscribe on its banners: 'From each according to his ability, to each according to his needs'.

Karl Marx, *Critique of the Gotha Programme* (1875)

Extract 2

The party aims to secure for the workers by hand or by brain the full fruits of their industry and the most equitable distribution thereof that may be possible upon the basis of common ownership of the means of production, distribution and exchange and the best obtainable system of popular administration and control of each industry and service.

Clause IV, part V of the Labour Party constitution, 1918 (written by Sidney Webb of the Fabian Society)

Analyse, evaluate and compare the arguments made in the above extracts about socialism's view of capitalism. In your answer, you should refer to the thinkers you have studied. (25 marks)

Edexcel

Essay questions

4 To what extent are reformist and revolutionary socialists more united than divided? You must use appropriate thinkers you have studied to support your answer and consider differing views in a balanced way. (24 marks)

5 To what extent does socialism endorse the state in capitalist society? You must use appropriate thinkers you have studied to support your answer and consider differing views in a balanced way. (24 marks)

6 To what extent is socialism committed to equality? You must use appropriate thinkers you have studied to support your answer and consider differing views in a balanced way. (24 marks)

BURKE

Conservatism

Learning outcomes

This chapter will enable students to:

- understand the contrast between conservatism and the two other 'core' ideologies
- understand there is more to conservatism than conserving
- understand that conservatism is an ideology that bends according to circumstance
- understand the continuities between 'ancient' and 'modern' conservative thinkers.

Key thinkers

This chapter will frequently reference the key conservative thinkers cited in A-level exam specifications:

- Thomas Hobbes (1588–1679)
- Edmund Burke (1729–97)
- Michael Oakeshott (1901–90)
- Ayn Rand (1905–82)
- Robert Nozick (1938–2002).

Introduction: a paradoxical ideology

As we shall see in the course of this chapter, conservatism is a durable ideology that has responded to a series of remarkable changes over two centuries. Yet, despite its durability, conservatism is widely misunderstood. This may arise from a number of paradoxes that are worth explaining at the outset.

The first paradox is that conservatism is *a form of change*. In other words, conservatism is not just about conserving; and it is certainly not about avoiding change at all costs. Instead, it champions the cause of changing to conserve. In this sense, it is useful to distinguish between conservative politics and reactionary politics: whereas the latter seeks to resist all change, to restore what has been lost and 'turn back the clock', conservatism argues that such objectives are futile and counterproductive.

Key term

Change to conserve
This is the fundamental principle of conservatism and one that distinguishes a conservative from a reactionary. It indicates a belief that, for something valuable to be preserved, it has to be continuously updated and maintained.

Like liberals and socialists, conservatives see change as inevitable and indeed essential. What matters for conservatives is that *change occurs in a certain manner*; one that will draw upon, rather than dismiss, concepts like tradition, experience and continuity. Furthermore, conservatives assert that change, when conducted in a certain way, is the *only* way to conserve what is best about the status quo. As **Edmund Burke** (Key thinker 2) observed: 'A state without the means of change … is without the means of its conservation'.

To understand this paradox, we need only recall that few things survive by remaining unchanged: much of what endures will have had ongoing attention, nurture and renewal. For this reason, **Michael Oakeshott** (Key thinker 3) liked to describe conservatism as a 'doctrine of maintenance'; a philosophy that rejects *iconoclasm* (the destruction of that which has traditionally been respected and praised) but which nonetheless embraces reform. What distinguishes most conservatives is their belief that change should be about repair and careful adjustment, rather than breezy demolition and a wish to start from scratch. As **Oakeshott** explained:

> The preservation of an ancient building, or perhaps a venerable vehicle, will not be achieved through inaction and inertia … preservation demands constant attention, harnessed to a keen awareness of what has gone before.

Another paradox to consider is that *conservatism is not always the same as Conservatism*. In other words, conservatism, particularly the orthodox or 'traditional' conservatism described later in this chapter – is not always synonymous with the ideas of the UK Conservative Party. However, it is useful to understand *why* this is the case. One of the most important reasons is that the Conservative Party advocates not just the principles of traditional conservatism (outlined below) but also many of the ideas previously championed by classical liberalism. This distinction, between the philosophical principles of orthodox conservatism and the party-political principles of Conservatism, became especially marked during the mid-to-late twentieth century when the Conservative Party exploited the decline of the UK Liberal Party by absorbing many of the ideas associated with nineteenth-century Liberal politicians – notably support for individual freedom and free-market economics. That said, the advent of New Right conservatism in the 1970s (also outlined later in this chapter) did reflect to some extent the union of liberal and conservative values within the Conservative Party.

Key terms

Radical A reform which involves 'root and branch' change and which shows little sympathy for past practices and opinions.

Progressive Linked to the values of other ideologies, notably liberalism and socialism, this denotes a belief that problems can usually be eliminated, rather than merely contained or endured, and that the future can and will be better than the past and present.

The final paradox attending conservatism is that *conservative instincts are not only found within the Conservative Party.* Many of those who fear drastic change, for example, are especially fearful of free-market capitalism and globalisation, neither of which have much respect for tradition (a key theme within conservative ideology). Yet the sternest opposition to such developments has usually come not from the Conservative Party (which has often championed them) but from left-wing parties like Podemos in Spain and Syriza in Greece. Likewise, withdrawal from the European Union, one of the most **radical** changes undertaken by any UK government since 1945, and pursued after 2016 by successive Conservative prime ministers, was strenuously opposed by many **progressive** politicians from parties like Labour and the Liberal Democrats. Indeed, such politicians – for example, Labour's Sir Keir Starmer and the Liberal Democrats' Sir Ed Davey – frequently denounced the 'Brexit' phenomenon as 'reckless' and a threat to 'stability' and 'continuity': fears historically associated with the essence of orthodox conservatism.

Clearly, conservatism is a more subtle and complex doctrine than many might imagine. It is therefore helpful to examine its provenance.

Knowledge check

1 What is the difference between conservatism and Conservatism?
2 Which radical or drastic changes might be feared by anti-Conservative politicians?

The origins of conservatism

Like liberalism and socialism, conservatism is a by-product of the Enlightenment. This was an intellectual movement of the seventeenth and eighteenth centuries which encouraged greater scrutiny of religion, politics, science and other aspects of the human condition. However, compared to the other core ideologies, conservatism's relationship with the Enlightenment is more complicated and nuanced.

Key liberal thinkers like **Mary Wollstonecraft**, and recent socialist thinkers such as **Anthony Crosland**, were inclined to argue that conservatism was a reaction *against* the Enlightenment. Indeed, **Wollstonecraft** even suggested that conservative thinkers like **Thomas Hobbes** (see Key thinker 1) and **Edmund Burke** were seeking to *reverse* the central principles of Enlightenment philosophy. For example,

Hobbes was in favour of concentrated political power while Burke denounced 'abstract' notions like equality in favour of aristocratic privilege. Yet the **Wollstonecraft/Crosland** argument – that conservatism is a reactionary doctrine – is misplaced and overlooks the vital contribution made by both **Hobbes** and **Burke** to Enlightenment thinking.

Prior to his historic work *Leviathan* in 1651, **Thomas Hobbes** was already noted for his attempts to apply Enlightenment principles, like reason and logic, to disciplines such as physics and mathematics. Indeed, it was this same, rationalist approach which led **Hobbes** to conclude that the 'divine right of kings', as advocated by contemporary scholar Robert Filmer, was an intellectually flimsy basis for modern government. Instead, **Hobbes** contested that divine right should be replaced by the principle of 'government by consent', where the authority of government rests ultimately with *the governed* rather than any monarch or god. Just like the liberal thinker **John Locke**, **Hobbes** therefore insisted upon a 'social contract' as the basis of any 'rational' state: a deal whereby governments were only legitimate if they served the pre-identified interests of the governed. For this reason alone, **Hobbes** might be seen not as an opponent of the Enlightenment, but as one of its earliest spokesmen.

Likewise, prior to writing his critique of the French Revolution, which erupted in 1789, **Edmund Burke** was seen as a progressive, rather than reactionary, figure. As a Whig MP, **Burke** had endorsed the economic liberalism of Adam Smith (emphasising laissez-faire economics), criticised the effects of British imperialism in India, and famously supported the rebels' cause during the American War of Independence. Indeed, in his *Reflections on the Revolution in France* (1790), **Burke** insisted that 'Man is by nature reasonable', in addition to making the assertion (quoted earlier) that states hoping to survive must find ways to reform.

However, while neither **Hobbes** nor **Burke** wished to halt or reverse the Enlightenment, they were concerned that its pursuit could have dire consequences. **Hobbes** was especially keen to ensure that, when a traditional model of government is scrapped, its replacement quickly guarantees public safety. **Hobbes** claimed that, without such guarantees, lofty notions such as 'liberty', 'tolerance' and 'reason' are illusory and unsustainable. It was therefore no accident that **Hobbes** conceived *Leviathan* during the English Civil War: a period of terrifying disorder and

Key term

Laissez-faire economics based on the theories of Adam Smith's *The Wealth of Nations* (1776), this involves governments allowing market forces and economic competition to operate freely. Laissez-faire capitalism will normally involve low levels of taxation, public spending and state regulation.

anarchy, caused largely by an emphatically progressive idea: the defiance of monarchical rule.

Edmund Burke offered a further important caveat to Enlightenment thinking: that progress requires not just a passion for improvement, but also a respect for tradition and experience. This caveat also helps explain one of the great paradoxes of **Burke**'s career: namely, his loud support for the American Revolution in 1775 and his vehement opposition to the French Revolution just fifteen years later.

From **Burke**'s perspective, the American Revolution was a noble attempt to conserve or restore an established pattern of colonial life, one that had 'organically' evolved during the previous century. Consequently, he argued that the American rebellion was a clear case of 'changing to conserve'. By contrast, **Burke** noted that the French Revolution aimed to impose a new and wholly untested way of life, based on nothing more than theory, and contemptuous of experience and tradition. According to his later supporters, **Burke**'s belief that the French Revolution was a terrible mistake – one that would lead to 'fearsome darkness' rather than enlightenment – was powerfully vindicated by the repression and genocide that soon engulfed the new French Republic.

It must be remembered that the views of **Hobbes** and **Burke** were not inseparable. **Burke**, for example, disliked the concentrated power prescribed by **Hobbes** and was keener than **Hobbes** on the concept of a 'natural' ruling class, or aristocracy. As such, the differences between *Leviathan* and *Reflections* provide an early example of how conservatism is an evolutionary creed, with different points of emphasis from one generation to the next. As we shall see later in the chapter, the changeable nature of conservatism was again demonstrated, in both the UK and USA, by the emergence of the New Right in the 1970s. Indeed, by combining elements of conservative *and* liberal thinking, the New Right offered a fresh example of how conservatives can both embrace and criticise 'progressive' ideas.

In summary, conservatism does not come from either a rejection of the Enlightenment or a rejection of 'progress' generally. Instead, it is rooted in a wish to ensure that progress is compatible with both experience and security. To adapt the nautical metaphor coined by **Michael Oakeshott**, conservatism does not seek to abandon or disable the vessel of Enlightenment; merely to slow it down from time to time, occasionally alter course, and always ensure the voyage continues safely.

Knowledge check

3 When and what was the Enlightenment?
4 Who was Adam Smith and what is economic liberalism?

Thomas Hobbes

Comparing ideas

The Enlightenment

Whereas liberalism and socialism have clear links to the Enlightenment, as shown by their stress on both liberty and equality, conservatism's relationship with the Enlightenment is more opaque – due mainly to **Hobbes'** support for concentrated political power, and **Burke**'s preference for aristocratic societies. However, like liberal thinkers, **Hobbes** endorsed the principle of government by consent, while **Burke** defended constitutional government and free-market capitalism.

Key thinker 1

Thomas Hobbes (1588–1679)

Thomas Hobbes is considered one of England's most important political thinkers. Although widely seen as a 'conservative' philosopher, he is also linked to the liberal principle of government by consent and the philosophical idea of a 'state of nature', later used to different effect by the liberal philosopher **John Locke**.

■ In his most famous work, *Leviathan* (1651), Hobbes took a profoundly sceptical view of human nature, arguing it was ruthlessly egotistical and likely to commit cruel and destructive acts. Hobbes also asserted that, prior to the emergence of a state, there was no co-operation or voluntary arrangements between individuals and therefore none of the 'natural rights' later cited by liberals. Instead, the Hobbesian state of nature was a place of scarce resources where individuals would be driven by unflinching self-interest. Human nature was thus shaped by a restless desire for the acquisition of goods, an immovable distrust of others and a constant fear of violent death. In Hobbes' own words, life in this state of nature would be 'solitary, poor, nasty, brutish and short'.

■ For Hobbes, such 'natural chaos' stemmed from the absence of any formal authority, which could enforce an unquestioned code of right and wrong. In its absence, Hobbes noted, mankind in the state of nature was left to form its own version of acceptable conduct. Yet because each person's version of this was likely to be different, uncertainty and war were inevitable.

■ Because Hobbes did not consider mankind irrational, he believed it would eventually recognise the state of nature as being contrary to self-interest and agree to a 'contract'. Under this contract, individuals would render to a 'sovereign' (the state) the right to make laws which restrained everyone and allow the order and security that were absent in the state of nature. This would eventually lead to a 'society', where individuals could enjoy some security and progress.

■ For the state to accomplish its side of the bargain, Hobbes claimed its power must be concentrated. If it were dispersed, Hobbes argued, then the conflicts within the state of nature would soon be replicated.

■ In summary, Hobbes argued that the principal reason for the state was the creation of order and security; that without such a state there could be no civil society; and for the state to be effective, it would have to be awesome and forbidding.

Edmund Burke (1729–97)

As a Whig MP, Edmund Burke was known as the champion of numerous progressive causes during the mid-to-late eighteenth century. He was a firm supporter of the American Revolution after 1775, defended Irish tenants in their clashes with extortionate landlords, demanded the impeachment of the governor general of Bengal (Warren Hastings) for alleged cruelty towards Hindustanis, and was a fervent advocate of Adam Smith's call for free trade. Yet despite this radical pedigree, Burke is widely considered the father of conservatism and one of the Enlightenment's most important critics. How did this arise?

- The answer lies in Burke's impassioned opposition to the French Revolution of 1789, via his famous text *Reflections on the Revolution in France* (1790). It was in this book that Burke defined various tenets of conservative thought, including human imperfection, empiricism, organicism, tradition, aristocracy and localism.
- In respect of human imperfection, Burke stressed mankind's fallibility and its tendency to fail more than succeed. He therefore denounced the idealistic society that the French Revolution imagined, claiming it was based on a utopian – and thus unrealistic – view of human nature.
- Burke argued that, while change was necessary to conserve, change should proceed on the

basis of fact and experience rather than theory and idealism. Burke duly criticised the French Revolution for discarding what was 'known' in favour of an entirely new society based on 'philosophical abstraction'. This was a very different rationale, Burke argued, from that of the American colonists, whose own revolution stemmed from a practical desire to conserve an established way of life that had evolved organically.

- Burke claimed that both society and the state were complex, based on history and slow, evolutionary change. He therefore insisted that future change must also be cautious and organic, and denounced the French Revolution for discarding history and tradition.
- Burke was scathing about the French Revolution's stress on equality, asserting that within all 'organic' societies, a ruling class was inevitable and desirable. However, this class had a clear obligation to govern in the interests of all. For Burke, it was the French aristocracy's failure to do this that had led to revolution.
- Burke condemned the new French republic for its highly centralised structures, praising instead a society of 'little platoons': a multitude of small, diverse and largely autonomous communities, which would 'acknowledge, nurture and prune … the crooked timber of humanity'.

Knowledge check

5 Why might the work of Hobbes be seen as an example of Enlightenment thinking?
6 Why might the work of Hobbes be seen as a challenge to Enlightenment thinking?
7 Why might the work of Burke be seen as an example of Enlightenment thinking?
8 Why was Burke thought to be challenging Enlightenment thinking?
9 Why is Burke thought to have a contradictory view of revolutions?

The core ideas of conservatism

View of human nature

Fixed and flawed

The conservative view of human nature is defined largely by its response and opposition to the views of rival ideologies, especially liberalism and socialism. Whereas these 'progressive' ideologies take a generally upbeat view of human potential, asserting that human beings have the capacity for endless achievement and improvement, conservatives are inclined to restrain such optimism by stressing human frailty and human imperfection.

Likewise, conservatism rejects the malleable or 'plastic' view of human nature offered both by socialists such as **Karl Marx**, who looked forward to dispelling 'false consciousness', and by liberals like **John Stuart Mill**, who spoke of 'man as a progressive being'. Equally, conservatism denies that humanity can be positively reshaped within the 'correct' environment or society. Rather, it sees human nature as constant and imperfect. As a result, traditional conservative philosophers, such as Anthony Quinton (1925–2010) and **Michael Oakeshott**, have described the conservative view of human nature as 'a philosophy of imperfection'. This imperfection has been depicted in various ways by different conservative thinkers.

Cynical

Thomas Hobbes took a famously cynical view of human nature, arguing that life in the 'state of nature' – the imagined world before formal law and government emerged – was sharply different from that outlined by liberal theorists like **Locke**. Whereas **Locke** judged human nature to be egotistical yet respectful of others, **Hobbes** was more pessimistic, viewing it as *egotistical and ruthless* in pursuit of self-interest. Consequently, **Hobbes** argued that within the state of nature, where formal restraints on human conduct were absent, relations between human beings were marked by 'envy, hatred and violent conflict' and that life itself was 'solitary, poor, nasty, brutish and short'.

Yet, for **Hobbes**, the human condition would eventually be redeemed by our capacity for reason (another reason why **Hobbes** should be seen as an example, rather than a critic, of Enlightenment philosophy). He theorised that warring individuals would eventually reason that the state of nature was an obstacle, not a pathway, to their self-interest and self-fulfilment. This, in turn, would lead them to establish a formal

> **Key term**
>
> **Human imperfection**
> A shorthand term for conservatism's view of human nature, one that stresses our frailty, fallibility and limited capacity for self-improvement.

state which ensured order and security. Such a state would then enable individuals to pursue their self-interest far more efficiently — and far less hazardously.

Sceptical

Edmund Burke's view of human nature was at the heart of his response to the French Revolution after 1789. The revolution had offered the vision of a utopian (near-perfect) society in which human misery was erased. The joyous mood prompted by the Revolution, at least in its early stages, was encapsulated by the poet William Wordsworth, who proclaimed: 'Bliss was it in that dawn to be alive. But to be young was very heaven!'

Burke, however, was dismissive of such ideas, claiming they were based on an implausibly upbeat view of human potential. He offered a more sceptical view, one which advertised 'the warts and foibles that mark each man'. **Burke** also emphasised 'the timeless chasm' between human aspiration and achievement, using this 'chasm' as grounds for opposing the French revolutionaries' pursuit of perfection. **Burke** argued that, precisely because of our tendency to fall short, change should normally be slow and gradual. This cautious approach would then allow us to reset, back-track and revise, should we find we have misjudged our capacity to improve.

Forgiving

In contrast to the rather negative interpretation of human nature offered by **Hobbes** and **Burke**, **Michael Oakeshott** offered one that was more hopeful and forgiving. Insisting that humanity generally was 'fallible not terrible', and 'imperfect not immoral', **Oakeshott** argued that while we often fail to meet our targets, we are still capable of kindness, fellowship, generosity and solidarity with others.

With **Oakeshott** in mind, it has therefore been argued, by recent conservative scholars such as Roger Scruton (1944–2020), that conservatives actually take a *tolerant* view of human nature; recognising its faults, certainly, but also highlighting its many redeeming features. Scruton even argued that conservatives such as **Oakeshott** are more positive about human nature *as it is* than liberal thinkers like **John Stuart Mill** or socialist thinkers like **Karl Marx**, both of whom seemed positive only in respect of what human nature *could be* as a result of social and political reform.

According to **Oakeshott**, human nature was not, as **Hobbes** claimed, driven by brutally selfish rationalism. Instead, **Oakeshott** portrayed human beings as creatures of habit, instinct, impulse and emotion, with a fondness for the *communal* pleasures of 'family, friends, gardens and games'. For this reason, **Oakeshott** argued that human nature was rarely motivated by visionary ideological projects, of the sort associated with socialism and liberalism. Instead, he argued, most people preferred:

> ... the familiar to the unknown ... the tried to the untried, fact to mystery, the actual to the possible, the limited to the unbounded, the near to the distant, the sufficient to the superabundant, the convenient to the perfect, present laughter to utopian bliss.

Key thinker 3

Michael Oakeshott (1901–90)

Michael Oakeshott is regarded as one of the most important conservative philosophers of the twentieth century, bringing a fresh perspective to the core themes of traditional conservatism. Oakeshott's key text on the subject, *On Being Conservative* (1962), is renowned for its fresh interpretation of how conservatives regarded human imperfection. In particular, it is remembered for its argument that a 'philosophy of imperfection' need not be a 'philosophy of pessimism' or indeed unhappiness.

- First of all, Oakeshott wished to qualify the negative view of human nature associated with **Thomas Hobbes**. Most men and women, he argued, were 'fallible but not terrible' and 'imperfect but not immoral'. Though incapable of the 'perfect' societies linked to other ideologies, humanity was still able to secure 'both pleasure and improvement through the humdrum business of everyday life'.

- From this perspective, Oakeshott tried to make conservatism seem more optimistic than ideologies such as liberalism and socialism. He argued that such ideologies, with their clear views of how society 'should' be, simply led to impatience, intolerance and frustration. By contrast, Oakeshott claimed that conservatives are reconciled to human imperfection and thus have a greater appreciation of the pleasures that already exist in life – such as families and friends.

- Being dismissive of 'normative' politics, with its 'simplistic' visions that overlook 'the complexity of now', Oakeshott affirmed the merits of an empirical and pragmatic approach to both politics and life generally. He argued that it was through experience, trial and error, rather than abstract philosophy, that wisdom was achieved.

- These perspectives on human nature informed Oakeshott's views about the state. In his final work, *The Politics of Faith and the Politics of Scepticism* (published in 1996, six years after Oakeshott's death), he argued that the state existed to 'prevent the bad rather than create the good', restating that the best things in life normally emerge from routine, apolitical activity. This also led him to offer his celebrated 'nautical metaphor': that, during our lives, 'we all sail a boundless sea, with no appointed destination' and that the job of government is to reflect this by:

  > keeping the ship afloat at all costs ... using experience to negotiate every storm, stoicism to accept necessary changes of direction ... and not fixating on a port that may not exist.

- Oakeshott's critics, especially conservative critics on the New Right, claim his philosophy is too fatalistic and underestimates our ability to shape circumstances. For New Right philosophers like **Robert Nozick**, the 'Oakeshott mentality' was 'lazy' and allowed socialist ideas to advance unchallenged after 1945.

Knowledge check

14 Why was Oakeshott not downbeat in his view of human nature?

15 Why did Burke and Oakeshott think communities were important?

Communal

While **Hobbes** depicted human nature as mercilessly individualistic, this view was rejected by both **Burke** and **Oakeshott**. They insisted that human beings, mindful of their own imperfection, were *sociable* creatures, drawn to the security of local communities and the 'sense of belonging' they provide. **Burke** referred to such communities as 'little platoons', and they will be examined later in relation to conservatism and society.

The New Right perspective

Hobbes's more individualistic view of human nature, however, is not isolated or eccentric within conservative thought. Indeed, it was significantly updated following the advent of New Right conservatism in the 1970s. Drawing upon the New Right's neo-liberal dimension, key thinkers like **Ayn Rand** (Key thinker 4) and **Robert Nozick** (Key thinker 5) stressed our yearning for individual freedom, autonomy and self-determination. As the central character in **Rand**'s novel *The Fountainhead* (1943) declares, 'I recognise no obligation towards men except one: to respect their freedom.'

Echoing **Hobbes**, the New Right emphasised human nature's *egotism* – or what **Nozick** termed 'our restless quest for self-betterment'. However, unlike **Hobbes**, who thought such characteristics were likely to produce conflict, New Right thinkers believed egotism inspired a vibrant capitalist economy, the enrichment of society, and general contentment: an idea reflected in the title of another **Rand** book, *The Virtue of Selfishness* (1964). However, in a nod to the traditional conservatism of **Burke** and **Oakeshott**, the New Right agreed that even the most dynamic individuals need the periodic restraint of formal authority and the support of communities; a key difference from the unchecked individualism of anarcho-capitalists like Murray Rothbard (1926–55).

Ayn Rand

Key thinker 4

Ayn Rand (1905–82)

The sharp differences between traditional and New Right conservatism were highlighted by the writings of Ayn Rand, one of the USA's most provocative New Right thinkers.

■ Rand's defining work, the novel *Atlas Shrugged* (1957), secured her status as a highly influential

libertarian. Its theme was that talented individuals, rather than ambitious governments, lay at the heart of any successful society. The novel suggested that without the energy of such individuals, a society would quickly wither – no matter how much activity was expended by governments.

- This theme was restated in a non-fictional way through Rand's works of philosophy. *The Virtue of Selfishness* (1964) explained a philosophical system that Rand described as 'objectivism' – its core belief being that we should all be guided by self-interest and 'rational self-fulfilment'.
- For this reason, Rand became associated with the New Right's **atomism**, the term for a society defined by millions of autonomous individuals, each independently seeking self-fulfilment and self-realisation. Indeed, Rand's work provided a philosophical justification for the idea that society did not exist in any practical form; it was just a loose collection of independent individuals.
- Although Rand's ideas are consistent with both classical liberalism and **neo-liberalism**, they gained political traction on account of New Right politics in the 1970s. Her 'objectivist' philosophy became strongly linked to the New Right's support for a more laissez-faire brand of capitalism and its renewal of 'negative liberty', thus providing a philosophical justification for 'rolling back the frontiers of the state' via policies such as tax cuts and privatisation.
- Rand was proud to call herself a libertarian, in that she defended not just free markets but also an individual's 'right to choose' in areas like homosexuality and abortion. However, Rand dismissed the rights of native Americans, and argued they had no right to property that was 'primitive' or ancestral.
- In her later work, Rand strengthened her connection to conservatism by stating that liberty was impossible without order and security, which only a state could provide. Her conservative credentials were highlighted by her support for the ultra-conservative Republican candidate Barry Goldwater in the 1964 US presidential election, during which she wrote: 'The small state is the strong state.'

Key terms

Atomism Denotes the New Right/neo-liberal view that human beings prioritise autonomy and 'space', leading to only a vague awareness of 'society'. Traditional conservatives reject this view, arguing that individuals are both defined by and connected to their communities.

Neo-liberalism Linked to the work of philosopher Friedrich von Hayek, this updates the principles of classical liberalism by emphasising individual liberty within the context of minimal state interference. It therefore argues that liberty can only be secured if state intervention is significantly reduced.

Knowledge check

16 What is meant by 'neo-liberalism'?

Robert Nozick (1938–2002)

During the 1970s, Robert Nozick emerged as one of the key thinkers for New Right conservatism. His key work, *Anarchy, State and Utopia* (1974), remains a vital reference for modern conservative philosophy.

- Nozick developed many of the themes first raised by neo-liberal philosopher Friedrich von Hayek in *The Road to Serfdom* (1944). Like Hayek, Nozick argued that the growth of government was the gravest contemporary threat to individual freedom. More specifically, Nozick thought that the growth of welfare states in western Europe fostered a 'dependency culture'.

- Despite the title of his most famous work, Nozick was not a 'true' anarchist in that he believed in a 'minarchist' state – one that mainly involved outsourcing public services to private companies.

- This minarchist prescription owed much to Nozick's optimistic view of human nature, which seems very different from that of **Thomas Hobbes** and **Edmund Burke**. Indeed, some have suggested that Nozick's philosophy has less in common with conservatism than with strands of anarchism. For example, his claim that 'tax, for the most part, is theft' indicates an upbeat view that individuals have self-ownership, that they are the sole authors of their talents and abilities, and that they should be left alone to realise those talents without intervention from government. However, there are reasons why Nozick is considered a conservative:

- First, Nozick's view of human nature was not wholeheartedly positive. He argued that, while dishonesty, theft and violence were not the main characteristics of humanity, the preservation of life, liberty and property 'could not be taken for granted' without some formal authority enforcing laws: a vital concession to the legacy of **Hobbes**.

- Secondly, the purpose of Nozick's limited state was not simply to facilitate raw individualism and free-market capitalism. For Nozick, the minarchism he prescribed would allow a multitude of self-sufficient communities to emerge alongside the extension of individual freedom. In Nozick's minarchist society, each of these communities would be free to practise its particular values, including values which might be seen as culturally unorthodox. This arguably represents an updated version of **Burke**'s view that the best form of society is one comprising a variety of 'little platoons'.

Knowledge check

17 How does the New Right's view of human nature differ from that of earlier conservatism?

Comparing ideas

Human nature

Whereas liberals and socialists believe human nature can be infinitely improved, conservativism is inclined to see it as fixed and fallible. Like socialists, traditional conservatives believe we are naturally drawn to the support and solidarity of communities. New Right conservatives, however, share liberalism's view that human beings are motivated by a desire for self-reliance.

View of society

Rejection of 'natural' society

Unlike many liberal and socialist thinkers, traditional conservative thinkers like **Thomas Hobbes** and **Edmund Burke** dismiss any notion that society is 'natural', or that it somehow predates the state. Given their sceptical view of human nature, and mindful that 'society' involves the peaceful interaction of individuals, neither **Hobbes** nor **Burke** thought society possible without law and order – which only a state could provide. With reference to the English Civil War and French Revolution respectively, **Hobbes** and **Burke** argued that, once law and order collapse, the various trappings of society, such as individual rights and a respect for personal property, quickly disappear. For this reason, conservatism sees 'natural rights', 'natural laws' and 'natural society' as dangerous fantasies. This belief forms a big part of its opposition to liberalism, socialism and anarchism.

The 'little platoons'

Rather than viewing society as a single entity, traditional conservatives such as **Burke** and **Oakeshott** see it as an assortment of local, voluntary and largely apolitical mini communities – what **Burke** described as 'little platoons'. These 'platoons' are exemplified by local churches, clubs, teams and families, and are unified by an attachment to what was later termed 'one nation'. According to **Michael Oakeshott**, these voluntary units provide their members with security, fellowship and a sense of purpose, while 'helping us help one another'.

These 'little platoons' also perform a vital, moderating purpose. First, they moderate the competitive egotism of individuals which, as **Hobbes** argued, can prohibit society. Secondly, they moderate the power of the state. As **Oakeshott** explained, 'a strong society protects us from an over-mighty government' by providing individuals with much of the support they might otherwise need from remote and impersonal bureaucracies. This notion was given wider circulation by David Cameron, shortly after he became Conservative prime minister in 2010. Promising a 'big society and a small state', Cameron duly emphasised that 'there *is* such a thing as society; it's just not the same thing as the state'.

Key term

Tradition Linked to opinions and practices that have been handed down from one generation to the next. Supporters of tradition argue that such opinions and practices have been 'tried and tested' and therefore remove any need for radical change.

The 'organic' society

For traditional conservatives, the kind of society extolled by **Burke** and **Oakeshott** cannot be planned or created; it is something that can only emerge gradually and *organically*. Conservatives therefore view society as less like a machine, responding to levers pulled by human hands, and more like a plant, emerging and growing in a way that can never be wholly foreseen. However, conservatives freely admit that their 'organic' society still requires discipline and attention, and is therefore only possible once law, order and authority are established.

Importance of tradition

The notion of an organic society helps explain the conservative view that a good society values **tradition**. As Scruton observed:

> Just as a plant's new leaves are connected to, dependent upon, and explained by its roots and branches, so a society's present course stems ineluctably from its past locations.

In a similar vein, **Burke** described the best kind of society as a 'partnership ... between those who are living, those who are dead and those who are to be born'. For **Burke**, however, this 'partnership' was not a sentimental one; it had a current, practical purpose:

> When ancient opinions and rules of life are taken away, the loss cannot possibly be estimated. From that moment, we have no compass to govern us, nor can we know distinctly to what port we steer.

Consequently, a conservative society would not proceed according to abstract ideas, devised by our imperfect intelligence. Instead, it would be guided by practical experience and (in **Oakeshott**'s words) 'that which is known'. On the other hand, neither **Burke** nor **Oakeshott** seemed averse to the abstract ideas of traditional Christian religion. Indeed, they argued that, with its stress on Original Sin, Christian teaching had a sure understanding of human nature and was therefore the best moral basis of society. By contrast, **Burke** despaired of the atheism fostered by the French Revolution, and its certainty that the 'age of religion' had given way to a new 'age of reason'.

Paternalistic inequality

Given **Burke**'s claim that humanity is akin to 'crooked timber', the conservative view of society is one that defends inequality

Key terms

Paternalism This refers
to the obligations that
society's stronger and richer
classes have towards the
less fortunate and, indeed,
society as a whole – akin to
the responsibilities that a
father or parent might have
to younger members of a
family.

One nation Dating from
the 1870s, and linked to
leading UK Conservatives
like Benjamin Disraeli,
this term denotes a belief
that conservatism should
prioritise national cohesion
by attending to the condition
of society's poorer classes.
It has since been used to
justify conservative support
for greater state intervention
in both society and the
economy.

Knowledge check

22 What, according to Burke
and Oakeshott, was the
'familial' duty of society's
upper class?

Key term

Private property This
usually refers to land,
buildings or other
possessions that are owned
not by the state but by
individuals, businesses or
voluntary organisations.

of outcome, seeing unequal wealth and power as natural and desirable. **Burke** thus argued that the French Revolution's bid to reshape society, in the name of *égalité*, was at best futile and at worst disastrous.

However, **Burke** and **Oakeshott** argued that the beneficiaries of inequality had a crucial responsibility to the majority of society. As **Burke** explained:

> The wiser, the more expert and the more opulent ... should enlighten and protect the weaker, the less knowing and the less provided with the goods of fortune. When the multitude are not under this discipline, they can scarcely be said to be in a civil society.

This relationship is usually described as **paternalism**, in that it resembles the power and responsibility falling to parents within a family. According to **Burke**, if the upper classes neglect this 'familial' responsibility, it will unleash tensions that can overturn existing society – the obvious explanation, he thought, for the French Revolution and its overthrow of an indulgent French aristocracy. For later conservatives, like the Tory leader Benjamin Disraeli, effective paternalism was also vital to the cohesive, '**one nation**' society he and others commended.

Property

Like socialism, traditional conservatism both recognises and appreciates the importance of society and human interaction. However, unlike socialism, a conservative society is more likely to stress the value of **private property**. This does not, of course, make conservatism unique: private property will also be at the heart of a liberal society. What makes conservatism's support for property distinct are its justifications. Whereas liberals see property as a 'natural right', and a vehicle for individualism, conservatives see it as complementing several aspects of a conservative society. For example:

- As something that is often bequeathed and inherited, property is a perfect example of **Burke**'s 'partnership' between the dead, living and yet to be born.
- As something often linked to local institutions, such as churches or schools, property provides a tangible basis for **Burke**'s 'little platoons'.
- As something often associated with wealth, property is often the basis for paternalism.
- As something its owners think worth preserving, property is a force for stability and the avoidance of revolution.

Key term

Social conservatism
Denotes support for conventional family structures and codes of conduct that reflect traditional Christian morality. It is concerned by rising levels of divorce, abortion and 'alternative' lifestyles, seeing them as regrettable effects of social liberalism.

Knowledge check

23 What kind of government policies might exemplify social conservatism?

24 What do New Right conservatives mean by a 'dependency culture'?

25 What do New Right conservatives mean by an 'enterprise culture'?

26 How does the New Right's view of society differ from that of traditional conservatism?

The New Right perspective

Reflecting the influence of neo-liberalism, New Right conservatives like **Ayn Rand** and **Robert Nozick** take a more 'atomistic' view of society, seeing it not as a collection of communities and classes, but as what **Rand** termed 'a kaleidoscope of autonomous individuals'. Following certain comments by Margaret Thatcher in the 1980s, the New Right even seemed to be suggesting that there was 'no such thing' as society – a notion which David Cameron (quoted earlier) was eager to refute.

Given their faith in individualism, New Right conservatives are unimpressed by the concept of paternalism, linking it to a patronising attitude among the wealthy and a 'dependency culture' among the majority. Instead, the New Right seeks to promote an 'enterprise culture', involving greater self-reliance and self-determination. As **Rand** remarked in 1957, 'a surplus of obligation spawns a deficiency of innovation'. Likewise, although New Right conservatives share traditional conservatism's tolerance of inequality, they insist its beneficiaries must always be those who have earned, not inherited, their privileges. For the New Right, unequal societies must therefore be *meritocratic* not *aristocratic*, and therefore more like the modern USA than the historic UK.

Like traditional conservatives, the New Right sees private property as essential to the good society; **Rand** and **Nozick** thought it vital for property rights to be enjoyed by the majority of individuals. However, consistent with the New Right's neo-liberal aspect, both **Rand** and **Nozick** saw property ownership more in terms of self-realisation and self-determination than of tradition and continuity.

As will be explained later in the chapter, the New Right is not merely about neo-liberalism. It also promotes social conservatism – stressing the importance, for example, of heterosexual marriage and traditional family units. In the UK, this was demonstrated after 1979 by the Conservative government of Margaret Thatcher, which rewarded traditional marriage through

Comparing ideas

Society

Like socialists, traditional conservatives acknowledge 'society' and see it as vital to the well-being of individuals. Like socialists, but unlike liberals, traditional conservatives also recognise different classes within society. However, unlike socialists, traditional conservatives support paternalism and do not think inequality precludes a good society. The New Right's view of society is more individualistic and therefore closer to that of classical liberalism. However, all forms of conservatism endorse a society that promotes 'traditional' family values and other expressions of social conservatism.

steady increases in the marriage tax allowance. Via Section 28 of its Local Government Act 1988, Thatcher's government also prohibited schools from 'promoting' homosexual relationships.

View of the economy

Given their support for a society which defends private property and inequality, it is unsurprising conservatives back an economy that is fundamentally *capitalist* in nature. However, conservatives differ over the *type* of capitalism they prefer.

Cautious support for market forces

Traditional conservatives generally support capitalism and private enterprise – largely because they can provide a level of material prosperity, which then cements society. Yet traditional conservatives also acknowledge that laissez-faire capitalism can damage and destabilise society by exacerbating inequality. Once again, this connects to traditional conservatism's view of human nature. As Anthony Quinton observed, 'behind the forces of the market lie the forces of human imperfection'.

Many traditional conservatives would reluctantly agree with **Karl Marx** that 'raw' capitalism is the enemy of continuity and, indeed, conservation. In other words, unchecked capitalism is an iconoclastic economic system and therefore troubling to many orthodox conservatives. **Michael Oakeshott**, for example, complained that the historic charms of rural areas and village communities were frequently threatened by 'the remorseless rhythms' of market forces – an argument recently updated by those seeking to protect England's green-belt areas from property developers, or by those seeking to protect ancient woodlands from the HS2 rail project (a project mainly informed by capitalist, not conservative, imperatives).

Moderated capitalism

For this reason, traditional conservatives tend to endorse a more regulated *or moderated* form of capitalism, similar to that associated with modern liberal economist John Maynard Keynes. According to Harold Macmillan, Conservative prime minister 1957–63, the best economy is one representing a compromise between free-market capitalism and socialist state ownership – what Macmillan termed a 'middle way'. The resulting 'mixed economy' would supposedly preserve capitalism, while sustaining full employment and rising levels of public spending on public services – both of which were thought vital to the maintenance of a 'one nation' society.

Knowledge check

27 What is meant by a 'mixed economy'?

103

Free-market economy A form of capitalism where private companies and economic competition are largely unchecked by governments and the state. It is therefore closely linked to the notion of 'laissez-faire' capitalism.

Thatcherism Essentially a synonym for New Right conservatism in the UK. Between 1979 and 1990, the Thatcher governments pursued a controversial mixture of neo-liberal policies (e.g. privatisation and tax reduction) and neo-conservative policies (e.g. strengthened police powers, curbs on immigration and tax breaks for 'traditional' families).

The New Right perspective

Influenced by neo-liberal philosophers such as Friedrich von Hayek (1899–1992), New Right conservatives like **Robert Nozick** generally have a more sympathetic view of market forces and free-market economies. Indeed, during the 1980s, free-market capitalism was widely dubbed 'Thatcherism' or 'Reaganomics', on account of policies pursued by Conservative prime minister Margaret Thatcher (1925–2013) and Republican president Ronald Reagan (1911–2004). As a result, New Right economics is strongly linked to the privatisation of state-owned industries, the deregulation of state-owned utilities, and a more enthusiastic view of capitalism generally.

New Right politicians: Ronald Reagan and Margaret Thatcher

Debate 1

Is conservatism compatible with capitalism?

Yes

- Capitalism is based on private property, which all conservatives support.
- Capitalism generates hierarchy and inequality, which conservatives see as natural and 'organic'.
- In states like the UK and USA, capitalism is the established economic system and therefore consistent with conservatism's support for tradition.
- New Right conservatives see capitalism as a precondition of liberty and self-fulfilment.

No

- Capitalism generates inequality and tensions within society; it therefore threatens the traditional conservative goal of 'one nation'.
- Capitalism and market forces are often dynamic and volatile, at odds with the stability and continuity that traditional conservatives crave.
- Capitalism is linked to economic liberalism. It therefore advances competitive individualism, often at the expense of the communities valued by traditional conservatives.
- Modern capitalism tends towards 'globalisation' and the erosion of national identity.

Evaluation check: To what extent are conservatives relaxed about capitalism?

Knowledge check

28 What is meant by the UK's 'mixed economy'?
29 How does the New Right's view of the economy differ from that of traditional conservatism?

New Right conservatives usually justify such measures as practical responses to difficult economic circumstances – particularly the recession of the late twentieth century, which they saw as an indictment of Keynesianism and 'mixed' economies. But free-market economies have also been defended on wider philosophical grounds, with **Nozick** citing them as allies of individual freedom and a brake on state power.

To those who suggested that New Right economics were 'unconservative', Thatcherites and Reaganites usually offered two responses. First, it was recalled that **Edmund Burke**, as an admirer of Adam Smith, was a firm defender of free trade and a laissez-faire approach to the economy. Secondly, the New Right argued that, if the state withdrew from the economic arena, the state would be much better equipped for its true, conservative purpose – an issue we shall now examine more closely.

Comparing ideas

The economy

Like liberalism, but unlike orthodox socialism, conservatism supports capitalism and private enterprise. New Right conservatism is particularly close to the neo-liberal economic theories of Friedrich von Hayek. However, like socialism and modern liberalism, traditional conservatism has concerns about the 'divisive' effects of free markets and untamed capitalism.

View of the state

Primacy of order

Conservativism's view of the state's purpose is distinct from that of liberalism and socialism. Whereas the other core ideologies see it as serving 'progressive' goals, such as the promotion of 'natural rights' or greater social justice, conservatives see the state's role in more *preventative* terms. For conservatives, the state's main role is to ensure safety and security and, in **Michael Oakeshott**'s words, to 'prevent the bad rather than create the good'.

Upholding the theories of **Thomas Hobbes**, conservatives argue that safety and security are simply impossible without authority and law and order. And, given their 'Hobbesian' disdain for 'natural laws', 'natural society'

Key term

Authority A recognised right for those 'in authority' to make decisions others must accept (or face penalties for not accepting). Conservatives claim such authority is essential to order and security; that the only effective authority is 'formal' authority; and this can only be provided by a state.

105

and 'natural authority', conservatives believe there can be no authority, and no law and order, without a state. As a result, conservatives see the formal authority provided by the state as the precondition of society and, therefore, the precondition of liberty and individual rights.

Once again, this connects to the conservative view of human nature and its fear that human beings can behave in irrational and frightening ways. As **Edmund Burke** explained:

> Government is a contrivance of human wisdom to provide for human wants. Among these wants is … the want … of a sufficient restraint upon their passions. Society requires that … the inclinations of men should be frequently thwarted, their will controlled, and their passions brought into subjection.

Limited hierarchy

In terms of the state's *structure*, traditional conservatives again take a different view from that of liberals and socialists. Thinkers like **Hobbes**, **Burke** and **Oakeshott** were much more comfortable with a state that is openly hierarchical and elitist — reflecting, perhaps, the unequal society they defended. **Hobbes** further argued that, in order to maintain peace and security, the state's power would have to be *concentrated* — thus turning the state into an awesome 'leviathan' that ensured order. If power were dispersed, **Hobbes** insisted, it would merely reproduce the horrific divisions that had made the state necessary.

However, among conservatives generally, support for concentrated power is unusual. Far more common has been support for an *aristocratic* state limited by clear, formal rules and a robust society. **Burke** was certainly keen on the notion of a 'natural' hierarchy or 'ruling class' — one that was born and bred to rule the state, while exercising a paternalistic responsibility for society generally. However, as a Whig who generally supported the Enlightenment, **Burke** also stated that aristocratic and hierarchical government must be limited by a *constitution*, of the sort that had been established in England since its Glorious Revolution of 1688.

Aristocratic rule should be further constrained, **Burke** argued, by the existence of a strong, confident society, guaranteed by the myriad of 'little platoons' mentioned earlier. This relationship between society and state was later described by **Oakeshott** as 'the limiting of Leviathan'. As **Oakeshott** explained, by putting an end to anarchy, where life is 'nasty and brutish', the state does indeed allow society to emerge. Yet, once it has emerged,

Knowledge check

31 What, according to conservatives, checks the power of a hierarchical state?

32 What is meant by Oakeshott's 'nautical metaphor'?

in the shape of many small communities, it is then the role of society to ensure the state does not become ubiquitous – and potentially 'nasty and brutish' itself.

Empiricism, experience and consensus

Both **Burke** and **Oakeshott** believed the state should not be guided by dogma or doctrine, or by 'normative' views about the kind of society which 'should' exist. Instead, the conservative state is one guided by *empiricism* – or, to quote **Oakeshott**, 'a preference for what is *known* rather than *envisaged*'.

Such sentiments gave rise to **Oakeshott**'s celebrated 'nautical metaphor': one that compares the state to a ship that has 'no agreed port of destination', but whose principal aim is merely to 'stay afloat' by charting whichever course seems safe and conducive to steady sailing. According to **Oakeshott**, socialists and liberals see the state mainly as the means to an end, such as greater equality or individual liberty. Conservatives like **Oakeshott**, however, see the state as *an end in itself*: a sturdy and spacious 'vessel' that rescues its 'passengers' from the 'fatal waters' of anarchy, provides them with a vital sense of safety, and allows them enough 'deck space' to pursue their own, various interests with like-minded 'seafarers'.

In terms of navigating this 'ship of state', in a way that 'avoids tempestuous seas', **Oakeshott** echoed **Burke** by citing the importance of experience rather than abstract theory. He duly endorsed **Burke**'s view that change pursued by the state should be slow, cautious and respectful of what **Oakeshott** termed our 'love of the familiar'. By rejecting dogma, **Oakeshott** argued, the state would also be better equipped to aggregate and reconcile society's various interests and thus promote consensus. The outcome, he believed, would be a state that could secure harmony, stability and what Disraeli termed 'one nation'.

The New Right perspective

The reluctance of a conservative state to adopt experimental policies, its preference for the tried and tested, and its willingness to defend a state's traditional structures, are predictable sources of ridicule among conservatism's opponents. **Karl Marx**, for example, stated that conservative states are based on 'the democracy of the dead' (or an excessive reverence for tradition) rather than the urgent ambitions of the living.

Key term

Empiricism An empirical approach to politics indicates a preference for evidence over theory and tends to emphasise 'what is' over 'what should be'. By contrast, a normative approach is more theoretical, stressing the need for change and 'what should be' in the future.

Yet contempt for **Oakeshott**'s 'nautical metaphor' is not confined to Marxists. New Right conservatives, such as **Robert Nozick**, thought that **Oakeshott**'s views were too passive and accommodating, leading to a state that was easily blown off course by the enemies of conservatism. The New Right state is therefore likely to be less empirical and pragmatic, more rigid and certain in its objectives, and more explicitly ideological. After 1975, this new approach would be signalled by Margaret Thatcher's claims to be a 'conviction politician not a consensus politician', by her government's commitment to a 'resolute approach' that rejected 'U-turns', and by its readiness to confront various 'enemies within' (such as 'Marxist' trade union leaders).

Debate 2

Is conservatism merely 'the politics of pragmatism'?

Yes

- **Edmund Burke**'s attack on the French Revolution was also an attack on what he termed 'abstract' politics, claiming that political ideas were a poor substitute for political experience.
- **Burke** and **Michael Oakeshott** both praised an 'empirical' approach to politics, based on 'what is' and 'what has been', rather than 'what should be'.
- Traditional conservatism prides itself on 'flexibility', which has supposedly allowed it to remain relevant despite centuries of dramatic change.
- New Right theorists such as **Robert Nozick** insisted that their ideas were in fact a pragmatic response to serious social and economic problems, caused largely by the 'failure' of previous governments.

No

- **Oakeshott** asserted that traditional conservatism was not 'philosophically empty'. Instead, he argued that conservatism drew upon certain principles linked to key aspects of human nature – notably our 'love of the familiar' and 'fear of the unknown'.
- In their view of state, society and economy, New Right thinkers like **Nozick** sought to update the overtly ideological approach of philosophers such as Friedrich von Hayek, while New Right politicians like Margaret Thatcher were proud to proclaim themselves 'conviction politicians'.
- Liberals like **T.H. Green** argued that traditional conservatism was based on a certain view of reform that was itself 'ideological'. As **Green** pointed out, the argument that cautious reform is always preferable is actually quite dogmatic – especially in situations where radical action is urgently required.
- Socialists such as **Beatrice Webb** argued that traditional conservatives took a far from 'pragmatic' view of society. Instead, she argued, they were driven by a consistent political principle: namely, that radical economic change should be avoided, so that those with a vested interest in the status quo were protected.

Evaluation check: To what extent are conservatives unprincipled?

In terms of the state's scope and structure, the New Right's prescription seems at first paradoxical: one that involves strengthening the state by shrinking the state. As **Ayn Rand** argued, 'The small state is the strong state.' Yet the New Right's logic is as follows: when the state is 'overloaded' by social and economic obligations, it is less able to focus on its essential conservative functions – namely, the maintenance of order and security. During the 1970s, for example, Thatcherites asserted that the post-war social democratic consensus had 'overloaded' the UK state, with both loss-making nationalised industries and a burgeoning welfare state. According to this argument, the state was thus gravely weakened: its police and security forces became underfunded, leaving society vulnerable to terrorism and disorder, while its armed services became marginalised, leaving the nation exposed to potential external enemies (such as the former Soviet Union).

For **Nozick** and others on the New Right, the solution was clear. In respect of economics and welfare, the aim should be to 'roll back the frontiers of the state', via radical policies like privatisation and deregulation. This, in turn, would allow the state to refocus and 'roll forward' in respect of areas such as law and order, security and defence. For those on the New Right, the outcome would be a state that was 'leaner but fitter'.

Comparing ideas

The state

Whereas liberals and socialists believe the state's role is to promote 'progressive' ideas like human rights and social justice, conservatives think the state's main task is merely to provide order, and thus avert a life that is 'nasty, brutish and short'. Like socialists and modern liberals, traditional conservatives are often prepared to extend and enlarge the state. However, New Right conservatism echoes the classical liberal preference for minimal government in economic policy.

Different types of conservatism

Traditional conservatism

The key thinkers of traditional conservatism span several centuries and include **Thomas Hobbes** (mid-seventeenth century), **Edmund Burke** (late eighteenth century) and **Michael Oakeshott** (mid-late twentieth century). This huge time-span points to traditional conservatism being an ideology that has constantly *evolved*, making it a culmination of responses to shifting circumstances and unexpected challenges.

Four of these responses are examined below. As we shall see, their concerns, methods and legacies are variable. But there are certain constant aims, such as:

- to ensure that change is orderly and non-revolutionary
- to ensure that private property is preserved
- to ensure that tradition and custom are respected wherever possible.

Response to the English Civil War: a stress on authority

For **Hobbes**, the violent chaos of the English Civil War (1642–51) demonstrated the dire consequences of a society where the state and authority have collapsed. **Hobbes** was no defender of monarchical rule and wished to exalt 'reason' and 'logic' over faith and religion. However, amid the violence and bloodshed of civil war, he was anxious to stress that there could be no freedom or progress without law and order. In this way, **Hobbes** gave to conservatism its firm belief that the principal purpose of government is the maintenance of peace and security.

Knowledge check

35 Why did Hobbes fear the collapse of authority?
36 What sort of change did Burke recommend?

The English Civil War: crucial to Hobbes's thinking.

Response to the French Revolution: a stress on evolutionary change

Given his earlier support for the colonists during the American Revolution, **Burke** might have been expected to applaud the French Revolution of 1789. Instead, he foresaw the mayhem and violence that eventually disfigured it, arguing that change should be evolutionary and always mindful of humanity's imperfection. **Burke** therefore bequeathed to conservatism the notion of 'change to conserve': a recognition that change was inevitable, but something that should normally be pursued slowly, carefully and with a reverence for tradition. Radical or revolutionary reform, such as that sought by the American colonists after 1775, was defensible only if there were serious threats to what was established, customary and of proven efficiency.

Response to industrialisation: a stress on 'one nation'

The industrialisation of the late eighteenth and nineteenth centuries gave rise to new and grotesque forms of class-based inequality, and predictions of revolution in advanced industrialised societies like Britain and Germany. While liberals such as **John Stuart Mill** were inclined to deny such class differences, maintaining that society still comprised largely autonomous individuals, conservative politicians like Otto von Bismarck (1815–98) in Germany, and Benjamin Disraeli (1804–81) in Britain, offered a rather different analysis.

Disraeli and Bismarck thought the best way to avoid revolution was first to recognise, and then reconcile, the class differences arising from industrialisation. This involved two approaches. The first emphasised 'the nation' – a concept which had previously been associated with revolution and the rejection of monarchical empires (French revolutionaries had described themselves as 'patriots'). Disraeli and Bismarck, however, adjusted this concept into a more conservative vision of 'one nation'. Within this vision, the various classes of society were part of one 'national family', with society's richer classes having a parental or paternalistic responsibility for the poorer classes. This, in turn, would serve the conservative aim of a stable society by moderating class differences, while highlighting the obligations of the wealthy. As Disraeli warned, 'The palace is not safe when the cottage is not happy.'

Disraeli and Bismarck's second approach involved greater state intervention, designed (in Disraeli's words) "to elevate the condition" of the poorer classes. In the UK, this had been encouraged by the widening of the franchise in 1867 – a development which exposed

111

new distinctions between traditional conservatives and classical liberals like **Mill**. While **Mill** continued to support the principle of laissez-faire, Disraeli's government of 1874–80 acknowledged that unfettered capitalism produced dangerous levels of deprivation, while heightening tension between classes. Reforms like the Factory Act 1874 and the Artisans' Dwellings Act 1875 (restricting factory owners and landlords respectively) were therefore enacted, largely to avert enthusiasm for Marxist revolution. In this way, Disraeli and Bismarck bequeathed to conservatism a stress on 'one nation' and a readiness to legislate for social reform within industrialised societies.

Response to democratic socialism: a stress on 'the middle way'

During the early twentieth century, traditional conservatism faced further challenges from those who would challenge inequality and hierarchy. In the UK, the Representation of the People Act 1918 made age (rather than property) the main criterion for voting, paving the way for universal adult suffrage and an electorate that was overwhelmingly working class. This naturally posed a threat to parties like the Conservatives, while offering a clear opportunity to the new Labour Party: a democratic socialist movement, formally committed to common, not private, ownership of the economy.

In the event, it was the Conservative Party that governed for most of the century that followed – and for reasons that owed much to the adaptable nature of conservatism. Prominent inter-war conservatives, such as future prime minister Harold Macmillan (1894–1986), spoke of a new 'middle way' between capitalism and socialism: one that would address economic inequalities, while respecting property rights, national identity and other themes chiming with traditional conservatism.

Macmillan did not become prime minister until the late 1950s. Yet, as early as the 1930s, it was clear that conservatism was prepared to sanction further state intervention in order to stifle both socialism and fascism. Between 1935 and 1937 alone, Conservative ministers sponsored Public Health, Housing and Factory Acts, all of which checked market forces in the name of 'one nation'. After 1945, conservatism evolved again, this time by embracing (or, according to **Anthony Crosland**, 'plagiarising') the more compelling ideas of rival ideologies – notably a 'welfare state' (as championed by modern liberals like **John Rawls**), and the 'mixed economy' (as advocated by social democrats like **Crosland**).

Political Ideas for A Level: Liberalism, Socialism, Conservatism, Feminism, Anarchism

However, post-war conservatives denied that such shifts were an abandonment of traditional conservatism. As a former Conservative home secretary, R.A. Butler, argued in 1971:

> Our support for state welfare, and an economy promoting full employment, was simply a renewal of our historic concern for national unity. We have never been a party of unbridled capitalism; we have never given uncritical support to laissez-faire economics.

It was also significant that Butler's memoirs were entitled *The Art of the Possible*: a crisp illustration of traditional conservatism's 'empirical' approach to politics and government. It is an approach which still resonates with mainstream conservatives across western Europe, including the Christian Democrats in Germany (see Boxes 3.1 and 3.2).

Box 3.1: Traditional conservatism today – an advocate's prescriptions, 2020

- A recognition that 'capitalism works best when harnessed to strong, voluntary communities'.
- A reassertion of 'civic capitalism … profit should serve the community as well as individuals'.
- A subsequent willingness to 'check the power of global markets through enhanced state regulation'.
- A reassertion of family values, but 'a recognition that families are varied … and include families with same-sex parents, and families underpinned by ethnic minority religions'.
- Tolerance of ethnic, sexual and gender minorities, but rejection of identity politics and multiculturalism.
- 'Leftwards economically; anti-leftwards culturally'.

Source: N. Timothy, *Remaking One Nation* (2020)

Box 3.2: European conservatism today – the German CDU–CSU manifesto, 2021

Ahead of the 2021 German elections, the German Christian Democratic Union (CDU), in alliance with the Christian Social Union (CSU) in Bavaria, issued a manifesto that included the following commitments:

- variety of tax cuts for high earners, plus a 5 per cent reduction in corporation tax
- commitment to higher welfare spending, harnessed to tighter restrictions on eligibility
- tightening of rules for asylum and immigration, including capacity to deport refugees who commit criminal offences in Germany
- construction of 1.5 million new homes through tax relief and reduced regulation for building companies
- strengthening of links with both the EU and Biden's US administration in a bid to combat climate change, terrorism and growing threats from China and Russia.

Source: *Die Welt*, 5 October 2021

Knowledge check

40 Why did the New Right believe, in the mid-1970s, that the UK and US economies were failing?

41 Why did the New Right believe, in the mid-1970s, that UK society was 'dysfunctional'?

New Right conservatism

The New Right critique

Influenced by thinkers such as **Ayn Rand** and **Robert Nozick**, New Right conservatism emerged in the 1970s and was practised in the 1980s by Conservative governments in the UK and Republican administrations in the USA. The New Right was largely a response to various political 'failures', which seemed especially acute by the mid-1970s. These included:

- *'Failing'* economies – involving extensive state intervention, state ownership and public spending, and higher taxation. Within the UK, the failure of such economies was thought to be evidenced by spiralling inflation, rising unemployment and wastefully inefficient nationalised industries.
- *'Failing'* societies – involving 'bloated' welfare states, a 'dependency culture' and 'irresponsible' lifestyles, arising from the 'permissive society' of the 1960s. According to **Rand**, individuals within such societies had become 'over-indulgent', 'over-reliant on state welfare' and therefore 'indifferent to notions of self-reliance and individual initiative'. This, in turn, supposedly contributed to rising levels of public spending on welfare, 'crippling' rates of taxation, and serious obstacles to capitalist enterprise and dynamic individualism.
- *'Failing'* states – involving a sense that western democracies were becoming 'ungovernable'. In the UK, for example, the economic policies of both Conservative and Labour governments were seriously obstructed in the 1970s by trade union strike action, sparking **Nozick**'s fear that the UK was 'ripe for Marxism'. During the 1970s, such fears were also sparked by wider global developments, including the USA's loss of the Vietnam War and the advance of Marxist forces in south-east Asia and southern Africa.

The New Right solution

As we have seen, the New Right was not the first example of conservative thought adapting to new circumstances. What made the New Right unique, and distinct from previous variants of conservatism, was its enthusiasm for elements of classical liberalism. Consequently, New Right conservatism can be seen as a hybrid ideology, which aims to combine two distinct philosophies:

- a robust reassertion of certain traditional conservative principles, otherwise known as *neo-conservatism*

Knowledge check

42 How does neo-conservatism update two of the themes associated with traditional conservatism?

- a bold update of certain classical liberal principles, otherwise known as *neo-liberalism*.

Neo-conservatism

Neo-conservatism is associated with American scholars like Irving Kristol (1920–2009) and British philosophers like Roger Scruton. In response to the alleged problem of 'ungovernability' mentioned earlier, it wished to channel the spirit of **Thomas Hobbes** by reasserting the importance of order, authority and a strong, formidable state. Yet, in response to concerns about social liberalism, it also wished to reassert the Christian morality and social conservatism associated with **Edmund Burke**; and it was equally keen to revive the sense of national identity fostered by Disraeli.

As a result, neo-conservatism is linked to a variety of approaches, all of which found expression in the Thatcher and Reagan governments of the 1980s:

- a tougher approach to law and order, involving more powers for the police and stiffer sentences for offenders
- a more robust approach to national defence, including a less conciliatory approach to the nation's potential enemies (principally the former Soviet Union)
- a less tolerant approach to immigration, based on a perceived threat to traditional national identity
- a less tolerant approach to issues like abortion, homosexuality and 'the permissive society'
- a more committed approach to the promotion of marriage and 'traditional' families, via taxation, welfare benefits and education.

Neo-liberalism

Neo-liberalism is principally associated with Austrian philosopher Friedrich von Hayek, whose book, *The Road to Serfdom* (1944), is regarded as the 'bible' of neo-liberal thinking. Hayek's views were endorsed in the UK by think-tanks such as the Adam Smith Institute (ASI) and were echoed by the libertarianism and 'minarchism' of **Nozick** and **Rand** (see Key Thinkers 4 and 5).

Updating the individualism of **John Locke**, and the 'negative liberty' associated with **John Stuart Mill**, the ASI wished to 'roll back the frontiers of the state' so as to 'set the people free' from state interference, expand individual freedom, diminish the 'dependency culture' and advance a free-market economy. As with neo-conservatism, such neo-liberal ideas were

Knowledge check

43 Give two examples of how neo-liberalism aims to expand individual liberty.

44 What is meant by 'negative liberty'?

reflected by the Thatcher and Reagan administrations, which emphasised:

- the reduction of personal taxation (reflecting **Nozick**'s complaint that 'tax is theft')
- the containment of government spending
- the deregulation and privatisation of industries and services, thus transferring control and ownership of the economy from the state to the private sector.

A contradictory doctrine?

New Right conservatism proved one of the most controversial ideologies of the late twentieth century, and some of its fiercest critics were supporters of traditional conservatism. In his book *Dancing with Dogma* (1992), Ian Gilmour contested that, because they mixed neo-liberalism and neo-conservatism, New Right policies were 'a series of contradictions' that made for 'incoherent government'. For example:

- While neo-liberalism wished to 'roll *back* the frontiers of the state' (hence the Thatcher government's promotion of privatisation), neo-conservatism wished to roll *forward* 'the frontiers of the state' (hence the Thatcher government's restrictions on trade unions and local authorities).
- While neo-liberalism wished to *advance* individual liberty (hence Thatcherism's commitment to income tax cuts), neo-conservatism wished to *restrict* it, both in the name of 'law and order' (hence Thatcherism's extension of police 'stop and search' powers) and through an **anti-permissive** agenda designed to restore traditional moral values.
- While neo-liberalism was *relaxed* about immigration (**Nozick** saw it as an expression of free markets and individual choice), neo-conservatism was much more *wary* (hence Thatcher's fear that immigration might 'swamp' British culture).
- While neo-liberalism was keen to *contain* state spending and taxation, neo-conservatism was content to *increase* state spending on police, security and the armed forces (hence the Thatcher government's upgrading of the UK's nuclear deterrent and its firm commitment to the defence of the Falkland Islands).

A subtle blend?

Despite Gilmour's derogatory view, however, many would argue that the New Right's twin components are perfectly compatible.

Key term

Anti-permissive The New Right's social policies were often described as 'anti-permissive' in that they were critical of many of the reforms associated with the 'permissive society' of the 1960s (e.g. the laws that relaxed divorce, abortion and homosexuality).

Knowledge check

45 Give two examples of how neo-liberalism and neo-conservatism are apparently in conflict.

One of the most incisive studies of Thatcherism was Andrew Gamble's *The Free Economy and the Strong State* (1988), the title of which provides a neat summary of New Right thinking. Though not a supporter of the New Right, Gamble argued that, far from being contradictory, neo-conservatism and neo-liberalism subtly complement each other – for two main reasons.

First, Gamble noted that a 'strong' neo-conservative state may be enhanced by a 'free' neo-liberal economy. The reasoning here was that, if the state withdraws from the economic arena and is no longer burdened by nationalised industries and the hefty costs of state welfare, New Right governments can then devote more funds to policing, defence and other features of a strong 'Hobbesian' state. As **Rand** observed, the state would then be 'smaller in scope but stronger in effect'.

Secondly, Gamble noted that a 'free' neo-liberal economy may be served by a 'strong' neo-conservative society. In this respect, we can recall Irving Kristol's argument that, if disciplined by the codes of social and moral conservatism, fewer individuals are likely to 'go off the rails' in a way that makes them recipients of state welfare (Kristol cited 'unmarried teenage mothers' as an example of those who become 'casualties' of 'permissive societies'). Furthermore, in a socially conservative society, those who are genuinely unfortunate might have strong families and communities to support them, thus reducing their reliance on state welfare. Freed from the obligation to support society's growing number of unfortunates – the unexpected by-product of social liberalism – New Right governments could then trim welfare spending, cut taxation and more effectively pursue a neo-liberal economic agenda.

This second argument helps explain Kristol's taunt that a New Right conservative was simply 'a liberal mugged by reality' – the 'reality' being that economic liberalism is hampered by social liberalism. Kristol insisted that the relaxation of traditional social mores, and the normalisation of 'alternative' lifestyles, merely added to the cost of state welfare, while fanning a culture of dependency on the state.

Box 3.3 provides a recent example of New Right principles as stated by the US Libertarian Party.

Knowledge check

46 How do neo-liberal economics help to promote neo-conservatism?
47 How does a neo-conservative society help to promote a neo-liberal economy?

Box 3.3: New Right conservatism today – the US Libertarian Party, 2019

- 'We promote a political ideology more culturally conservative than that of the Democrats, and more fiscally conservative than that of the Republicans'.
- 'Free trade and minimal regulation of markets'.
- 'Minimal taxation' and the 'abolition of the Inland Revenue Service'.
- Opposing 'any movement to European-style welfare states'.
- 'Maintenance of gun-ownership rights'.

Source: Libertarian Party, *Statement of Principles,* December 2019

Debate 3

Is Brexit compatible with conservatism?

Yes

- The decision to leave the EU was an attempt to restore national self-governance and a greater sense of 'one nation'.
- The ability to take back control of immigration helps restore national identity.
- To a large extent, the EU was an idealistic project, based on abstract goals like 'European political union'. Such goals, however, were not approved by UK voters, who were not allowed a referendum on either the Maastricht Treaty, which created the EU in the early 1990s, or the crucial Lisbon Treaty of 2007, which strengthened EU powers. As a result, the EU's relationship with the UK was never likely to be durable and thus failed a vital condition of traditional conservatism.
- The EU represents supranational authority – an audacious attempt at 'big government' which is at odds with the 'leaner and fitter' state advocated by the New Right.
- As Edmund Burke argued, radical political action *is* sometimes required to maintain or restore key conservative principles. In addition to threatening national identity, or the ideal of 'one nation', the EU lacked institutional accountability to those it governed, and was therefore at odds with the traditional, representative nature of the British Constitution. Brexit was therefore an act of pragmatic necessity, designed to salvage principles that had historically 'worked' for the UK.

No

- Leaving the European Union was a 'leap in the dark' – a radical change with highly uncertain consequences.
- Rejecting David Cameron's 'renegotiated membership' was a rejection of gradual, incremental change.
- Leaving the EU was a rejection of an arrangement which, though imperfect, had 'worked' for over four decades.
- Leaving the EU was sometimes tied to faith in global, laissez-faire capitalism – an historically liberal form of economics that defied the scepticism of many traditional conservatives.
- Brexit exacerbated social and cultural divisions and therefore threatened 'one nation'.

Evaluation check: Was Brexit an act of radicalism or conservatism?

Conclusion: conservatism today

An ideology preaching order, stability and incremental change will always have some appeal. Yet it is likely to have even greater appeal during periods of economic, social and global uncertainty. For this reason, it can be argued that conservative values are increasingly relevant as the twenty-first century proceeds.

One illustration of this has been the refocusing of the state in many advanced societies. During the late twentieth century, it seemed that, within such societies, the state's concerns were increasingly liberal and individualistic. In the UK, for example, there were various reforms – such as civil partnerships for same-sex couples and fresh anti-racism laws – that forbade discrimination against individuals with 'minority' characteristics. Likewise, there was a flurry of constitutional reforms, such as devolution, which aimed to disperse political power in the manner prescribed by **John Locke** and other apostles of classical liberalism.

During the twenty-first century, however, such liberal concerns appear to have been downgraded in favour of other priorities, which seem more attuned to the philosophy of **Thomas Hobbes**. The surge of terrorism after the destruction of the World Trade Center in 2001, the growing concerns about our economies after the financial crash of 2008, the increased anxiety about climate change and migration, the effects of a global pandemic in 2020 and the outbreak of a European war in 2022 all served to undermine confidence and optimism. In the UK and elsewhere, the state therefore felt obliged to place greater emphasis on order, safety and security, often at the expense of liberty and individual rights. In short, as the world became more akin to **Hobbes**' state of nature – marked by fear, tension and conflict – the state's role became increasingly conservative.

These gloomy developments also led to growing interest in traditional, conservative concepts of society. According to 'post-liberal' commentators like David Goodhart and Nick Timothy, this interest was fuelled by a reaction against the 'egotistical' and 'narcissistic' culture arising from decades of 'hyper individualism'. In this respect, 'post-liberals' have been critical of both the New Right and New Labour, noting that both placed huge faith in neo-liberal, free-market economics. This neo-liberal approach, they argued, nourished soulless consumerism, the globalisation of our economy, increased migration and the steady decline of traditional white communities. All this

David Cameron: advocate of 'Big Society, Small State'.

Key term

Globalisation A term that emerged in the late twentieth century, following the end of the Cold War and the collapse of the Soviet Union. It denotes the spread of capitalism and consumerism and points to a diminished difference between the economies and societies of advanced nation-states.

Key term

Populism A term denoting voters' rebellion against liberal norms and conventional political values. It has been linked to both right-wing politics (exemplified for many by Brexit and Donald Trump) and left-wing politics (exemplified by ex-Labour leader Jeremy Corbyn and French presidential candidate Jean-Luc Mélenchon).

Knowledge check

48 Give two examples of events this century that have strengthened the conservative view that the state's main aim is to secure peace and order.

contributed, Goodhart and Timothy argue, to an erosion of local and national identity, a growing number of voters who were 'citizens of nowhere', and an equally large number who were 'left behind' by economic change.

For this reason, support for Brexit and other forms of **populism** may be seen as a straightforward yearning for the kind of societies praised by **Burke** and **Oakeshott**. Such societies, it will be recalled, value tradition and custom, embody a strong sense of 'us' rather than 'me', promote both local and national pride, and connect to what Goodhart termed 'somewhere not anywhere'. In the wake of the Brexit referendum, and during the UK general elections of 2017 and 2019, commentators even began to discuss a political and electoral 'realignment' based on culture and social attitudes. It was argued that this realignment would highlight the substantial sympathy that still existed, particularly among non-metropolitan voters, for timeless conservative values such as patriotism and the upholding of local customs and traditional family structures.

This supposed realignment may have helped to explain the result of the UK's 2017 and 2019 general elections and was crucial to understanding why Conservatives progressed in many provincial urban areas (widely referred to as Labour's 'Red Wall'). Many of the voters in such seats were low paid and economically insecure. But they were also sympathetic to Brexit and increasingly alienated by aspects of social liberalism – particularly its relaxed attitude to immigration and its commitment to what were perceived as 'minority' or 'woke' causes. In other words, social liberalism just seemed to make voters more aware of their own social conservatism: a new form of political consciousness which, between 2016 and 2019, served to benefit the Conservative Party. Consequently, if other parties are to prosper in future, they too may need to show a greater appreciation of socially conservative values: a point often made by Maurice Glasman and advocates of Blue Labour (see Chapter 2).

Meanwhile, conservatism remains an adaptable and therefore durable ideology, rooted in the importance of habit, community and kinship. Change may be constant and inevitable, yet the desire to change in a particular way – one that shows respect for tradition and national identity – has a timeless appeal to many voters. As the twenty-first century proceeds, amid various forms of turbulence, the appeal of conservatism shows little sign of receding.

Summary: key themes and key thinkers

	Human nature	The state	Society	The economy
Thomas Hobbes	Cynical: individuals are selfish, driven by a restless and ruthless desire for supremacy and security.	The state arises 'contractually' from individuals seeking order and security. To serve its purpose, the state's power must be concentrated and awesome.	There can be no 'society' until the creation of a state brings order and authority to human affairs. Life until then is 'nasty, brutish and short'.	Constructive and enduring economic activity is impossible without a state guaranteeing order and security.
Edmund Burke	Sceptical: the 'crooked timber of humanity' is marked by a gap between aspiration and achievement. We may conceive of perfection but are unable to achieve it.	The state should be constitutional, but driven by an aristocratic elite, reared to rule in the interests of all.	Society is organic, comprising a host of small communities ('little platoons') which check the power of the state.	Trade should involve 'organic' free markets and laissez-faire capitalism.
Michael Oakeshott	Forgiving: humanity is mainly benevolent, especially when focused on the routines of everyday life.	The state should be guided by tradition and practical concerns. Pragmatism, not dogmatism, should be its watchword.	Localised communities are essential to humanity's survival and well-being.	Free markets are volatile and unpredictable; they may require pragmatic moderation by the state.
Ayn Rand	'Objectivist': we are guided by rational self-interest and the pursuit of self-fulfilment.	The state should confine itself to law, order and national security. Any attempt to promote 'positive liberty', via further state intervention, should be resisted.	In so far as it exists, society is atomistic: the mere sum total of its individuals. Any attempt to restrict individuals in the name of society should be challenged.	Free-market capitalism is an expression of individualism and should not be hindered by the state.
Robert Nozick	Egotistical: individuals are driven by a quest for 'self-ownership', allowing them to realise their full potential.	The 'minarchist' state should merely outsource, renew and reallocate contracts to private companies providing public services.	Society should be geared to individual self-fulfilment. This may lead to many small, variable communities reflecting their members' diverse tastes and philosophies.	The minarchist state should detach itself from the economy, merely arbitrating disputes between private economic organisations.

Tensions within conservatism

- **Human nature:** traditional conservatives, such as **Edmund Burke** and **Michael Oakeshott**, take a sceptical view of human nature, drawing attention to the gap between aspiration and achievement while warning against the grand, utopian schemes of progressive politicians. For them, the horrors of supposedly idealistic movements – such as the French and Russian revolutions – are not tragic accidents; they arise from a misreading and overestimation of human potential. By contrast, New Right thinkers take a more optimistic view, emphasising the opportunities for individuals with initiative and liberty. Key thinkers like **Robert Nozick** and **Ayn Rand** take an especially positive view of what individuals can achieve in the economic sphere, arguing that the key to unlocking human potential lies in fostering a pro-capitalist environment where individual energies are unleashed.

- **Society:** traditional conservatives see society as a collection of small communities (what **Burke** termed 'little platoons'), overseen by a hierarchical structure in which paternalistic elites exercise inherited power in the interests of the majority. Such communities are considered organic, in that they emerge in a natural and unplanned way, and place great store upon tradition and continuity. By contrast, New Right conservatives are ambivalent about society's very existence, drawing upon the libertarian belief that society is a mere collection of atomised individuals seeking self-determination. New Right conservatives are also more sceptical of paternalistic communities, preferring a society defined by those who have achieved, rather than inherited, power, status and property.

- **State:** traditional conservatives like **Burke** defend a state where political power is wielded by those 'born to rule'. Traditional conservatives therefore believe that the best states have a natural 'ruling class', reared according to the principles of duty and sacrifice, and instilled with a sense of responsibility towards the governed. Traditional conservatives are pragmatic about the reach of the state and are prepared to enlarge it in the name of social stability and 'one nation'. By contrast, New Right conservatives wish to 'roll back the frontiers of the state' so as to advance individual freedom and reverse the 'dependency culture'. New Right conservatives are hostile to the principle of aristocratic rule – they fear that ruling classes have too much stake in the status quo and are therefore reluctant to admit the need for radical change by New Right governments.

- **Economy:** traditional conservatives are happy to defend an economy based on private ownership, but are sceptical about free-market capitalism. They are fearful that its dynamic effects exacerbate inequality, threaten 'one nation' and fuel support for socialism. As capitalism becomes more globalised, traditional conservatives also fear that market forces promote a more cosmopolitan society that erodes national identity and national culture. As a result, traditional conservatives have been prepared to allow state intervention via Keynesian economics, higher taxation and high public spending on state welfare. By contrast, New Right conservatives such as **Nozick** zealously advocate free-market economies where state functions are privatised and deregulated, and where levels of taxation and state spending are significantly reduced.

Further reading

Politics Review articles

Gallop, N., and Tuck, D. (2020) 'Conservatism and the Conservative Party', *Politics Review*, vol. 30, no. 1.

Kelly, R (2023): 'One Nation Conservatism', *Politics Review*, vol. 32, no. 4.

Tuck, D. (2021) 'Paternalism and conservatism', *Politics Review*, vol. 31, no. 2.

Books

Goodhart, D. (2017) *The Road to Somewhere: The New Tribes Shaping British Politics*, Penguin.

Timothy, N. (2020) *Remaking One Nation: The Future of Conservatism*, Polity Press.

Exam-style questions

AQA

Short-answer questions

1 Explain and analyse three reasons why conservative thinkers defend capitalism.   (9 marks)

2 Explain and analyse three ways in which conservative thinkers support tradition.   (9 marks)

Extract question

3 Read the extracts below and answer the question that follows.

Extract 1

Government is a contrivance of human wisdom to provide for human wants. Among these wants is ... the want ... of a sufficient restriction upon their passions ... Yet a state without the means of change is without the means of its conservation. Without such means, it might even risk the loss of that part of the Constitution it most religiously wishes to preserve. But it is with infinite caution that any man ought to venture upon pulling down an edifice which has answered to a tolerable degree for ages the common purposes of society ...

Edmund Burke, *Reflections on the Revolution in France* (1790)

Extract 2

How then are we to construe the disposition to be conservative in politics? It is the observation that the duty of government is not to impose other beliefs and activities upon its subjects, not to tutor or educate them, not to make them better or happier, not to direct them or galvanize them into action. The office of government is merely to govern ... its business is not to inflame passion but to inject into the activities of already too passionate men an ingredient of moderation; to restrain, to deflate, to pacify and reconcile.

Michael Oakeshott, 'On being conservative', in *Rationalism in Politics* (1962)

Analyse, evaluate and compare the arguments made in the above extracts about conservatism's view of the state. In your answer, you should refer to the thinkers you have studied. (25 marks)

Edexcel

Essay questions

4 To what extent is conservatism 'a philosophy of imperfection'? You must use appropriate thinkers you have studied to support your answer and consider differing views in a balanced way. (24 marks)

5 To what extent does conservatism conserve? You must use appropriate thinkers you have studied to support your answer and consider differing views in a balanced way. (24 marks)

6 To what extent is New Right conservatism distinguishable from traditional conservatism? You must use appropriate thinkers you have studied to support your answer and consider differing views in a balanced way. (24 marks)

Chapter 4

Feminism

Learning outcomes

This chapter will enable students to:
- understand how feminist ideas developed in the twentieth century
- understand the core values of feminism as a political ideology
- understand the various types of feminism, how they differ from each other and the tensions that exist within the movement
- understand the ideas of feminism's key thinkers.

Key thinkers

This chapter will frequently reference the key feminist thinkers cited in A-level exam specifications:
- Charlotte Perkins Gilman (1860–1935)
- Simone de Beauvoir (1908–86)
- Kate Millett (1934–2017)
- bell hooks (1952–2021)
- Sheila Rowbotham (1943–).

Feminism is the belief that women are entitled to the same legal, political, economic and social rights as men. The feminist movement was necessary because centuries of discrimination meant that women had a lesser place in society, and were denied the respect and opportunities given to men. Feminist campaigning began in earnest in the late nineteenth century. Since that time, women have seen both their rights and the choices open to them increase tremendously (see Table 4.1). This means that the nature of the feminist struggle has changed. The focus today is less on legal change and more on protecting women from discrimination and violence. Raising awareness of the consequences of prejudice against women has also become an important feature of modern-day feminism.

Table 4.1 Feminism: a timeline of legal landmarks for women in the UK

Year	Legal landmark
1870	The Married Women's Property Act allowed single, married and divorced women to own property in their own right.
1907	The Qualification of Women Act enabled the election of women to borough and county councils and as local mayors.
1918	The Representation of the People Act gave women aged 30 or over the right to vote provided either they or their husband met the property qualification.
1918	The Parliamentary Qualification of Women Act gave women the right to become MPs.
1918	Constance Markiewicz of Sinn Féin became the first woman elected to the UK Parliament. She refused to take her seat because of her opposition to British rule in Ireland.
1922	The Law of Property Act allowed a husband and wife to inherit property equally.
1928	The Equal Franchise Act gave both men and women the right to vote from the age of 21.
1967	The Abortion Act made abortion legal in Britain under certain circumstances.
1975	The Sex Discrimination Act made it illegal to discriminate against women in the workplace or educational establishments.
1975	The Employment Protection Act made it unlawful to sack a woman because she was pregnant.
1985	The Prohibition of Female Circumcision Act was passed. This made female genital mutilation a crime.
1990	Independent taxation for women was introduced. This meant that married women were for the first time taxed separately from their husbands.

Feminists have taken a variety of approaches in their struggle for equal rights. Liberal, radical and socialist feminists have not always agreed in their methods and priorities. All want to see an end to patriarchy (rule by men), but liberals have advocated reform to achieve this, while radical and socialist feminists have pushed for revolution. The similarities and differences between the feminists will be explored further in this chapter.

The origins of feminism

Mary Wollstonecraft's *Vindication of the Rights of Woman* (1792) was written in the immediate aftermath of the French Revolution (see Chapter 1). It was a call for women to be recognised as 'human creatures' and given the same chances as men to fulfil their potential. **Wollstonecraft** called for a co-educational school system to allow girls and boys the same opportunities. She also wanted women to be able to pursue careers in fields such as medicine. The chains that confined women needed to be broken, so that they could live alongside men in 'fellowship'. Finally, women should have not only the right to vote but also their own elected representatives.

Harriet Taylor, who published *The Enfranchisement of Women* in 1851, was more explicit than **Wollstonecraft** in her demands. She called for women to be given 'political, civil and social' equality with men. She also argued that all of society would benefit if married women worked outside the home. **John Stuart Mill** (see Chapter 1) credited Harriet Taylor, whom he married in 1851, with influencing his own thinking on women's rights. His 1869 book *The Subjection of Women* was more cautious in its demands than Taylor's book but still argued that women were as deserving of freedom as men, and equally entitled to vote.

Wollstonecraft, Taylor and **Mill** influenced the campaign for women's suffrage, which started to gain momentum in the 1890s. In the USA, the National American Woman Suffrage Association was formed in 1890 by the merger of two existing organisations, the National Woman Suffrage Association and the American Woman Suffrage Association. **Charlotte Perkins Gilman** (Key thinker 1) became one of the most effective public speakers for the organisation and advocated for women's suffrage in front of the House of Representatives' Judiciary Committee in 1896. In Britain in 1897, the National Union of Women's Suffrage Societies brought together many smaller, local groups that had been pressing for the franchise. They campaigned peacefully for the vote. The Women's Social and Political Union, founded in 1903, took a more militant approach, using direct action to raise publicity for their cause.

Knowledge check

1   What did first-wave feminists hope to achieve?

It was a while before either American or British suffrage campaigners saw their aims achieved. Married women over 30 were awarded the vote in 1918 but women in the UK only won the vote on equal terms with men in 1928. In the USA, all women were enfranchised in 1920, although discrimination meant that black women, like black men, often found it hard to exercise this right.

Those who had campaigned for women's right to vote came to be known as first-wave feminists. They were admired for their contribution to the women's movement, even though it quickly became clear that the impact of giving women the vote was more limited than had been anticipated. First-wave feminists thought the changes in the law would see large numbers of women seeking and winning political office. The hope was that this new generation of women politicians would then use their authority to pass a raft of measures to extend women's rights. It was because these things did not happen that a new generation of feminists, calling themselves the second wave, were spurred into action.

Charlotte Perkins Gilman

Key thinker 1

Charlotte Perkins Gilman (1860–1935)

Charlotte Perkins Gilman advocated for women's rights in her writings and was also an active campaigner for female enfranchisement through her involvement in the National American Woman Suffrage Association.

■ Gilman's best known piece of writing, her 1892 short-story, *The Yellow Wallpaper*, was inspired by her personal experience as a new mother. It is the tale of a young woman suffering a mental breakdown following the birth of her baby. Denied the right by her doctor husband to take the positive action she thinks will improve her well-being – for example, the right to work, exercise or socialise – the woman sinks deeper into depression and madness. By highlighting the consequences for one woman of excessive male power, the story suggested a much broader message.

■ This broader message was articulated more directly by Gilman in her non-fiction writings. In her 1898 book *Women and Economics*, Gilman argued that it was time to overturn the pattern of male/female relations. In early societies, it made sense for women to seek the protection of the strongest men, even though this also entailed accepting that these men would control them, sexually and socially. Modern society rendered such relationships redundant. To Gilman, the existing 'sexuo-economic relation' between men and women entrenched inequality because it left women oppressed by the expectation and reality of performing menial household chores. Confining women in this way hindered the development of a fully productive society. What women needed was economic independence, and there was no logical reason to deny them this. As Gilman noted, 'There is no female mind. The brain is not an organ of sex.' You might 'as well speak of a female liver'.

- Economic equality could only be achieved, Gilman wrote, if the right to work outside the home was extended to married as well as unmarried women. Granting women an equal right with men to work would require a rethinking of marital relations. Gilman suggested that this be achieved not by an equitable division of labour in the home but by hiring professionals to cook, clean and raise the children.
- In her 1900 work *Concerning Children*, Gilman proposed that children be cared for in communal nurseries and have their meals provided by communal kitchens. She wanted to distance women from childcare because she felt that there was nothing innate about maternal feelings or instincts. In their communal nurseries, boys and girls should be raised wearing the same clothes and playing with the same toys. Society should have the same aspirations for girls as for boys.

- Liberating women economically, politically and socially would also involve freeing their bodies from the restrictive and over-sexualised costumes they were expected to wear. Gilman made this point in her 1887 article 'A protest against petticoats', and emphasised it in her daily life by refusing ever to wear a corset. In her desire to see women escape from fashions imposed by wider society, Gilman's thinking chimes with that of mainstream feminism, but some of her ideas, particularly those on childcare, sound as radical today as they did when she first committed them to paper.

Knowledge check

2 What did Charlotte Perkins Gilman think was the problem with existing male/female relationships?

3 List the changes Gilman wanted to see in society.

The core ideas of feminism

Key term

Sex This is determined by a person's biological organs. Traditionally, an individual's sex was regarded as designated at birth and unchangeable but today many countries acknowledge the right of anyone who has had a sex-change operation to be recognised as belonging to their chosen sex.

View of human nature

Sex and gender

It was psychologists considering transsexuality who were the first to provide the definitions of **sex** and **gender** that feminists find so useful. They defined sex as biological. Whether a person was male or female depended on their reproductive organs. Gender, by contrast, they saw as resulting from the balance within a person of masculine and feminine qualities. Feminists have refined this definition of gender, explaining that it was nurture and societal norms that were responsible for constructing a person's gender

Key terms

Gender This is a social construct and refers to the behaviours, perspectives and characteristics considered by society to be either masculine or feminine. The gender with which a person identifies may not match their biological sex and today some people identify as non-binary, which means that they see themselves as being neither wholly male nor wholly female, while other people prefer not to have an assigned gender and refer to themselves as genderless, non-gendered or gender-free.

Discrimination This exists when a person is subject to prejudice or unfair treatment on the basis of personal characteristics, such as their race, ethnicity, gender, sexuality or physical ability.

identity. Extending this argument to its logical conclusion, feminists have proposed that those who were biologically female should be given the same upbringing, choices and opportunities afforded to those who were biologically male. This would blur the differences between the two groups.

In separating a person's sex from their gender, feminists were putting themselves at odds with established thinking on the male and female character. At its most extreme, established thinking did not even recognise that gender was a necessary category. Instead, it assumed that a person's biology predetermined how they would develop. Women, it argued, had natural inclinations towards femininity and men towards masculinity. Feminists point out that such thinking served women badly. It had been used to claim that the right and proper roles for women were as mothers and homemakers. Men, by contrast, were seen as belonging to the public sphere of political and economic life. Inevitably, this removes the opportunities available to women, which is a source of considerable frustration to feminists.

By stressing that a person's sex should not make a difference to the opportunities available to them, feminists are attempting to undermine the basis for **discrimination** against women. A recent example of feminist action against discrimination in the workplace is given in Box 4.1.

Box 4.1: Feminism in action – a sexual discrimination claim

In 2019, sales manager Alice Thompson asked her employer, the estate agent Manors, to consider her request for flexible working. Thompson wanted to leave work at 5 p.m. rather than 6 p.m. each day so that she could collect her daughter from nursery. Manors refused the request, saying it could not afford to retain Thompson unless she was working full time. Thompson resigned and brought a sexual discrimination case against Manors. In October 2021, an employment tribunal ruled that Manors had failed to consider that women are more likely than men to need to change their hours of work to fulfil their childcare responsibilities. In expecting Thompson to continue working until 6 p.m. each evening, they were discriminating against her. The employment tribunal awarded Thompson £185,000 in damages.

Knowledge check

4 What determines a person's gender?

Comparing ideas

Nurture versus nature

Conservatives regard our personalities as shaped by nature. They also see human nature as flawed. Feminists, like socialists, believe that it is nurture, not nature, that determines how people develop. Feminists believe that, provided with the right upbringing, anyone can become a caring and responsible member of society.

Key terms

Gender stereotype Views about what characteristics men and women have, or what they can do, based only on their sex (e.g. women are the best care givers and should therefore look after children).

Androgyny The belief that a person can have both male and female characteristics because, biological sex aside, there are no major differences between men and women. This encourages the idea of 'personhood', rather than separate male and female identities, and stresses that men and women are equally capable in all walks of life.

Liberal, radical, socialist and cultural feminists have different approaches to issues raised by the sex/gender divide.

Liberal feminist views on the sex/gender divide

Liberal feminists do not want women restricted by gender stereotypes.

■ **Simone de Beauvoir** (Key thinker 2) did not talk explicitly about sex and gender, but she was clear that the physical differences between men and women did not indicate any deeper distinctions between the sexes.

■ For **Betty Friedan** (see Chapter 1), emphasising the sex/gender divide was a way to underpin her demand for equal rights. She reasoned that, since the categories of man and woman were merely biological classifications, they should not be used to draw conclusions about the intellectual abilities of women. Society needed to accept that all the scientific evidence showed that women were as capable as men and to reject the idea that their sex predisposed them to exclusively masculine or feminine ways of being. Instead they should aim for androgyny – a life unbounded by gender.

■ At the same time, liberal feminists acknowledge that women might feel a strong inclination towards motherhood, and defend the right of women to make traditional choices about how to live their lives. If a woman wants to be a housewife and mother, that is a private matter. It is not a decision that wider society should seek to influence.

Recent feminist action against gender stereotypes is described in Box 4.2.

Box 4.2: Feminism in action – Pinkstinks

Pinkstinks is a pressure group dedicated to stamping out gender stereotyping. Pinkstinks' founders, sisters Emma and Abi Moore, want to eliminate gender stereotyping because they believe it limits girls' thinking and ambitions. The pressure group produces 'Pinkstinks Approved' – a list of companies that make and sell toys without gender labelling. Pinkstinks can count among its successes persuading John Lewis, Marks and Spencer and Sainsbury's to stop marketing toys specifically to boys or girls.

Knowledge check

5 Why did Betty Freidan say that people should aim for androgyny?

Pinkstinks pressure group successfully persuaded many supermarkets to stop marketing toys to a specific gender

Key thinker 2

Simone de Beauvoir (1908–86)

De Beauvoir's *The Second Sex* was published in 1949 but it was not until 1972 that she publicly described herself as a feminist. In 1977, de Beauvoir banded together with other feminists to found the journal *Questions Féministes*. It was to *The Second Sex*, however, that many continued to look for their own answers to questions on the role and status of women.

■ The first big question de Beauvoir explored in *The Second Sex* concerned how and why women had come to be regarded as lesser members of society when compared to men. A study of history would not, she concluded, answer this question because although it furnished a range of examples of male dominance, it provided no rational justification for men's superior position. Equally, biology listed ways in which men and women were different but had discovered no proof that what was distinctively male was better than what was distinctively female.

■ What women needed, de Beauvoir wrote, was to cease to be 'the other' in society. She took the idea of a society consisting of 'subjects' and 'others' from the German philosopher Georg Hegel, who had used it to describe the relationship between enslavers and slaves. De Beauvoir argued that a woman's situation was similar to that of a slave, in that she was confined to a lower rank in society. And men, like enslavers, justified their superior status by reference to what they considered to be women's natural deficiencies. The trouble with such reasoning, as de Beauvoir pointed out, was that in characterising something as a deficiency, men were assuming that they were the ideal type of human, and this did not stand up to scrutiny. Even the 'fact' that men are stronger than women was problematic, de Beauvoir explained. Strength was measured according to criteria such as body size, which tended to favour men, rather than, for example, how long a person lived, a criterion that would have favoured women. The oppression of women by men was, therefore, wholly unjust and women needed to achieve liberation from it.

■ Achieving liberation would involve rejecting the false notion that women were predisposed to certain behaviours and instincts. In *The Second Sex*, de Beauvoir wrote, 'One is not born, but rather becomes, a woman.' This expressed the idea that a person's sex was distinct from their gender, although without using those words. Girls were raised to be meek, subordinate and unquestioning, but this was not their natural

state. Society needed to accept that women were entitled to economic independence and women needed to engage in intellectual pursuits.

■ To liberate themselves, women needed to do more than simply ask men for their freedom. They needed to join together and work actively for change. De Beauvoir recognised that this would not be easy because women were oppressed, and often identified with their oppressors rather than with each other. Working-class women, for example, often had more in common with working-class men than they did with women of different social classes.

■ The fight for change would inevitably pit men and women against each other, but de Beauvoir thought that this would be a temporary state. She took the optimistic view that in time men would accept that women deserved their freedom and come to respect them as different but equal beings.

Simone de Beauvoir, an early French feminist

Key term

Patriarchy A male-dominated society in which men have the upper hand in political and economic life and women are discriminated against and denied opportunities.

Knowledge check

6 Define 'otherness'.
7 What did Simone de Beauvoir mean by 'One is not born, but rather becomes, a woman'?

Radical feminist views on the sex/gender divide

Radical feminists believe that the false idea of sex and gender being linked has been used by the patriarchy to undermine and marginalise women.

■ Radical feminists, such as **Kate Millett** (Key thinker 3), argue that their liberal counterparts have underestimated the depth of the problems caused by pre-existing prejudices about sex and gender.

■ They also see the liberal response to these problems as inadequate. Radical feminists believe that gender stereotypes are at the root of the repression of women in all aspects of their lives and advocate a sexual revolution to overthrow the institution responsible for this repression, the patriarchy.

- To participate in this sexual revolution, women will need to reject inferior, submissive roles in both their private and their public lives. Involved in this would be an insistence that men take equal responsibility for housework and childrearing, so that women can have the same opportunities as men to build their careers outside the home.

Socialist feminist views on the sex/gender divide

Socialist feminists argue that the sex/gender divide has made life worse for women both in the home and in the workplace.

- To socialist feminists the problems caused by the sex/gender divide are part of a larger system of discrimination caused by patriarchal capitalism. This works to the advantage of employers who can hire women more cheaply than men to do menial, low-status jobs.
- The fact that childcare and housekeeping were traditionally done by women was helpful to employers because it freed up male workers from all obligations except wage earning. This enabled them to put in long hours at their places of employment.
- This meant that women suffered at two levels. They faced worse treatment than men at work, including a greater chance of being sacked during an economic downturn. They were also exploited at home, where they did jobs that were largely unappreciated and entirely unpaid.
- To Marxist feminists, the solution to this situation is a rebellion to overthrow capitalism and establish a society that guarantees complete equality between men and women.
- More moderate socialist feminists believe that reform of capitalism is sufficient to eliminate the problems caused by the sex/gender divide. Among the reforms they advocate is equal pay for women. They also want to see women given a legal entitlement to the same consideration as men for roles for which they are qualified. In the long run, they hope that this will see as many women as men in senior roles and win women the same respect in the workplace that men enjoy.

Knowledge check

8 List the problems that socialist feminists see as caused by the sex/gender divide.

Key thinker 3

Kate Millett (1934–2017)

Kate Millett deserves to be remembered as the first academic to examine the writing of others through the lens of feminist theory. The feminist ideas that lay behind her analysis were largely ones she acquired rather than invented, but because she expressed these ideas so powerfully she became a figurehead for second-wave radical feminism.

- Millett called her 1970 bestselling book *Sexual Politics* to highlight that traditional definitions of politics were too narrow. Political activity took place in the public sphere, but politics also regulated the domestic relations of men and women. The personal was political because men and women did not form equal partnerships. Men dominated and women submitted.

- Only if the patriarchal power structure in society was overthrown could women be truly free. The revolution to eliminate patriarchy needed to happen in people's minds, as much as in their homes, workplaces and civic institutions. Changing the thinking of men and women about their roles in society would be hard. The oppression of women was, Millett wrote, more entrenched and complete than any other form of division in society. Furthermore, each new generation started to be inducted into their traditional roles before they were old enough to understand what was happening. These roles were arbitrary because they were based on the inaccurate assumption that some personal characteristics, such as cleverness and brutality, were masculine, whereas others, including docility and kindliness, were feminine.

- All around children was confirmation that the positions assigned to them were normal and natural. Boys and girls were given different toys and expected to enjoy different leisure activities. Religious texts, literature and television programmes tended to confirm stereotypes of the male and female character. Or, worse, they perpetuated 'Adam and Eve'-style myths of women as domineering creatures, possessed of demonic qualities, who corrupted blameless men and presented a danger to wider society.

- It was also problematic for those who sought radical change within society that the extent of male power was rarely acknowledged. Holding this power up to scrutiny was seen as subversive, rather than being viewed as a valid subject for debate. The armed forces, manufacturing, political, economic and academic institutions were all just accepted as male domains. Without open discussion of the extent of male control, it was hard to win public sympathy and support for an alternative to patriarchal power.

- An alternative was required because political reform in the public sphere had failed women. At the time that Millett was writing, women had had the vote in the USA for fifty years but were still very under-represented in political office. Nor had granting women the vote done much to improve their material circumstances. Women were still judged by their looks, encouraged to make marriages in which they would be undermined, and denied economic opportunities.

- In order to transform the public and private lives of women, Millett wanted people to realise that sex was distinct from gender. This insight would allow for the total rejection of repression, persecution and subjugation because these behaviours did not belong to anyone. Instead of placing themselves in false categories, men and women could strive to create a community in which respect, honour and esteem were extended equally to all citizens.

Kate Millett

Knowledge check

9 Why did Kate Millett think the 'personal is political'?
10 List the factors Millett saw as contributing to the oppression of women.

Comparing ideas

Tradition

Conservatives have a strong belief in tradition, which they think provides familiarity and helps hold society together. They also see traditional family units as the heart of society and the best way to raise children. Feminists reject tradition, which they see as having kept women confined to the household and excluded from the workplace.

Key term

Essentialism The belief that biology dictates not only a person's sex but also their behaviours and psychological make-up. Essentialists see men as predisposed to be aggressive and domineering and women as imbued with softer characteristics which make them naturally empathetic, tender-hearted and nurturing. For some essentialists, women's qualities are not only different from men's but also superior.

Knowledge check

11 What makes cultural feminists different from other feminists?

Cultural feminist views on the sex/gender divide

Cultural feminists believe that sex and gender are linked.

- The response of cultural feminists to the sex/gender divide sets them entirely apart. Rather than seeing the connection between sex and gender as artificial, they argue that men and women have different inclinations and seek to honour their contrasting masculine and feminine characters. This is known as **essentialism**.

- For cultural feminists the problem is not that sex and gender have been artificially connected. The problem is that the roles performed for society by women have been treated as of lesser importance.

- To remedy this, cultural feminists emphasise the value of motherhood and highlight those feminine qualities that they think give women an advantage over men – for example, the fact that women tend to be more socially adept than men.

In her 1990 book, *Gender Trouble: Feminism and the Subversion of Identity*, gender theorist Judith Butler presented a different view of the sex/gender divide. She argued that by using the terms 'sex' and 'gender' feminists were bolstering the idea of gender as binary. Feminists should, Butler suggested, focus less on definitions and more on analysing the power structures in society. This change of emphasis would allow gender to be seen as open-ended, rather than rigid.

Judith Butler

The personal is political

Feminist thinking is concerned with both the public and the private spheres. The public sphere is the domain of political, economic and legal activity within a state. It encompasses a state's governing institutions and its workplaces. The **private sphere** consists of the home and the family.

The main aim of liberal feminists is for women to enjoy equality with men in the public sphere. They want to achieve this through political and legal reform, which will extend the same rights to women as men. Included among these have been the right to vote and to run for political office. In addition, liberal feminists have worked to remove barriers to female progression in the public sphere, such as laws requiring women to resign from their jobs if they got married. They have also campaigned for equal pay, as well as particular rights for women, including paid maternity leave.

Liberal feminists do not concern themselves with what happens in the private sphere. They believe that women should be able to make their own decisions about how to conduct their lives behind closed doors, and take the view that how women behave in private has little bearing on their lives outside the home. Radical feminists disagree completely with liberal feminist reasoning on the significance of the private sphere. The phrase 'the personal is political', made famous by the writings of Carol Hanisch, summed up the radical feminist view that the way women behave at home has an impact on their lives in the public sphere.

There are several reasons why radical feminists believe this to be true. First, they feel that women who are submissive at home will find it difficult to assert themselves in the public sphere. Secondly, they argue that if women do most of the housework and childcare, this limits the time they have to advance their careers, while at the same time freeing up men to spend more time at work. A third strand to their argument is that if the greater part of the household chores and parenting is done by women, this models a pattern of unequal gender relations to the next generation. This will encourage the continuation of the problematic idea of male/female roles. All this explains why the fight for equality at home is crucial to the success of the continued struggle in the public sphere. According to radical feminists, liberal feminists have failed because they have not realised this.

Socialist feminists agree with radicals that repression within the home matters. The unpaid work performed by women in

Knowledge check

12 What is the reason for the liberal feminists' focus on reform in the public sphere?

Knowledge check

13 What do radical feminists mean by 'the personal is political'?

Key terms

Equality of opportunity A situation in which everyone is given an equal chance to succeed. Early feminists tended to believe that equality of opportunity could be achieved simply by removing barriers to female achievement and progression. When it became clear that the removal of barriers was insufficient in facilitating rapid or radical change, feminists began to campaign for legal and political measures to support and promote women's equality.

Gender equality A situation in which men and women have complete parity in all aspects of society. Achieving gender equality is the key goal for liberal feminists.

Knowledge check

14 List the ways liberal feminists have tried to stop discrimination against women.

private props up the exploitative, capitalist state. Without it, men would not have been fed or cared for, nor the next cohort of industrial labour raised to adulthood. The major problem for socialist feminists remains, however, patriarchal capitalism in the public sphere, and it is on the reform or overthrow of this that they have focused their efforts.

View of the state

Disappointment with the patriarchal state has driven much feminist thinking. A shared sense that women have been badly served by governmental structures and policies has not, however, translated into a single set of solutions about how to address this problem. Liberals and moderate socialists have sought reforms that would eliminate discrimination and extend women's rights, whereas radical and Marxist feminists have advocated revolution to bring about wholesale change.

Liberal feminists have worked for changes that would enshrine in law fair and equal treatment for women in all aspects of life. Initially, liberal feminists focused on reversing discrimination against women. This involved making changes that allowed women to exercise the same rights as men, and to compete equally with them in, for example, political contests and the workplace. As time progressed, liberal feminists came to feel that the state needed to do more than extend **equality of opportunity** to women. They began to campaign for more specific pieces of legislation that would offer increased protection or new rights to women.

Among the laws which liberal feminists in the UK worked to get onto the statute book were those that criminalised rape in marriage, afforded greater rights to women facing domestic violence, and guaranteed access to contraception and abortion. The reformist approach taken by liberal feminists to altering the balance of state power requires patience. It also involves working with the patriarchal state to achieve change. At the same time, it enables liberal feminists to look to a future in which women are as well represented as men in and by state institutions.

Radical feminists are appreciative of the changes brought about by liberal feminist campaigns. It is impossible to deny that women's lives have improved, but radical feminists believe that liberals should have been bolder and more uncompromising. Radicals argue that patriarchy is so ingrained into the fabric of the state that it can only be eliminated if the existing structures of government are dismantled. This would allow for the creation of state systems designed for the new era of **gender equality**.

It is socialist feminists who have written most about state power. It is their view that patriarchal capitalism emerged from, and is upheld by, the state. As long as that state exists, genuine freedom will be denied to most citizens. Marxist feminists have sought a revolution that will overthrow the state. In line with traditional Marxist thinking, they expect this to be followed by a short period of dictatorship of the proletariat (see Chapter 2). This will embed a society of complete social and gender equality in which the state will eventually wither away. Other socialist feminists see an ongoing role for the state in defending citizens' rights, and managing the means of production, distribution and exchange in such a way as to guarantee equality of outcome to men and women alike.

Feminist action to highlight the restrictions on women's freedom resulting from male violence, and the need for action by government and the judiciary to remedy the situation, is described in Box 4.3.

Box 4.3: Feminism in action – Reclaim the Night

Started in 1977, Reclaim the Night organises annual marches through towns and cities to draw attention to the low conviction rates for rape and sexual assault. The marches occur during the hours of darkness in order to give women an opportunity to feel safe on the streets for at least one night a year. The importance of Reclaim the Night's work was underscored by the abduction and murder of Sarah Everard by a serving police officer in Clapham on the evening of 3 March 2021.

Reclaim the Night march in London, 2021

Knowledge check

15 Which feminist groups have sought a revolution to overthrow the state?

Comparing ideas

Importance of the state

Liberals, conservatives and socialists have very different ideas about how the state should operate, but their views on the state are central to their ideology. Feminists are less concerned about the state than they are about society. Even liberal and socialist feminists, who want liberal democracy or a socialist government respectively, tend not to dwell on this in their writings. Their focus is on creating a more balanced and harmonious society for both men and women.

View of society

Patriarchy

Patriarchal societies are found the world over and the beliefs on which they are constructed are deeply entrenched. The vast majority of power within economic, political, religious, educational and social institutions is held by men. Patriarchal societies have the following features:

- Men hold positions of authority in politics and business. Women have more junior roles. This implies that men are more suited to top jobs than women.
- Senior men favour other men when making appointments and promotions. Women are overlooked.
- Men run media outlets, which reinforce patriarchal norms in their articles, news bulletins, programming and advertising.
- Men design academic curriculums and these neglect women's history, literature and cultural contributions.
- Most scientific research is carried out by men and centred around male concerns.

Liberal feminists seek to reform patriarchal societies through political, social and cultural change. Radical and socialist feminists take a more confrontational approach. They attack patriarchal values. Some of their number even encourage women to live entirely separately from men, so as to sidestep patriarchal power altogether.

Knowledge check

16 What type of feminist seeks gradual change?

Equality and difference feminism

Equal rights or **equality feminism** is the desire for a society in which men and women have complete parity. The view of equality feminists is that where inequalities have existed in the

Key terms

Equality feminism A branch of feminism with the goal of eradicating legal, political and cultural differences between the sexes so that men and women have the same status in society and command the same level of respect.

Difference feminism This is based on the belief that there are fundamental differences between men and women. Some difference feminists argue that women are different but equal, and others that women are superior to men.

Knowledge check

17 What are the key ideas of difference feminism?

Key term

Intersectionality This emphasises that every individual has a variety of identities (e.g. a person can be simultaneously a woman, middle class, an Arab and a Muslim). To understand anyone properly, one must consider their race, ethnicity, social class, sexuality and gender. If a person has a religious affiliation, lives with physical or intellectual disabilities or has a condition such as Autism, this also needs to be taken into account.

past they have worked to the advantage of men. Any inequalities that are allowed to remain will continue to give men the upper hand. Most liberal and radical feminists believe in an equal rights society, though they differ on how this should be achieved.

Difference feminism takes a different approach, arguing that men and women are different and that this should be accepted. For example, Susan Griffin argues that society benefits more from nurturing these differences than from encouraging women to behave like men. Most difference feminists view women as different but equal to men, although a small number think of women as better than men or argue that some of their personal characteristics are superior. Eco-feminist Vandana Shiva has stressed women's greater connection to nature as a positive quality. She has written that empowering women now is the best way to protect the environment for future generations. Difference feminists also state that a society with women at its helm would provide superior care for its children. Another common belief among difference feminists is that a society led by women would be more peaceful and harmonious than patriarchy.

Intersectionality

Intersectionality arises from an understanding that all members of society are complex individuals, with multiple identities. It is not possible to address the needs of women because the needs of each individual woman will vary according to a range of factors, such as social class, race, ethnicity, religion and gender identity. More broadly, intersectional theory recognises that people can face multiple sources of oppression, including those that arise from capitalist forces, the patriarchy and racist attitudes.

Intersectional theory was developed by Kimberlé Crenshaw. She was inspired in her thinking by **bell hooks** (Key thinker 4), who had explained in her 1981 book *Ain't I A Woman?* that black women were discriminated against as blacks, as women and as black women. At times, they would suffer from racial prejudice. At others, they would encounter gender discrimination. They would also be treated worse than both white women and black men.

Crenshaw saw the wider application of this argument. The experience within society of a wealthy, black, heterosexual woman would vary even from that of a poor, black, heterosexual woman, and the more non-mainstream elements a person had in their make-up, the more difficulties they would encounter. A woman who was poor, a lesbian, had physical disabilities and belonged to a minority ethnic group would face discrimination on each and all of these grounds.

141

International Women's Day celebrations

Crenshaw's insight was enormously important. It showed that a more multi-faceted approach was needed in dealing with discrimination against women. It highlighted the fact that white, middle-class feminists had made assumptions about women's needs. They presumed to speak for all women when they often understood little about the additional difficulties particular women faced. For white feminists, the equal pay struggle was about ensuring that women and men earned the same. For black women, it involved fighting for the same wage levels as white women. Intersectionality led to more scrutiny of the specific needs of women from minority groups. It encouraged women from all parts of society to campaign on issues important to them. In doing these things, intersectionality broadened the scope and appeal of feminism.

bell hooks (1952–2021)

When Gloria Jean Watkins adopted the pen name 'bell hooks', she decided to write it using only lower-case letters. She did this because she wanted the emphasis to be on the arguments in her books, not her identity.

■ bell hooks was spurred on to write her first book, *Ain't I A Woman?* (1981), by a sense of disappointment at the liberal feminist movement. First- and second-wave feminists were largely white, middle-class, university-educated women, with a narrow focus on achieving equality with the men they lived and worked alongside. That black women had completely different experiences of discrimination and thus different needs was barely considered. White women, bell hooks explained, only faced prejudice based on their gender, whereas black women were also discriminated against because of their race. The concrete impact of this double whammy of discrimination was economic. Black women not only earned less than their white counterparts but also less than black men.

■ The insight that discrimination could operate at more than one level was at the heart of bell hooks' classification of the problem black women faced: the imperialist-white-supremacist-capitalist-patriarchy. bell hooks herself admits that this is a rather unwieldy term but sees it as a strength because it highlights the multifaceted nature of the discrimination black women need to overcome. In recognising that discrimination operates at many levels, hooks was giving first voice to an idea that would later be described by Kimberlé Crenshaw as intersectional feminism, and which emphasised the diversity of the female experience.

■ These arguments made difficult reading for feminists who thought it crucial that the movement maintained a united front and pursued common goals but, as hooks was quick to note, their talk of unity was often at variance with their actions. Middle-class, white women often freed themselves from housework and constant childcare by paying less well-educated women low wages to do these undesirable jobs for them. The liberation of middle-class, white women was thus bought at the price of continued exploitation of more vulnerable women.

■ hooks' dismay at the behaviour of some feminists was tempered by her appreciation of those who responded positively to her thoughts on where feminism was going wrong. She thanked white people who had not only changed their own minds but also helped to alter wider feminist thinking and activism. In hooks' eyes, feminism had become a more inclusive movement because feminists were more willing than most political activists to engage in reflection and self evaluation.

■ hooks continued to push for change within the feminist movement until the end of her life. One of her final hopes was to embed a 'feminist masculinity' within modern society. This would involve feminists speaking directly to boys and men, and helping them to forge identities free from the taint of sexism. 'Feminist masculinity' would stress that men have value because of who they are, not what they do. It would also make it clear to men that their strength comes from their ability to take responsibility for both themselves and others, not from their dominance within society. Engaging in a dialogue with men has value too as a way of reinforcing hooks' contention that feminism has the ability to improve the lives of all people across all societies.

bell hooks

View of the economy

Women have always worked outside the home but traditionally they did so only out of economic necessity. The jobs they were allowed to do tended to be undervalued. Women earned less than men and the positions they held commanded less respect than those occupied by men. Some roles were closed to women entirely. Even if a particular career path was theoretically open to women, they were rarely considered for promotion. Women's jobs also tended to be less secure than men's, meaning that they were more likely to be made redundant if a company's circumstances changed. Many of these forms of economic discrimination continue to exist and feminists have campaigned against them. They want to see:

■ An end to the gender pay gap, which sees women earn less than men for the same or similar work. An example of the latter is female cleaners earning less than male refuse collectors. In 2010 the Supreme Court ruled that Sheffield County Council had breached the Equal Pay Act 1970 by paying bonuses to refuse collectors but not to cleaners. Their work is considered to be similar because it involves clearing up after people. A more recent case of feminist action against unequal pay is described in Box 4.4.
■ Women being promoted to the highest levels in organisations. Achieving this is thought of as smashing the 'glass ceiling', the invisible barrier that prevents women advancing beyond a certain level in their careers.
■ No jobs considered off limits for women. Physically and psychologically, women are as capable as men of tough jobs such as front-line army service.

Box 4.4: Feminism in action – an equal pay claim

In June 2021, thousands of current and former employees of Tesco brought an equal pay claim against the supermarket. Tesco had been paying the staff in its distribution centres, who were mostly men, £3 per hour more than its shopfloor workers, who were mostly women. The shopfloor workers claimed that this was discrimination because their work was of equal value to that done by those working in distribution centres. The European Court of Justice found in favour of the shopfloor employees. This ruling forced Tesco to equalise its pay rates and will see the company paying compensation to employees affected by past discrimination.

Reserve army of labour
A term used by socialist feminists to refer to members of society who are economically inactive but ready and able to step into employment at a moment's notice. The 'reserve army' can be called upon when employers want to boost productivity following an increase in demand and dispensed with when demand falls.

For socialist feminists, the problem is not just that women have been denied equality of opportunity by the market economy. They view capitalism as the root cause of female oppression. In this view, they are influenced by the ideas of **Friedrich Engels** (see Chapter 2), who argued that in the pre-capitalist world the work done by women had been considered equally vital to that performed by men. It was the capitalist mindset, **Engels** wrote, that had led women to be considered the property of men, rather than full members of society. Within capitalist economies, women were treated as a reserve army of labour, employed when male workers were in short supply. The existence of a reserve army of labour enables employers to keep wages low because their current workforce are so easily replaceable that they have no political or economic leverage. Once the number of men available to work became sufficient, the women would be replaced by male workers.

Socialist feminist **Sheila Rowbotham** (Key thinker 5) claimed that this meant that an end to capitalism would benefit women more than men. She hoped this would inspire women to organise for a post-capitalist future.

Sheila Rowbotham, leading socialist feminist

Sheila Rowbotham (1943–)

Shelia Rowbotham became actively involved in the British women's liberation movement in the 1960s. Her 1969 pamphlet, *Women's Liberation and the New Politics*, summarised her key ideas on what she called the 'women's question'.

- Rowbotham felt that complete equality between men and women could only be achieved through a social revolution. Liberal feminism, she argued, had been effective in raising awareness of women's subjugation in the public sphere, but it was predominantly an upper-middle-class movement. It had done little to address the oppression of working-class women or housewives.

- Some women, Rowbotham pointed out, had the misfortune to occupy both of these roles in a society which accorded little value to either. Recognition was needed of the fact that the capitalist system exploited working-class women more completely than it did working-class men. Like men, they had to sell their labour to their employers and accept a lack of autonomy in the workplace. Unlike their male counterparts, they also had to work for free within homes controlled by men.

- Rowbotham wanted it to be easier for women to work part time and to choose hours of work which suited them. She proposed that employers provide crèches to care for the children of both male and female workers. Rowbotham also suggested that the greater availability of nursery schools, laundrettes and cheap restaurants would free working women from some of the day-to-day drudgery of their domestic lives.

■ Alongside these practical changes, Rowbotham wanted the phrases 'girls' work' and 'women's work' to be banished from the English language. Such terms implied that the work was of lesser value and were used to justify lower rates of pay. Rowbotham rejected the argument made by employers such as Ford Motors that, because they allowed women to take time off work to have children, it was acceptable for them to discriminate against women in other ways. Granting women the same rights as men would not address this problem. What women needed were 'unequal' rights, which would recognise that their circumstances were different from those of men.

■ Rowbotham thought that housewives suffered more than workers. The home was not a woman's domain; it was a prison. A pregnant housewife had it worst of all because she was 'unable to escape from her femininity' and 'economically, socially and psychologically dependent on the man'. The wider importance of housewives' care for their husbands and children went unacknowledged by society. Instead, women had to rely on the allowances their male partners chose to pay them. A better system would be for housewives to be paid a wage by the state for their work.

■ Crucial to the transformation of society would be revolutionary groups. Rowbotham thought that, at first, it would be acceptable to exclude men from such organisations and allow women to gain confidence in their role as political activists. The exclusion of men should only be temporary because women's freedom could not be obtained in a society in which men did not abandon their sexism and patriarchal attitudes. A revolution in men's thinking was a necessary part of the wider revolution to abolish patriarchal attitudes.

Knowledge check

23 Why did Sheila Rowbotham think that capitalism had worse consequences for women than for men?
24 List the social changes Rowbotham wanted.

Different types of feminism

Liberal feminism

Early feminists tended to approach the issue of women's rights from a liberal perspective. Thinkers such as **Mary Wollstonecraft**, **John Stuart Mill** and **Charlotte Perkins Gilman** wanted women seen as individuals, entitled to enjoy the same rights as men. They demanded that women be able to:

■ Exercise the same democratic rights as men, such as the right to vote or to run for political office.
■ Enjoy equality of opportunity with men, including full access to education and the right to enter any career or profession.

Key terms

Political and legal equality
The main demand of early feminists, consisting of an equal right to participate in elections and run for political office, and laws that treat men and women in the same way.

Otherness In a patriarchal society, women are subject to control by men, who have the upper hand because of their greater economic and political power. Being considered 'other', rather than equal members of society, forms a major barrier to women achieving equality with men.

Reformist feminism Liberal feminists have a reformist approach, in that they seek to work within existing political structures to achieve change, as opposed to trying to overthrow those structures.

Knowledge check

25 Name two key liberal feminist thinkers.
26 What action did liberal feminists want to take against the patriarchy?

- Claim the same civil rights as men. This meant that the rule of law needed to apply to women as well as to men, so that the law never discriminated against women.
- Inherit and own property on the same terms as men.
- Direct their own lives inside and outside of the home, rather than have to follow the dictates of men.

By the mid-twentieth century, women had been granted a large measure of **political and legal equality** with men, as well as equal access to education. These changes did not prove to be transformative. Women continued to be discriminated against and denied opportunities open to men. To those puzzled about the reason for this, the work of **Simone de Beauvoir** and **Betty Friedan** had answers. **De Beauvoir** explained that men continued to assume that they were superior. Since men had established how society operated, they saw all around them confirmation of their own elevated status. Girls, meanwhile, continued to be raised in a way which prepared them to be wives and mothers, rather than full members of society. The moulds into which men and women were fitted would need to be broken if women were to make progress. **De Beauvoir** called the problem women faced 'otherness'. **Friedan** used the term 'patriarchy' to describe the entrenched system of male dominance and female oppression.

Liberal feminists were troubled by patriarchal power but they also wanted individual women to be free to choose how to live their lives. Deciding to be a housewife and mother was a legitimate choice, but women should also be able to fulfil their potential in the public sphere should they choose to pursue a career. Liberal feminists proposed that two main forms of action be taken to combat the patriarchy:

- Cultural attitudes which demeaned women and reinforced women's perceived inferiority had to be combated. This would require education, propaganda and opposition to sexist attitudes and language.
- Political and legal equality had to become a reality in all aspects of life through legislation to protect and extend women's rights.

The 1960s were the heyday of liberal **reformist feminism**. After that it faced an increasing challenge from radical feminists, who believed that liberals were insufficiently ambitious in their aims and mistaken in their approach to the patriarchy.

Radical feminism

Radical feminists focus on the patriarchy and have some key characteristics in common:

Comparing ideas

Reform versus revolution

Liberals and liberal feminists are reformists. They agree that the best way to improve society is through gradual change. Socialist and radical feminists, on the other hand, share socialism's desire for revolution to bring about quick and dramatic change in society.

Knowledge check

27 What goals and ideas do radical feminists share?

- They propose the dismantling of patriarchy and the transformation of society into a completely new form.
- They are revolutionary in their outlook. Even though they normally reject the idea of violent revolution, this sets them apart from liberal feminists who are reformists.
- They stress the importance of raising female consciousness in both their critique of patriarchy and their proposals for a new social order. By raising female consciousness they mean making women aware of the ways in which they are oppressed in patriarchal societies.

Underlying these similarities are important differences between radical feminists on both the exact nature of the problem with patriarchy and how this should be addressed.

Radical perspectives on patriarchy

In her exploration of the patriarchy, **Kate Millett** looked first at the family. She argued that in marriage women are exploited both sexually and economically. Her bestselling work, *Sexual Politics*, published in 1970, was a criticism of the role of men in patriarchal society. Men, she wrote, oppress women in the home, in the economy and in life in general. Their domination is political in nature because it involves the exercise of power. **Millett** did much to popularise the idea of male chauvinism, the tendency for men to exercise and celebrate their power over women.

Germaine Greer's *The Female Eunuch*, which also appeared in 1970, took a harder line than *Sexual Politics*. Greer contended that men actually hate women and that is why they oppress them. Women, who have been taught to hate themselves, willingly accept an inferior position assigned to them by men. In *The Female Eunuch* she asserted that women must understand and then throw off the inferiority imposed on them by men. Only when they have done this will they become fully human.

Another 1970 publication was Shulamith Firestone's *The Dialectic of Sex*. Firestone saw the history of civilisation as a struggle between men and women, just as **Marx** had seen history in terms of a class struggle. The origins of the gender struggle lay

Germaine Greer, a controversial and challenging feminist

in the biological differences between men and women, and the limitations which women encountered by being confined to life in the home. Patriarchy had persisted because women, constrained by childbirth and housework, had become enslaved to men.

The most controversial of all modern radical feminists was perhaps Andrea Dworkin (1946–2005), who produced her first book, *Woman Hating*, in 1974. She campaigned against the sexual oppression of women, and in particular saw pornography as symptomatic of men's view of women as little more than sex objects. Dworkin believed that the only way this could be successfully combated would be for women to form themselves into lesbian communities. As long as women allowed themselves to be sex objects for men, they would never achieve true liberation.

Millett, Greer and Firestone have in common their stress on the importance of how women perceive patriarchy. They felt that women's consciousness of their own inferiority, which had often confined them to the home, stemmed partly from their biological role. Significant too was that patriarchy had destroyed any ideas of potential liberation among women. Women needed to believe that they had the power to liberate themselves.

Radical responses to patriarchy

Radical feminists made a number of proposals to combat patriarchy and liberate women from its clutches. These solutions are based on radical perspectives on the nature of patriarchy. Their proposals include the following:

- The abolition of the nuclear family and its replacement by communal forms of childrearing and living in general. This will naturally remove the male domination of the family. **Millett** combined this vision with her support for the ideals of socialism.
- Sexual liberation was critical for many radicals, especially Greer. By escaping from the limitations of traditional male–female relationships, women could free themselves from male domination and, in Greer's terms, cease to hate themselves.
- The elimination of biological roles is perhaps the most radical solution of all. Firestone celebrated the potential of modern bio-technology to free women from their biological enslavement. Recommending androgyny, the removal of sex differences between men and women, she envisaged a world where women no longer need men to reproduce the species. This, she believed, would result in liberation of a fundamental kind.

149

Key term

Cultural feminism An attempt to increase the esteem in which 'feminine' qualities (e.g. caring and nurturing behaviours) are held by wider society. It is based on the essentialist belief that men and women are not just biologically different but also predisposed to different personal qualities. Some cultural feminists see 'feminine' qualities as superior to 'masculine' ones.

Knowledge check

28 What do cultural feminists believe?

Cultural feminism

The **cultural feminist** movement emerged from radical feminism but has its own distinct approach to the problem of patriarchy. The theory of essentialism is at the heart of cultural feminism. Essentialism is the belief that women are different from men in their nature as well as their biology. To cultural feminists, to be a woman is to be caring, empathetic and co-operative.

Cultural feminists have been accused of being naïve for accepting a definition of femininity devised by men for the benefit of men, and their way of thinking puts them at odds with liberal and radical feminists, who argue that to ascribe particular qualities to women reinforces gender stereotypes and encourages behaviours that prop up patriarchy. In response, cultural feminists argue that the problem is not that traditional societies assigned certain characteristics and roles to women. The problem is that under patriarchy, who women are and what they do is not sufficiently valued. Cultural feminists seek to redress this by celebrating the softer qualities they associate with women, as well as by pointing out that the aggressive and forthright behaviours men have a tendency to display are more likely to disrupt and destabilise society. Cultural feminists argue that men are, for example, more prone to start conflict, resort to violence and act selfishly. Women, on the other hand, are more likely to heal discord, promote dialogue and encourage understanding.

Some cultural feminists draw the conclusion that women's instincts and ways of being should be considered superior to those of men. A small number of cultural feminists, particularly those in the eco-feminist movement, have advocated replacing patriarchy with matriarchy on the grounds that societies run by women would be more conducive places for everyone to live.

The majority of other feminists are uncomfortable with the idea of female superiority. Liberal and radical feminists reject it because of their belief in androgyny, while socialist feminists seek equality with men, not the replacement of one socially stratified society with another. More general among other feminists is the concern that cultural feminism suggests that there is only one way to be a woman, a viewpoint with the potential to narrow down the choices and opportunities open to women.

Cultural feminists claim that one of the strengths of their approach is that it has the power to unite women regardless of their social, ethnic or racial group. This has proved a controversial claim, with intersectional feminists arguing that this is an attempt to gloss over the varying experiences and complex backgrounds that have shaped women in a multitude of different ways. Transgender women and their allies are equally dismissive of the idea that cultural feminism can unite all women because they have often felt disregarded and marginalised by a movement which suggests a close link between a woman's sex and her gender.

Cultural feminists have found themselves at odds with other feminists on both the problems facing women and how these should be addressed. They have, however, received acknowledgement within feminist circles for some of their practical work, particularly for taking a lead in setting up rape crisis centres and women's shelters to support and protect the vulnerable. In addition, the cultural feminist insistence that traditionally female roles be accorded great respect has, some suggest, increased the self-respect and sense of fulfilment felt by those who devote themselves to motherhood and homemaking.

Socialist feminism

Marxist feminists look back to the ideas of **Friedrich Engels**, **Karl Marx**'s close colleague, for their inspiration. **Engels** understood that women were becoming a key element in the future of capitalism. Women, he pointed out, had always been deprived of private property. This resulted in their being oppressed by property owners throughout history, just as property-less peasants and workers always had been. As capitalism developed and needed increasing quantities of workers, women became a vital source of available, low-paid labour. Their lack of property increasingly forced them into paid employment.

Modern Marxist feminists take a similar view but criticise **Engels** for over-stressing the importance of property. In modern society, women have increasingly come to own property independently, but their oppression has not ceased. They remain an exploited part of the workforce. Marxist feminists, therefore, see the destruction of capitalism as necessary for the liberation of women.

Other socialist feminists have rejected the idea that class is the only meaningful division in society. They argue that both class and patriarchy are sources of oppression. This leads socialist feminists to concentrate on the plight of working-class women. While liberal feminists focus on issues such as equal opportunities and equal pay for women, socialist feminists argue that only the extreme modification of capitalism will liberate women from their inferior economic position. For example, the state ownership of industry will eliminate the need for women to compete against men for employment.

Knowledge check

29 List the criticisms that have been made of cultural feminist ideas.

British feminist **Sheila Rowbotham** rejects the rigid economic determinism of **Marx**. For her, female oppression has economic roots, but it also stems from the traditional nature of the nuclear family and the cultural dominance of men. While the economic liberation and equality of women is necessary for the sexual revolution, it is not sufficient to raise the consciousness of women or to ensure their ability to define their own future.

Above all, socialists seek the liberation of women from their economic dependence on men. This dependence begins in the home but extends to the economic world in general. The Chicago Women's Liberation Union, which was founded in 1969, led the socialist feminist movement in the USA. It was committed to a two-pronged attack upon patriarchy. First, it wanted power more evenly distributed in society, so that even working-class women could exercise it. Secondly, it sought a change in the culture, notably in the education of women.

Comparing ideas

Capitalism

Liberals and liberal feminists are supporters of capitalism. Liberal feminists want to ensure that the benefits of capitalism are extended to women through equal rights legislation. Socialists and socialist feminists want capitalism at the very least reformed, if not entirely dismantled. Socialists emphasise the benefits this would bring to the working class. Socialist feminists believe that working-class women, who are particularly oppressed by both the patriarchy and capitalism, would benefit most from the end of capitalism.

Debate 1

Do feminists agree with the statement that 'biology is not destiny'?

Yes

- Most feminists agree that it is nature, not nurture, that shapes personalities. If children were raised in gender-neutral environments, the differences between boys and girls would vanish.
- Most feminists agree that the only differences between men and women are biological. There are no differences in ability. Men and women are not predisposed to think or act differently.
- Feminists agree that it is patriarchy with its expectations of women as mothers and homemakers that has held women back.

No

- Some feminists think that women have still not entirely escaped patriarchal thinking and this can restrict their ambitions and achievements.
- Liberal feminists acknowledge that women often have strong maternal feelings and instincts.
- Cultural feminists believe that there are distinct masculine and feminine personalities.

Evaluation check: To what extent do feminists see sex and gender as separate?

Knowledge check

30 Who invented the term 'third-wave feminism'?

31 What do third-wave and post-colonial feminism have in common?

Post-modern feminism

For the post-modern feminists of the 1990s onwards, diversity is all important. Inspired by the thinking of **bell hooks** and by intersectional theory, they start from the perspective that every woman's experience is unique. No single narrative or set of solutions can be universally applied. Tackling discrimination will require a whole range of solutions, some small, others on a wider scale. Rebecca Walker, one of the leading lights of post-modern feminism, referred to the movement she helped to launch as 'third-wave feminism'. She wanted to break with the past because she felt earlier waves of feminism had primarily served the needs of middle-class, white women from high-income countries. She wanted to create a more inclusive 'sisterhood', which welcomed those from across the racial, ethnic and class spectrum. The third wave also opened its arms to trans women and those identifying as queer or intersex.

Debate 2

Do feminists share the same view of patriarchal power?

Yes

- Feminists agree that patriarchy has existed for centuries and is entrenched in society.
- Feminists agree that patriarchal power oppresses women and restricts their freedom.
- Feminists agree that the problem is the system of patriarchy, not individual men.

No

- Liberal feminists believe patriarchy can be reformed. Radical and socialist feminists think patriarchy needs to be dismantled.
- Liberal and radical feminists tend to assume that patriarchy affects all women in similar ways. Post-modern feminists argue that different women are affected in different ways by the patriarchal power structure.
- Liberal feminists think that the biggest problem with patriarchy is that it limits women's freedom in the public sphere. Radical feminists see patriarchal power in the private sphere as more problematic.

Evaluation check: To what extent do feminists agree on the impact of patriarchal power on women?

Kimberlé Crenshaw, American civil rights advocate and scholar of critical race theory

Post-colonial feminism

Post-colonial feminism was another response to the feeling that liberal and radical feminism were rather narrow in their attitudes and outlook. As its name would suggest, post-colonial feminism sought to understand the socio-economic impact of imperialism on women. Armed with this knowledge, post-colonial feminists would be able to confront the racist and sexist attitudes entrenched by colonial rule. Post-colonial feminists argue that those they represent should embrace the unifying description of 'women' and not allow class, religious, ethnic or racial differences to divide them. Audre Lorde has written that differences among women are a strength. Women can use their diverse experiences and talents to create a community in which everyone can find support.

Key distinctions among the different types of feminism are summarised in Table 4.2.

Table 4.2 Key distinctions within feminism

	Liberal	Radical	Socialist	Cultural	Post-modern
Type of movement	A reform movement.	Revolutionary, seeking a social and cultural revolution.	Often revolutionary but proposes an economic transformation of society towards socialism.	Reformist, seeking to persuade people that feminine characteristics should be prized at least as much as masculine characteristics.	Revolutionary in that it rejects the earlier feminist idea that all women have the same needs, but reformist in that it supports small-scale changes.
View of patriarchy	Patriarchy is a modern phenomenon which can be combated through legal and cultural reform.	Patriarchy has long and deep historical roots. It has penetrated deep into male and female consciousness.	Patriarchy is largely economically based. Men dominate women generally because they dominate them economically.	The problem with patriarchy is that it has convinced people that masculine ways of doing and being are superior.	Patriarchy affects different women differently and a range of solutions are needed to combat its diverse impacts.
Main belief	If legal and economic equality can be achieved for women, they will achieve general liberation.	Male and female consciousness must change if liberation is to be achieved.	Patterns of employment and the economic structure of the family have to be transformed to achieve the economic liberation of women.	Women will be liberated once the ways in which they are different from men are fully valued by society.	The liberation of women cannot occur all at once because of women's different circumstances.

	Liberal	Radical	Socialist	Cultural	Post-modern
View of women's freedom	Women should be free to choose how they conduct their lives and their relationships with men.	It is not sufficient to create freedom for women – men's domination must be destroyed and their consciousness of superiority reversed.	Women cannot be genuinely free until they achieve economic freedom.	To be free, women need to live in a society where raising children or being a homemaker is accorded the same level of respect as working outside the home.	Freedom and rights must be extended to women from all backgrounds and to those who self-identify as women.

Debate 3

Do feminists believe that capitalist societies oppress women?

Yes

- Feminists think that, as long as men hold the key positions of power, women will continue to be discriminated against.
- Socialist feminists argue that women are doubly exploited in capitalist societies. Employers treat women as a cheap source of labour and men expect women to work without reward in the home.
- **bell hooks** wrote that capitalism works with other factors to oppress women.

No

- Liberal feminists are supportive of capitalism and want its benefits opened up to women.
- Moderate socialist feminists believe that reformed capitalist systems can be a good way of generating wealth. Flourishing societies in which the profits of capitalism are redistributed can benefit women as well as men.
- Third-wave feminists argue that the problems facing women vary. Some women do well in capitalist societies and others suffer.

Evaluation check: To what extent are feminists anti-capitalist?

Conclusion: feminism today

The feminist movement is an active one and its campaigns for women's rights are many and varied. The group #MeToo provides help to the survivors of sexual assault. Period Poverty supplies sanitary products to women and girls who cannot afford them. The Fund for Global Human Rights gives direct support to feminists across the globe working to advance women's equality. The Pink Protest, founded by Scarlett Curtis, is a vocal and active part of the campaign to end female genital mutilation throughout the world. Many of today's campaigns are internet based. #MakeWomenVisible aims to draw attention to the economic and social impact of the Covid-19 pandemic on women. Everyone's Invited, a website created by Soma Sara, allows girls and women to share stories of the sexual harassment and abuse they suffered at school.

Sara's hope is that shining a light on the problem will help to eliminate aggressive and exploitative male behaviour.

One of the more troubling question for today's feminist movement is around the granting of rights to transgender women. Some feminists want anyone who identifies as a woman, regardless of their biology, to be allowed access to women-only spaces, such as public toilets and refuges. These feminists believe that it is essential to respect a person's chosen gender identity and to promote inclusion. They characterise those who disagree with this position as TERFS (trans-exclusionary radical feminists). This is a label their opponents reject, preferring to describe themselves as gender-critical. Feminists who adopt a gender-critical position are wary of ignoring biology. They point out that discrimination against women has often arisen because of their ability to bear children. If women's biology is ignored, such discrimination will become hard to challenge. They acknowledge that the vast majority of attacks on both women and transgender women are committed by men, but feel that women-only spaces will be less safe for women if anyone declaring themselves female is allowed to use them.

#metoo march, San Francisco, 2018

One issue on which all feminists are agreed is that they would like nothing more than for their movement to become redundant. This goal is some way off because there is no country in which women have complete equality with men. The struggle for women's rights continues to be an important political movement.

Summary: key themes and key thinkers

	Human nature	The state	Society	The economy
Charlotte Perkins Gilman	The biological differences between men and women are irrelevant. Women can compete equally with men.	Gilman had no especially distinctive views on the state.	Society has always assigned inferior roles to women. In modern society this no longer has any justification.	The domestic servitude of women allowed men to dominate the outside economic world.
Simone de Beauvoir	Gender differences are created by men in society. They are not natural.	The state reinforces a culture that prevents women from expressing their true freedom and identity.	The expectations placed on all people (not just women) by the societies in which they live limit them. People need to be free to attain self-realisation and true freedom.	Men's domination of economic life restricts the life choices open to women.
Kate Millett	The only major differences between men and women are biological. There is no evidence that certain characteristics are male and others female.	The state is merely the agent of patriarchy. It is part of the problem, not part of the solution.	Modern society is completely characterised by patriarchy, which is all-pervasive and infests both the private and public spheres.	Millett was supportive of socialist economics but this was not fundamental to her feminism.
bell hooks	Women, in common with men, have multiple identities and therefore experience multiple forms of oppression.	The state is dominated by white males and therefore reflects and reinforces their dominant position in society.	Society is full of complex relationships between different minorities. In order to resolve social conflict, love between different minority cultures must be established.	Women living in poverty have problems that middle-class women do not face. The liberation of the poor is an economic as well as a social issue.
Sheila Rowbotham	Women's consciousness of the world is created by men.	The state is the servant of capitalism.	The nature of society is economically determined. Society reflects the dominant position of both capitalists and men in general.	Rowbotham has a Marxist perspective. Women are a low-paid reserve army of labour.

Further reading

Politics Review articles

Boss, G. (2014) 'Are all feminists radical?', *Politics Review*, vol. 24, no. 3.

Egan, M. (2018) 'Intersectionality and feminism', *Politics Review*, vol. 28, no. 1.

Graham, P. (2012) 'Why do radical feminists criticise liberal feminists?', *Politics Review*, vol. 22, no. 3.

Grant, M. (2016) 'Is feminism a coherent theory?', *Politics Review*, vol. 26, no. 3.

Grant, M. (2016) 'Fourth wave feminism', *Politics Review*, vol. 26, no. 4.

Grant, M. (2020) 'Feminism: the "personal is political" debate', *Politics Review*, vol. 29, no. 3.

Hammal, R. (2018) '#MeToo', *Politics Review*, vol. 28, no. 1.

Books

Criado Perez, C. (2020) *Invisible Women*, Vintage.

Given, F. (2021) *Women Don't Owe You Pretty*, Brazen.

Lorde, A. (2019) *Sister Outsider*, Penguin.

Ngozi Adichie, C. (2014) *We Should All Be Feminists*, Fourth Estate.

Solnit, R. (2016) *Men Explain Things to Me*, Changbi.

Exam-style questions

AQA

Essay questions

1 'Feminists are united in the view that the personal is political.' Analyse and evaluate this statement with reference to the feminist thinkers that you have studied.   (25 marks)

2 'Feminists agree on the forms of oppression faced by women.' Analyse and evaluate this statement with reference to the feminist thinkers that you have studied.   (25 marks)

3 'Feminism is an anti-capitalist ideology.' Analyse and evaluate this statement with reference to the feminist thinkers that you have studied.   (25 marks)

In your answers you should draw on material from across the whole range of your course of study in Politics.

Edexcel

Essay questions

4 To what extent do feminists argue that sex is irrelevant in shaping human nature? You must use appropriate thinkers you have studied to support your answer and consider differing views in a balanced way.   (24 marks)

5 To what extent do feminists agree on equality? You must use appropriate thinkers you have studied to support your answer and consider differing views in a balanced way.   (24 marks)

6 To what extent are feminists united in the belief that reform of the state is the best way to address patriarchal power? You must use appropriate thinkers you have studied to support your answer and consider differing views in a balanced way.   (24 marks)

Chapter 5

Anarchism

Learning outcomes

This chapter will enable students to:

- be aware of the early development of anarchism
- understand the core values of anarchism as a political ideology
- understand the various types of anarchism and how they differ
- be aware of the main tensions between the various anarchist traditions
- know how and to what extent anarchism still flourishes
- understand the ideas of anarchism's key thinkers.

Key thinkers

This chapter will frequently reference the key anarchist thinkers cited in A-level exam specifications:

- Max Stirner (1806–56)
- Peter Kropotkin (1842–1921)
- Mikhail Bakunin (1814–76)
- Pierre-Joseph Proudhon (1809–65)
- Emma Goldman (1869–1940).

Introduction: an anti-authoritarian ideology

Our word 'anarchism' comes from the Ancient Greek *anarkos*, which means 'without a ruler'. Anarchists believe that society can operate effectively without a government or any other state institutions. An anarchist society would provide its members with a huge amount of individual freedom. Anarchists reject the common characterisation of anarchy as chaotic. They believe that anarchism can be an orderly and peaceful system. Key events in the history of anarchism are summarised in Table 5.1.

Table 5.1 Anarchism: a timeline

Year	Landmark in anarchism
1840	**Pierre-Joseph Proudhon** (Key thinker 4) coined the term 'anarchism' in his book *What is Property?*
1848	The February Revolution took place in France. **Proudhon** and **Mikhail Bakunin** (Key thinker 3) were involved in this uprising, which overthrew France's constitutional monarchy and established the Second Republic. The events of the revolution convinced **Proudhon** that any future uprisings should seek to abolish authority, rather than to seize power.
1864–72	The International Workingmen's Association or First International was held. This was an attempt to unite a range of left-wing organisations, including collectivist anarchists. In 1872, the anarchist and Marxist factions split.
1871	Another revolution in France resulted in the Paris Commune being formed. The Commune, which lasted from March until May 1871 contained members who referred to themselves as anarchists.
1907	The International Anarchist Congress of Amsterdam took place, with delegates from across the world.
1918	The Anarchist Free Territory was established in Ukraine. It survived until 1921.
1936	An anarchist collective of peasants and workers seized control of Barcelona and sizeable parts of rural Spain and collectivised the land there.
1970–72	The anarcho-communist group the Angry Brigade carried out a series of bombings in the UK. They bombed banks, embassies and the homes of Conservative MPs.
1971	The Freetown Christiania commune was founded in Copenhagen, Denmark.
1994	The Zapatista Uprising in Chiapas in Mexico was partly motivated by anarchist ideas, particularly mutual aid.
1999	Anarchists were heavily involved in the Seattle protests against the World Trade Organisation.
2020	The Mutual Aid UK website was set up in response to the Covid-19 pandemic.

Key terms

Government The bodies and individuals that control the state at any given time, including traditional governments such as monarchies, as well as democracies and dictatorships. Anarchists see government as corrupted, arguing that governments also corrupt those they rule over and prevent individuals obtaining genuine freedom.

State An established authority able to exercise power over people. Its role is to maintain order, enforce laws and protect people from both each other and external threats. All anarchists oppose the existence of the state, seeing it as an instrument of class rule and a denial of individual sovereignty.

Anarchist philosophers would be disappointed that anarchism today so often has a bad name. Its association with violence and terrorism is not entirely unfair. Some anarchists have used violent methods to draw attention to their cause. Others have justified the use of violence to overthrow the state or achieve other aims, but anarchists do not necessarily support the use of aggression (see, for example, the account of the activities of the Animal Liberation Front in Box 5.1). Many anarchist thinkers, entirely reject violence. All anarchists want to create future societies which are conflict free.

Anarchists agree in their opposition to the existence of a political state but have a range of ideas on how an anarchist society should operate. This makes it hard to generalise about anarchism, as does the fact that no genuinely anarchist society has ever existed. Some small-scale communes in Israel (known in Hebrew as *kibbutzim*) could be described as partly anarchist in nature. These self-governing communities operate a form of internal democracy where every member has an equal say in decision making. However, *kibbutzim* rely to some extent on the existence of the Israeli state and maintain relations with its central authorities, which means that they are not wholly anarchist.

Knowledge check

1 What ideas do all anarchists share?

Box 5.1: Anarchism in action – the Animal Liberation Front

The Animal Liberation Front (ALF) was founded in the UK in 1976 and claims to have members in over 40 countries. Its small, non-hierarchical groups use direct action to highlight and prevent anything they class as animal cruelty. They focus their activities against butchers, slaughterhouses, farmers, those involved in the fur trade, fast-food outlets and laboratories that conduct experiments on animals. The ALF promotes non-violence but in 2006 ALF activist Donald Currie was found guilty of placing bombs outside the homes of people with links to Huntingdon Life Sciences, an organisation that used animals in medical experiments. Currie was sentenced to 12 years in prison for his actions.

Animal Liberation Front march

The origins of anarchism

There are four main strands within anarchism (see Table 5.2) These are very different from each other and reflect the varied nature of anarchism.

Table 5.2 Main strands of anarchism

Form	Description
Philosophical	Early anarchist philosophy was based on a positive view of human nature. It stresses the sovereignty of the individual and their ability to exercise that sovereignty rationally and with sympathy for others.
Communist	Anarcho-communists stress mankind's innate sense of social order, seeing people as social animals who prefer to cooperate than to compete with each other. This branch of anarchism proposes small, independent voluntary communities known as communes.
Collectivist	This form of anarchism is associated with the industrial working class. Collectivists propose the creation of associations of workers who will co-operate and trade with each other to their mutual benefit.
Individualist	Individualist anarchists are opposed to all social and political restrictions on free choice. They want individuals to be left alone to pursue what they view as their own best interests.

Philosophical anarchism

Philosophical anarchism developed in the eighteenth century. Its two key figures were **Jean-Jacques Rousseau** (1712–78) and William Godwin (1756–1836). They were critical of existing justifications of power and **authority**. **Rousseau** was not an anarchist himself, but his ideas influenced later anarchists. Particularly important was **Rousseau**'s argument that mankind is 'born free but is everywhere in chains'. This established the idea that people are born with the right to liberty but have to live under governments and within societies that unfairly restrict their freedom.

The activities of one anarchist group, the Empty Cages Collective, in response to the literal restriction on freedom of individuals in the prison system is described in Box 5.2.

Comparing ideas

Hierarchy and authority

Conservatives defend hierarchy and authority on the grounds that they provide a structure for society and help maintain law and order. Anarchists argue that no one has the right to exercise authority over another person. If a hierarchy is created in which some people have power over others, this will serve to corrupt both the holder of the power and those over whom that power is exercised.

Godwin developed **Rousseau**'s argument in an anarchist direction. He wrote that if governments unfairly restrict individual freedom, the logical thing to do is to abolish them. He believed that society could operate smoothly without a state. He based this belief on a positive view of human nature. With the help of education, Godwin argued, every individual could achieve moral perfection. This would mean that they would not need guidance from the law or a government when making decisions. They could be trusted to use their private judgement to make good choices.

Box 5.2: Anarchism in action – Empty Cages Collective

Founded in the UK in 2014, the Empty Cages Collective is an informal network of people who co-operate to oppose the expansion of the UK's prison capacity. In recent years, it has been involved in local protests against prison expansion in Bristol, Leicester, Liverpool, London, Manchester and South Wales. In 2021 it began a campaign against the building of a new prison at HMP Wellingborough, including blockading the site. The collective also opposes the detention of migrants and asylum seekers. Its long-term goal is the abolition of prisons, which it argues create more social problems than they solve.

Communist anarchism

Communism emerged in the nineteenth century. The movement is most strongly associated with **Karl Marx**, but there was also an anarchist communist movement. The anarcho-communists and the Marxists had a shared goal: they both wanted to create a stateless, self-governing communist society. The two groups also had some different ideas: the anarcho-communists insisted on the immediate abolition of the state, while Marxists envisaged a workers' state replacing capitalism in the short term. The key figure in the anarcho-communist movement was **Peter Kropotkin** (Key thinker 2).

> **Key term**
>
> **Communism** A society in which there is no government. Communist societies consist of small, co-operative communities. Within these communities, goods are equally distributed and the means of production are owned in common by all people.

> **Knowledge check**
>
> 2 What distinguishes anarcho-communists from Marxists?

Collectivist anarchism

Collectivism was a response to industrialisation and the negative consequences this had for the living and working conditions of the urban working classes. It appeared in various forms and has some characteristics in common with socialism. Collectivist anarchism has been described as decentralised socialism, or 'socialism without a state'. It flourished in the second half of the nineteenth century and into the first few decades of the twentieth century. **Mikhail Bakunin** was a leading member of this movement.

> **Key term**
>
> **Collectivism** The principle that the group is more important than the individual, and in political terms that land and the means of production should be owned jointly.

Individualist anarchism

Individualist anarchism took two different forms. In the USA it was a largely peaceful movement. Henry Thoreau (1817–62) is representative of American individualist anarchism. He withdrew from society to live in a cabin in the woods. His aim was to be self-supporting and free from the influence of others. European individualist anarchists, such as **Max Stirner** (Key thinker 1), advocated a more violent approach to achieving individual freedom. They urged people to revolt against and destroy the state. In more recent times, individualist anarchism has taken the form of anarcho-capitalism. Murray Rothbard (1926–95) was a key proponent of anarcho-capitalism. He argued for the creation of a stateless society in which free-market capitalism is allowed a complete free rein. This would mean that there would be no taxation and no regulation of the economic market.

Knowledge check

3 What thinkers are associated with nineteenth-century individualist anarchism?
4 List the main types of anarchism.

The core ideas of anarchism

View of human nature

Anarchists believe that throughout history people have had their character corrupted by states and governments. They argue that if the state is removed, human nature will be restored to its true form. The problem is that different anarchists have come to very different conclusions about what true human nature is. Three different ideas stand out:

- People are self-interested or egotistical and will cooperate with other people only if they believe it to be in their own interests.
- People are born without any imprinted characteristics. Each individual is a *tabula rasa* or blank surface on which society, with all its faults, writes our character. Put another way, human nature is environmentally determined.
- People are born 'good', in that they are sociable and rational. They take into account the interests of others when making decisions and prefer **altruism** to selfishness. Anarchists who believe this also see people as naturally social beings who prefer to live and work co-operatively rather than to compete. Altruistic action by one anarchist group to reduce world hunger is described in Box 5.3.

Key term

Altruism A personal characteristic shown by people who take into account the needs and feelings of others when making decisions. People who are altruistic will naturally help other people and might even put the needs of others above their own.

Food Not Bombs protest, California, 2020

Box 5.3: Anarchism in action – Food Not Bombs

Food Not Bombs is an international anarchist movement whose mission is to make vegan and vegetarian food available to anyone who wants it. Food Not Bombs volunteers are motivated by a dislike of seeing people going hungry when there is plenty of food in the world. They also want to reduce food wastage. Most of the meals they make are created from food that would otherwise be thrown away. Today Food Not Bombs operates in Africa, the Americas, Asia, Australia, Europe and the Middle East. Each of its different branches has freely decided to be part of the Food Not Bombs network and all are involved in consensus decision making for the wider organisation.

Among those who have benefited from food provided for them by members of Food Not Bombs are the campaigners for democracy who took part in the Orange Revolution protests in Ukraine during the winter of 2004–05. Other beneficiaries are those affected by Hurricane Katrina in New Orleans in 2005 and the anti-capitalist Occupy Wall Street protestors of 2011. Since 2021, Food Not Bombs London has been providing free vegetarian food every first and third Saturday of the month from its stall outside Seven Sisters underground station.

Key term

Ego The part of a person's character that is interested exclusively in itself. A person's ego will lead them to follow their self-interest, even if this clashes with the interests of others. It is associated with individualist anarchism.

Knowledge check

5 What did Stirner see as the difference between being

The egotistical view of human nature

The most striking advocate of the idea that human nature is self-interested or egotistical was **Max Stirner**. For **Stirner**, the ego was part of the essence of every individual. A person's ego told them that they were entitled to everything on earth. To be true to themselves, people should pursue the aim of acquiring all the things they want. **Stirner** did not think that this would necessarily lead to selfish behaviour in which people refuse to help others. An individual would, **Stirner** argued, take others into consideration if it were in their own interest to do so. **Stirner** imagined a world where increasing numbers of people would become egoists and eventually form themselves into 'unions of egoism' – groups of people united in pursuing their joint interests.

Max Stirner (1806–56)

Max Stirner was a German philosopher who became a political activist and revolutionary. He was a major influence upon both individualist anarchism and nihilism, which proposes the abolition of both state and society. In his best known work, *The Ego and His Own* (1844), he developed his idea of egoism. To Stirner, the key to understanding how anyone acted came from recognising that all people behave in a self interested way.

- Stirner opposed not only the state but also religion and ideology. He argued that ideologies deny people freedom of choice. Anything which threatens a person's ability to pursue their self-interest, Stirner described as a 'spook' or a 'ghost'. By this he was suggesting that states, religions and ideologies are shadowy illusions. They appear to promote individual liberty but in practice are suppressing it.
- In place of ideology and organised religion, Stirner advocated that each individual should develop their sense of ego. As egoism spread it would begin to challenge all forms of authority. This would not, Stirner thought, lead to a permanent conflict between individuals. Egoists would form themselves into 'unions of egoism'. These were groups of people who realised that co-operating with others was the best way to maximise their self-interest. These unions of egoism would gradually replace the state.

- Stirner believed that the individual is entitled to anything they can find in the world. An individual can even use other people for their own purposes. In *The Ego and His Own* he described a world in which people are interested in others for what they can provide. Relationships are formed based on how one person is useful to another, not on any sentimental basis.
- Stirner acquired a reputation as one of the most radical and revolutionary of nineteenth-century anarchists. He was determined to bring down the state by force. His view of human nature is often viewed as the most pessimistic in the movement. This is not an unfair view. Stirner wrote that people are capable of altruism and fellow feeling but only if such acts and emotions serve a person's self-interest.
- Stirner can also be seen as a champion of unrestrained individual liberty. The state and private property had to be abolished to establish the widest possible freedom. He also wanted to see an end to any moral restraints that might inhibit the individual. Morality, religion, ideology and philosophy should all be resisted by the free individual. Stirner shared the determination to resist morality with Georges Sorel (1847–1922), who believed that committing acts that outraged public morality was a positive step on the road to genuine liberty of the mind.

6 What did Stirner view as preventing complete freedom of the individual?

The blank slate view of human nature

The view that we are born without any innate characteristics led to the belief that state and society corrupt individuals. If a perfect, moral society could be established, individuals would become moral and altruistic. This rested on the belief that anarchist ideas of order were natural and not artificial constructs. **Mikhail Bakunin** took this view. For him, the only impulse we have when we are born is towards moral justice. We understand the difference between good and evil, but there is nothing that compels us to act in any particular way. It depends on our experience of life whether we follow the rules of natural justice.

The positive view of human nature

Some anarchists agree with liberals that people are naturally good when they are born. This outlook suggests that anarchist ideas of a 'perfect' order and society are feasible. Associated with this is the belief that people are naturally social and prefer to live in groups. William Godwin was an early advocate of the idea that people are capable of moral perfection.

Key to all anarchists is the idea that each individual is sovereign and entitled to their own liberty. Liberals believe this too, but liberals argue that the state and its laws are necessary to establish and protect liberty. Anarchists reject this view. True freedom for them means that there are no laws that restrict an individual's actions. This leaves anarchists needing to explain how, in a society without laws, individuals could be protected from one another.

Anarchists differ in their ideas on how a society without laws would work, depending on their ideas on human nature. Godwin argued that, if people were allowed to use their private judgement, they would not infringe the freedom of others. This would make laws unnecessary. **Peter Kropotkin** said that mankind was naturally sociable and people would find freedom within voluntary social groups. 'Are bees in a hive free?' **Kropotkin** asked. His answer was 'yes' because they voluntarily choose to live as part of a collective.

Anarchists have contrasting ideas about human nature, but all agree that individual freedom is the natural state of mankind and that such freedom can never be sacrificed to any kind of external authority.

Knowledge check

7 What are the ways in which liberals and anarchists disagree about freedom?
8 List the anarchist alternatives to the existence of a state.

Comparing ideas

Human nature

Conservatives have a pessimistic view of human nature. They view people as intellectually limited and psychologically flawed. Anarchists have a much more positive view of human nature. They believe people can be trusted to know what is best for them. Given the freedom to do so, individuals will make rational choices that will allow them to pursue their own best interests.

View of the state

All anarchists insist that the state is unnecessary and must be abolished. Some argue simply that the state is unnecessary. Others think that the state is also an evil and corrupting force.

The state is unnecessary

Anarcho-communists and some philosophical anarchists, including Godwin, argue that the state is not necessary. It can be replaced with voluntary associations of one kind or another. **Peter Kropotkin** argued that small communes were the best form of voluntary association. **Mikhail Bakunin** preferred the idea of large workers' federations. Both the small communes and the larger workers' federations would preserve individual liberty because people had freely chosen to live in these collective units. This contrasts them favourably with the state, which forces people into artificial political units, such as nations, and subjects them to laws that restrict their individual sovereignty.

Key thinker 2

Peter Kropotkin (1842–1921)

Peter Kropotkin was born into the Russian aristocracy but came to disapprove of the behaviour of his own class. By the 1870s he had been converted to anarchism. His conversion was mainly the result of his visit to the Jura Federation in Switzerland, where he observed an experiment in co-operative production and living among a community of watchmakers, who pooled their resources and the profits of their work.

- Kropotkin became interested in the theory of social Darwinism which flourished in the 1860s and 1870s. This theory drew inspiration from the animal kingdom. According to Darwin's theories, animals were engaged in a struggle based on the survival of the fittest. This promoted competition for scarce food resources. Only those able to adapt to a changing environment could survive. Under capitalism, it was argued, humans were engaged in a similar struggle, in which some would succeed and prosper while others would fail and remain poor. To supporters of social Darwinism this meant inequality was natural. Kropotkin challenged this belief. In most of the animal world, he argued, creatures are co-operative and not competitive. Most animals live in natural social groups and engage in mutual aid. In *Mutual Aid: A Factor of Evolution* (1902) he concluded that this was also the natural state of mankind.

- To Kropotkin there was no contradiction between a close-knit society and individual liberty. He believed that, in an ideal society, all would share the same sense of justice and natural law. This would make artificial enforcement of laws unnecessary.

- Kropotkin became increasingly radical in his views and began to involve himself in revolutionary movements. He travelled extensively in Switzerland, France and England, and his movements were tracked by the Russian secret service.

- Kropotkin's brand of anarcho-communism proposed the creation of natural communities. His argument was that if people were free to join whichever community they wished, they would not be subjected to any force. He looked forward to a time when these communities would be self-sufficient and prosperous. Without scarcity, he argued, there would be no competition, and without competition there would be no inequality. His plans were described in his 1898 book *Fields, Factories and Workshops*.
- When revolution broke out in Russia in 1917, Kropotkin returned home after years in exile. He saw this as an opportunity for some of his plans to be put into practice. Despite favouring the development of peaceful, natural communities, Kropotkin was a revolutionary who envisaged the overthrow of the state, by violent means if necessary. But when the Bolsheviks took over in Russia under Lenin, Kropotkin was disappointed. He feared the development of a new state to replace the old one. He had hoped that a popular uprising would destroy the state altogether and begin to build the small, natural communities that he supported. By the time he died in 1921, Kropotkin was very unhappy about what he saw in Russia under the Communist Party. He had wanted a very different kind of communism from that of Lenin and the Russian Bolsheviks.

Knowledge check

9 What caused Peter Kropotkin to believe in natural communities?
10 Who argued that states corrupt people?

The state is evil

Other anarchists were more critical of the state than Godwin and **Kropotkin**. **Mikail Bakunin** was among those who viewed the state as evil, corrupting and oppressive. He thought states should be resisted and ultimately destroyed, by either violent or peaceful means. For **Bakunin**, the state was the agent of the capitalist ruling class. It had to be destroyed and replaced if economic justice was to be established. He also claimed that those with leadership positions in a state would inevitably become corrupted by working for the state. In *God and the State* (1970), **Bakunin** wrote that even the most moral and upright man could not escape the corrupting influence of the state.

Pierre-Joseph Proudhon's critique of the state was different from **Bakunin**'s. It centred on how the state restricts, represses and limits the individual at every turn. People under state control are, **Proudhon** wrote in his *General Idea of the Revolution* (1851), 'spied upon … indoctrinated, preached at, controlled … [and] commanded'. **Proudhon** implied that all states have the same flaws. This is partly because all states are led by people without the skills or morals needed to govern well. Errico Malatesta (1853–1932) largely agreed with **Proudhon**. In his 1892 publication, *Anarchy*, Malatesta argued that in all states the majority are oppressed by a state that defends and enables the actions of the oppressors.

Power Anarchists argue that the exercise of power by one person over another is unacceptable. They believe that individuals should exercise power over themselves only. The exercise of power by the state must be resisted.

Mikhail Bakunin

Comparing ideas

Small state

Liberals argue that the existence of a small state is the best way to protect individuals' rights and freedoms. Anarchists believe that even a small state is oppressive and prevents individuals achieving genuine liberty.

The anarchist rejection of government by consent

Liberals argue that a state is legitimate if it is created with the consent of the people. Anarchists do not agree. They argue that individuals are sovereign and would never freely surrender any of their **power**. All states erode people's rights and no one with genuine freedom would consent to such a situation. Another problem is that, when one generation allows for the existence of a state, they set a precedent which tends to be followed unthinkingly by future generations. In these circumstances, people stop questioning the legitimacy of the state.

Knowledge check

11 What did Mikhail Bakunin think should replace the state?

Key thinker 3

Mikhail Bakunin (1814–76)

Like his anarchist colleagues **Kropotkin** and Leo Tolstoy, Mikhail Bakunin was born into a minor aristocratic family in Russia. He became radicalised after reading philosophical works as a young man and then became a revolutionary activist. In his early life his ideas were close to those of **Marx**. He opposed capitalism and the existence of private property, seeing both as oppressive. He agreed with the Marxists that the state was the agent of capitalism. Like **Marx**, Bakunin wanted both capitalism and the state to be abolished.

■ In 1872, Bakunin split with the Marxists during the Socialist International meeting. Bakunin's key objection to Marxism was that it proposed replacing the capitalist state with a workers'

state. Marxists saw this as temporary. The state would, they argued, wither away as socialism established itself in the consciousness of the people (see Chapter 2).

■ Bakunin could not accept this. It was at this point that he established the key distinction between socialism and anarchism. Anarchists, he insisted, must oppose any state, even one that claims to operate in the interests of the working class. Bakunin opposed the state on the grounds that power corrupts people, both government and the governed. Socialists might be well meaning in proposing the proletarian state, but it would end in disaster.

- Bakunin was strongly influenced by his experience of the Paris Commune in 1871. The Commune, which was a spontaneous uprising against the French state, seemed to show the way forward for revolutionaries. Bakunin believed it was an anarchist revolt rather than an example of socialist consciousness. It was the replacement of an oppressive state with a commune. In place of political rule there was to be economic equality, direct democracy and the common ownership of property. He believed strongly in the power of propaganda and the Paris Commune was the perfect example of 'propaganda by deed'. It served as an example for others to follow, even though it was destroyed after a few weeks.
- Order and a just society could, Bakunin argued, be achieved without a coercive state. For him there was no contradiction between an ordered society and individual liberty. In his book *God and the State* (1871), he wrote that freedom is achieved when a person decides to obey the laws of nature. No one can be forced to make this choice. They have to choose the option freely because they have come to realise that it is the best path in life. The laws of nature include such ideas as the sociability of mankind, natural empathy for each other, equality and respect for each other's freedom.
- Bakunin's vision of an ordered society, based on the laws of nature, was known as **federalism**. He saw groups of workers or peasants joining together in voluntary communities of any size. As long as people grouped themselves in such communes, with common ownership of property and equal distribution of rewards on a voluntary basis, there would be no coercion. The relationships between these communes or federations were to be conducted on the basis of mutual benefit. There was to be no capitalist market system, which would promote inequality, but rather a system of free negotiation and exchange on the basis of the true value of goods and services.

Key term

Federalism A theory of how a stateless society would operate, developed by **Mikhail Bakunin**. He defined federations as free, self-governing communes, based on the principles of equality and the common ownership of property. **Bakunin** thought that these federations would form naturally.

Key thinker 4

Pierre-Joseph Proudhon (1809–65)

Pierre-Joseph Proudhon is famous for the statement 'property is theft', which he made in his 1840 book, *What is Property?* He is also credited with being the first to use the term 'anarchist' and was a key figure in the development of the movement in the nineteenth century.

- Despite his words, Proudhon did not totally oppose private property. His objection was to property that was used to oppress workers or to promote inequality. Workers and peasants, he accepted, might own what they needed to manage their own production. These he called 'possessions' to distinguish them from 'property'. He was unusual among anarchists of his day in that he proposed the peaceful abolition of the state, even becoming a member of the French Parliament after 1848.

- Proudhon was something of a bridge between anarchism and socialism and is often described as a 'libertarian socialist'. He agreed with socialists that the means of production should be owned in common and that the capitalist system of exchange should be abolished. Unlike socialists he wanted the abolition of any kind of government. Socialists saw the state as a vital part of the creation and maintenance of workers' rights. Proudhon rejected the state on the grounds that it would become oppressive. He wanted a decentralised society, made up of co-operative communities of workers.

- Proudhon was also a bridge between individualist and collectivist anarchism. He was collectivist in that he proposed a federal system of communes. These would be backed by a 'people's bank' which could recycle surplus funds to these productive units. He was also individualist as he saw workers and groups of workers freely entering into contracts with each other for the exchange of labour and goods. He hoped for a reconciliation between individualist and collectivist anarchism. He wrote in

What is Property? that in a truly anarchist society there would cease to be a distinction between politics and ordinary life. What was good for the individual would also be good for wider society. Individual and collective goals would be the same and everybody would be satisfied.

- Proudhon is still regarded as the 'ultimate' anarchist. His ideas continue to have influence today. Aspects of his mutualism can be seen in the twentieth-century co-operative movements and in the commune movement of the 1960s and 1970s. The current 'fair trade' movement, which seeks to ensure that producers in developing countries receive the just reward for their goods, can also be seen as inspired by Proudhon's thinking. His ideas of decentralisation can still be seen in the aims of some non-governmental organisations: for example, those that persuade workers in developing countries to reject pressure from global corporations to produce cheap goods for western consumers. These non-governmental organisations encourage workers to put themselves first by producing what they need and want.

Pierre-Joseph Proudhon, who declared that 'property is theft'

Comparing ideas

Co-operation

Socialists argue that people are naturally inclined to co-operate with one another. They see humans as a social species. Collectivist anarchists agree with this. Individualist anarchists take a different view, starting that people will co-operate only if it is in their self interest to do so. They do not believe that people enjoy co-operation for its own sake.

The anarchist rejection of representative democracy

Anarchists acknowledge that representative democracies are a better option for their citizens than monarchies or dictatorships. However, this does not make them an acceptable alternative to

12 What aspects of Proudhon's thinking were individualist?

13 List the ways in which anarchists feel the state has a negative impact on individual rights.

anarchy. Among the problems anarchists have identified with democracies are the following:

■ Democracies divide people into artificially constructed nations to which people do not necessarily have any natural loyalty. Nations, anarchists believe, should be replaced by natural, self governing communities.

■ Democracies allow for tyranny of the majority. Anarchists argue that it is wrong for the minority to be constrained by the majority, even if that minority consists only of one person.

■ Democracies enable governments to make decisions which infringe on an individual's right to enjoy their own property and fulfil their own desires.

■ Democracies have promoted and defended a capitalist system which oppresses workers and entrenches inequality. In capitalist economies, those with property tend to exploit those without it, a situation unacceptable to anarchists.

■ Democracies encourage the view that democracy is the best form of government. This has hindered change that might have improved society.

■ Democracies assume that it is possible for elected politicians to represent others in a meaningful way, which anarchists dispute.

■ Democracies work in the interests of the elites who hold power, rather than all members of society.

Anarchists are even wary of the welfare states that tend to arise in democracies. They argue that these lead to inflated bureaucracies. They also infringe on individual freedom by requiring citizens to be registered and to share personal information with the state. Anarchists think that smaller systems of mutual aid would do a better job of supporting people within their communities and targeting help at those who most require it.

Anarchist rejection of direct democracy

Rousseau had argued that even **direct democracy** would rarely be workable in practice. Anarchists accepted **Rousseau**'s view that people would tend to vote out of their self-interest rather than in the collective interests of the community. This could only be guarded against, **Rousseau** suggested, in very small communities in which all individuals understood what would be in the interests of all. It was **Rousseau**'s thinking that inspired **Kropotkin** to advocate a world of small, independent, self governing communities.

Key term

Direct democracy A system of government in which the people make key decisions on behalf of the community. Anarchists reject direct democracy if it is organised by the state, but some collectivist and communist anarchists support the exercise of direct democracy in small-scale communities.

Knowledge check

14 List the reasons why anarchists have objected to socialist states.

Anarchist rejection of the socialist state

The main objection anarchists make to socialist states is that each one tends to be propped up by a vast state machinery which controls and manages the people. The government officials who run the machinery of the state become the elite within socialist states and are quickly corrupted by the system in which they work. They demonstrate this by putting their own desires ahead of the common good. Individualist anarchists feel that socialist states undermine individual responsibility by allowing people to rely on state aid when they should be falling back on their own resources. Collectivist anarchists object to socialist states on the basis that they undermine local communities and the mutual aid they provide.

Anarchist rejection of organised religion

For most anarchists, rejecting the state has gone hand-in-hand with a rejection of organised religion. Anarchists such as William Godwin and the Russian novelist Leo Tolstoy, who maintained their Christian faith, are exceptions. The most typical anarchist view is that organised religion is another unwanted and unnecessary source of authority in society. The argument that religion is unnecessary stems from the belief that religions have been constructed by mankind as a way of controlling the masses. Religious officials encouraged the poor to put up with terrible living and working conditions by promising a comfortable afterlife to those obedient to authority during their lifetime.

Bakunin, who felt particularly strongly about this issue, wrote in *God and the State* that 'If God really existed, it would be necessary to abolish him.' This expressed his belief that even the idea of God was oppressive because it was used to control people's behaviour.

Knowledge check

15 What causes anarchists to reject organised religion?

View of society

To the anarchist way of thinking, societies existed long before the creation of states or other political institutions. The extreme individualist anarchist **Max Stirner** rejected the need for society, but he is an exception. Most anarchists view societies as having evolved naturally and believe that, free from artificial interference, they would achieve a balance and harmony. These harmonious societies would bring out the best in their inhabitants by facilitating collaboration, partnerships and the provision of mutual aid. They can bring people closer together, foster empathy and caring behaviour, and provide order.

Knowledge check

16 What reasons do anarchists give for arguing that society would operate better if there were no state?

Anarchism and order

It may seem strange to see order as something anarchists want. The word 'anarchy' is often used as a substitute for disorder. This is an error. Virtually all anarchists want an ordered society. For anarchists, order promotes freedom and security. Most anarchists see private property as a threat to social order. By promoting inequality, private property causes social conflict. This view has led anarchists to support the common ownership of property and the equal distribution of everything produced by the community. Establishing equality also prevents different sections of society from coming into conflict with one another.

Even individualist anarchists wish to promote order, as they hope it will allow free individuals to co-operate in a mutually beneficial way. Anarchists' idea of the community stems from the belief that order cannot be created artificially. It must emerge naturally within a group of people from the peaceful sentiments of its members. **Bakunin** thought that order could emerge in large-scale communities. Malatesta and **Kropotkin** stressed the need for smaller-scale communities. They could not see **Bakunin**'s larger-scale federations working without rules being needed. In supporting small-scale communities, Malatesta and **Kropotkin** were inspired by the example of a watchmakers' commune in the Swiss Jura mountains. In this self-governing cooperative, workers operated without government and shared their profits equally.

One other anarchist vision of order is important. This was developed by modern anarcho-capitalists, Murray Rothbard and David Friedman (1945–). They proposed the retention of capitalism but the removal of the vast majority of the state's powers. They argued that capitalism could operate in an ordered way without regulation by the state. The functions of the state, including law and order, the enforcement of contracts and consumer protection, could instead be carried out by private organisations. As long as demand for something existed, they believed that the free market would supply it. An ordered society would emerge because the competing forces of capitalism would balance each other out.

Anarchism and utopianism

The idea of utopianism is that it is possible to create a society in which social harmony reigns and there are no conflicts. Some view utopia as achievable. Others believe that those who promote it are mistaking what is desirable for what is possible.

David D. Friedman

Key term

Utopianism A term used both positively, to mean a set of beliefs about how to create an ideal or perfect society, and negatively, to suggest beliefs that are impracticable and not based on rational thought.

Knowledge check

18 What are the differences between anarcho-communist and anarcho-capitalist ideas of utopia?

All anarchists have a vision of what they consider to be an ideal society. Different branches of anarchism have different visions but the precondition for all these visions is the abolition of the state and its replacement with a more natural form of social order. Individualist anarchists want the abolition of the state and any kind of economic and social organisation. Anarcho-communists and collectivist anarchists propose a new social system to replace both capitalism and the state. This new social system would be based on mutual aid, common ownership of property and economic equality. At its heart would be natural communities, which their members would be free to form with whatever structure they choose.

The anarcho-capitalist utopia is one in which there is a balance between individuals' competing interests. They see economic competition and property ownership as natural. They also believe that economic competition does not need any outside regulation. In their utopian version of capitalism, everyone will receive what they are entitled to as long as it is honestly obtained through their own physical or mental labour.

Debate 1

Are anarchists utopian?

Yes

- Collectivist anarchists have an over-optimistic view of human nature.
- Anarchists do not generally explain how to create the societies they want. Nor do they have specific ideas about how these societies will operate.
- There has never been a successful, established anarchist society.

No

- Individualist anarchists have a realistic view of human nature.
- People only think anarchism is unobtainable because they are conditioned to believe a state is essential to the smooth functioning of society. Once the corrupting influence of the state has been removed, anarchism's aims will be achievable.
- Anarchism is based on a rational evaluation of the problems of modern states, including the failures of democracy and the corrupting nature of power.

Evaluation check: To what extent is anarchism idealistic rather than realistic?

Criticisms of anarchist visions of society

A range of criticisms have been made of anarchist visions of society, including the following:

- Anarchists never explain exactly how their visions for society will be achieved.
- There have been small-scale experiments with anarchism, but no large-scale anarchist society has ever been created. This suggests that anarchism is a dream, rather than a realistic political goal.
- Anarchists have an over-optimistic view of human nature. This criticism tends to come from conservatives who see human nature as flawed. For conservatives, government is essential in ensuring that people act reasonably and responsibly.
- Collectivist anarchists misunderstand the importance of private property to individuals. The liberals who make this point argue that the desire to obtain and retain property is part of human nature. People will not cease to want property and this means collectivisation and shared ownership will only cause dissatisfaction.
- Socialists argue that collectivist anarchists are naïve in believing that equality can be achieved without a state to manage the economy and redistribute resources. They also see the state as essential in ensuring that the poorest in society are not exploited by those above them.
- Socialists also think that anarcho-capitalists (see below) could never create an orderly society because capitalism creates winners and losers. The latter will always be discontented but in a society with no welfare state they will be particularly unhappy.

View of the economy

Anarchist ideas about the economy fall into two broad categories:

- Communist and collectivist forms of anarchism seek to abolish capitalism.
- Modern anarcho-capitalists wish to free capitalism from regulation by the state.

Collectivism and economic freedom

Most collectivist anarchists argue that a key cause of conflict in society is capitalism. The problem for them is that capitalism creates a type of order of its own. Free markets are self-regulating. There may be booms and slumps in a capitalist economy but it

Knowledge check

20 List the ways in which mutualism would benefit working people.

is a system that has endured and promoted wealth. However, anarchists believe that the inequality created within capitalism is unacceptable. Any new economic order cannot be based on free-market values for goods and labour. Collectivist anarchists want to see labour being paid at its true value and goods exchanged according to how much work has gone into making them, instead of their market-determined value.

The economic structure proposed by **Pierre-Joseph Proudhon** conformed to these principles. His theory of mutualism, also known as 'contractualism', argued for the replacement of capitalism with a system of exchange based on contracts entered into on a free, mutually beneficial basis. **Proudhon** wanted workers and peasants to receive the true value of what their labour produced instead of its market value, which was determined by capitalist forces beyond the workers' control. He proposed a voucher system to indicate the 'real' value of goods. This 'real' value would be based on how much time and effort had gone into producing the goods. **Proudhon** also suggested a national bank be set up to provide interest-free loans to peasants and other workers.

Proudhon's idea of mutualism was influential among nineteenth-century anarchists, most of whom proposed variations on his scheme to replace capitalism. **Peter Kropotkin** wrote in *Mutual Aid* (1902) that the competitive economic world was not inevitable. With co-operation and communal living, mankind could free itself from the competition for scarce resources. **Mikhail Bakunin** also argued that economic freedom could go hand-in-hand with collective ownership.

Individualist anarchism and the economy

The anarchist **Emma Goldman** (Key thinker 5) campaigned for the abolition of capitalism without expressing any particular preference for what would replace it. All she was concerned with was that no one could be free within capitalism. In this sense she placed herself in the tradition of nineteenth-century individualist anarchists. Henry Thoreau and Josiah Warren (1798–1874) in the USA both advocated a withdrawal of the individual from the capitalist world. Rather than selling their labour to capitalist employers, people should obtain their freedom both from the state and from the economic system. Warren created a scheme in which all goods could be sold at a price which reflected the amount of labour that had gone into them. He hoped his ideas would spread and that more people would free themselves from capitalism and trade freely and fairly among themselves.

Knowledge check

21 Who argued for avoiding involvement in capitalist markets?

Warren's ideas did not take hold but there remained in the USA a tradition of self-sufficiency. Individuals followed the example of Thoreau, who had isolated himself from society to live in a cabin near Walden Pond in Concord, Massachusetts. The aim of the individualist anarchists inspired by Thoreau was to live a simple life of subsistence. Only by not having to interact with capitalism would they achieve true economic freedom.

The principal anarchist answer to the problems of capitalism lies with a modern movement which does not oppose capitalism but embraces it to the full. Its advocates are often known as anarcho-capitalists and two of its most prominent are Murray Rothbard and David Friedman. They have both argued for a world in which free-market capitalism can flourish without any regulation by the state. Both oppose the existence of any state at all. They believe that economic freedom can exist only in the context of free competition without any external interference. They see inequality as natural and eliminating it as unacceptable in a free society. Human beings should be entitled to retain for themselves anything they earn from their own labour. Private property which is legally gained can therefore be justified. Rothbard summed up his beliefs by saying: 'Capitalism is the fullest expression of anarchism ... you can't have one without the other'.

Emma Goldman

Knowledge check

22 What social reforms did Emma Goldman campaign for?

Comparing ideas

Capitalism

Socialists share with collectivist anarchists a hatred of capitalism. They see capitalism as an oppressive force which exploits the poorest in society. Individualist anarchists and liberals disagree. They view the free market as a liberating force, which allows individuals to make free choices and maximise their own economic benefits.

Key thinker 5

Emma Goldman (1869–1940)

Emma Goldman was Russian-born but spent much of her life in the USA. She frequently found herself in American prisons. Among the crimes with which she was charged were planning assassinations and inciting workers to riot. She was implicated in the assassination of US president William McKinley in 1901 but never convicted of the crime. She was probably not responsible for McKinley's death. Suspicion fell on her because she preached that assassination was a valid tactic for anarchists to use.

- Goldman was involved in a number of social causes. She campaigned for the emancipation of women and the tolerance of homosexuality, and championed the idea of free love. Some modern feminists have claimed that Goldman was a pioneer of feminist philosophy. Others see her as the first anarchist feminist because she fused anarchist ideas with the cause of women's rights.
- Goldman spent 1936–37 participating in the Spanish Civil War. She was involved in founding some anarchist communes in Spain. The communes were a short-lived but genuine realisation of anarchist ideals. She coined the term 'propaganda of the deed' to describe the idea that the best way to inspire others to join the anarchist cause was to engage in acts of violence against state and capitalist institutions. This attempt to prove that practical anarchism was realistic won Goldman few followers but was not her key focus.
- Goldman's work was mainly directed at exposing the exploitative nature of capitalism, the oppressive nature of the state, and the need for violent revolution to bring both of them down. She rejected the idea of political reform, arguing, like **Mikhail Bakunin**, that the exercise of power corrupts people, so any system involving such power must be abolished. In other words, her philosophy was in some ways very negative.
- In *Living My Life* (1931), she stressed that people should view the state as their enemy. The state and capitalism worked hand-in-hand and no good could come from either. The role of the state was, Goldman argued, to crush ordinary people and to trick them into obedience to those with power. Even left-wing politicians, she wrote, could not be trusted because they made alliances with others in power. These alliances served to keep the workers weak and oppressed. In addition to her criticisms of the state, Goldman raged against virtually every enemy of individual liberty. She condemned the modern state, religion, nationalism, Marxism, capitalism, patriarchy and all forms of bigotry.
- Goldman's main contribution to anarchism was to communicate its key ideas with clarity and energy. She also made clear the connection between anarchism and the complete emancipation of the individual. She offered her followers hope by promising that the exploitation of one individual by another could be replaced by mutual love that would bring an end to oppression.

Debate 2

Is anarchism merely socialism without a state?

Yes
- Collectivist anarchism and socialism are both highly critical of capitalism and seek its abolition.
- Collectivist anarchists and socialists share a positive view of human nature. They see people as caring and co-operative.
- Both collectivist anarchists and socialists propose economic equality and the common ownership of property.

No
- The key aim for socialists is the creation of equality in society. Anarchists are more concerned with ensuring the individual has the maximum possible degree of freedom.
- Individualist anarchists are supportive of capitalism and believe in the importance of private property.
- Some individualist anarchists encourage people to withdraw from society and achieve self-reliance. For socialists, being part of a wider community is crucial to human flourishing.

Evaluation check: To what extent is anarchism distinct from socialism?

Different types of anarchism

There are five main types of anarchism, which fall under two broad headings, collectivist and individualist anarchism (see Figure 5.1). This section will explore how these types of anarchism view human nature, the state, society and the economy.

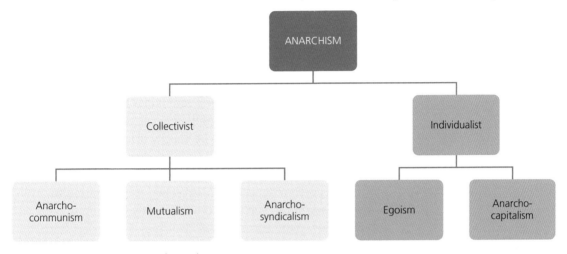

Figure 5.1 The different types of anarchism

Anarcho-communism and mutualism

The two traditions of anarcho-communism and mutualism are so closely related that they are treated together here.

Communist anarchists view man as a social animal. They do not agree with individualist anarchists who stress mankind's individuality and ego. Rather than believing people to be self-seeking and competitive, anarcho-communists see them as naturally empathetic and sociable. **Peter Kropotkin** likened human society to that of the animal kingdom, stressing that most species live in social groups. He rejected the social Darwinist view that people are competitive.

Anarcho-communists believe that people are capable of self-government. They do not need governments or rulers to live in peace and harmony. In his book *Mutual Aid* (1902), **Kropotkin** wrote that people should help and support each other, practically and emotionally. This mutual aid would ensure the security of all. Mutualism and mutual aid were, for anarcho-communists, a key aspect of human nature. They insisted that people would naturally seek to help each other and not compete. French anarchist Elisée Reclus (1830–1905) wrote that, whatever kind of social organisation might be adopted, mutual aid would ensure solidarity and

> **Key term**
>
> Solidarity A person shows solidarity when they express support for or agreement with someone else. Collectivist anarchists believe that social solidarity, the tendency for people to form mutually beneficial communities and to have empathy for each other, is a natural human instinct.

Knowledge check

23 What is the anarcho-communist idea of human nature?

24 List the anarcho-communist objections to capitalism.

progress. Through collaboration, people would gain greater understanding of each other, learn more and help society move forward.

Errico Malatesta, a close colleague of **Kropotkin** and Reclus, saw such solidarity and mutual aid as best served by people being grouped together on the basis of their occupation. By undertaking similar work, he believed, people would gain a greater sense of collective consciousness.

It is as a result of their belief in social solidarity that anarcho-communists see the state as unnecessary. If free individuals were allowed to form their own communities, they would naturally tend towards creating communes that were self-governing and well ordered. Mutual aid would replace the state. The rewards of labour would be equally divided because this is natural to mankind. Trust and interdependence among people would make law and coercion unnecessary.

Anarcho-communists see themselves as committed to democracy but define the word differently from those who follow more conventional ideologies. They reject both representative democracy and national direct democracy. They favour a system by which members of small communes debate and discuss issues until collective agreement is reached on what decisions to take.

Anarcho-communism is defined by its opposition to capitalism. All capitalist societies are inevitably oppressive, anarcho-communists argue. They pit people against each other in a competitive struggle. They encourage the strong to exploit the weak and this results in inequality. The mutually beneficial society that anarcho-communists want instead would create equality by ensuring that resources are collectively owned and produce shared. Capitalism, anarcho-communists believe, is an artificial creation, constructed by the ruling classes to maintain their own power. Communal living, on the other hand, is the natural state of man.

Anarchists share with **Marx** a belief that capitalism places too low a value upon labour and the goods produced by a person's labour. Under capitalism, workers' wages are determined not by their efforts or their output, but by their 'exchange value' or their place in the market. When labour is scarce it will be highly paid, but when there is a surplus of labour – the normal situation under capitalism – wages will be low. The same is true of goods and services. The capitalist class, who own the means of production, control the market. They use their control to ensure that they make high returns while workers are exploited.

Anarcho-communists propose the destruction of capitalism and its replacement by some form of common ownership of the means of production, including the land, factories and mines, and the financial system. This common ownership would be organised not by the state, but by smaller, natural communities. They would trade goods with each other based on the true value of the labour that has gone into making them, not their exchange value. The trade that takes place between the communities would be to their mutual benefit and would avoid wasteful competition. **Kropotkin** made his point forcefully in his well-known plea, 'Don't compete! Competition is always injurious to the species, and you have plenty of resources to avoid it!'

Anarcho-communism does not propose the kind of collectivisation which Marxist-inspired regimes promoted in the twentieth century which involved the enforced movement of peasants onto large, state-controlled agricultural units. For anarchists, this is unacceptable. The commune must be voluntary and free from the control of any higher authority.

Anarcho-syndicalism

This branch of anarchism stems from the idea that workers have a natural tendency to form groups with others in similar occupations. These groups advantage the workers because they enable them to act together to resist the oppression caused by capitalism. In their most developed form, these groups are trade unions. The French word for trade union is *syndicat* and that is why this type of anarchism is known as anarcho-syndicalism. It is different from socialist syndicalism because it seeks the abolition of the state, and stresses the value of trade union organisations. Anarcho-syndicalism is a philosophy of direct action, insurrection and violence.

The most important champion of anarcho-syndicalism was Georges Sorel (1847–1922). For Sorel, the main quality of the working class was its solidarity or unity of purpose. He argued that workers could use their solidarity to destroy both capitalism and the state. A key weapon the working class could use against their capitalist masters was the all-out strike. With this, workers could bring down the established order simply by refusing to do their jobs. If strikes were used alongside mass demonstrations and acts of violence, Sorel believed, the state's desire to power and its survival instinct would be destroyed.

After the revolution and destruction of the state, a new social order based on trade union or syndicate organisation would emerge naturally. Each trade union would be a self-governing federation of workers. The various federations would then exchange labour and goods. These exchanges would ensure that the needs of all individuals were met. The interconnected communities would promote the well-being of their members and create a wider society that was harmonious.

American philosopher Noam Chomsky (1928–) has claimed to be an anarcho-syndicalist, but he is far less radical than Sorel. For Chomsky, syndicalism represents the hope that workers can regain control of their own labour. He suggests that this could be done in a number of ways. What is important is that workers are able to free themselves from external control and take charge of their own workplaces. He shares the anarchist view that democratic workers' councils could be formed to allow for collective decision making.

Rudolf Rocker (1873–1958) led the anarchist reaction against the ideas of Marxist-inspired socialism in the first half of the twentieth century. The emancipation of workers, he argued, could not be realised through a powerful workers' state. It could only be achieved if the state were abolished and replaced by independent workers' communes.

Anarcho-syndicalists have a similar view of human nature to other collectivist anarchists, but they lay greater stress on mankind's capacity for social solidarity. The reliance they place on trade unions demonstrates that they see labour and creativity as key to the human condition. Work, they say, should be an expression of mankind's creativity, but this can only happen if the oppression of the state is removed.

Knowledge check

25 Name the thinkers associated with anarcho-syndicalism.

Noam Chomsky

Anarcho-syndicalists believe that the state and capitalism are tied together in the same web of exploitation. For that reason, capitalism can be abolished only if the state is removed, preferably by revolutionary means. Socialist syndicalists want to replace the capitalist state with a workers' state. In contrast, the anarcho-capitalist replacement for the state is a co-operative arrangement of independent, self-governing workers' federations or syndicates. However, the close relationship between syndicalism and socialism is demonstrated by the fact that anarcho-syndicalism is sometimes described as a form of decentralised socialism.

Like all collectivist anarchists, syndicalists see people as social animals and society as a natural phenomenon. They think that communities within society should be based upon occupation. The solidarity of groups such as miners, factory workers and construction workers make them natural groupings. The common circumstances of members of such syndicates mean they have the social solidarity needed for the creation of an ordered stateless society.

In an anarcho-syndicalist economy, workers' trade unions or syndicates would become the owners of their own means of production. Miners would collectively own their mines, farmers the land they worked and factory workers their factories. Trade between the syndicates would take place but not on a competitive, free-market basis. The price of goods and services would be determined by the real value of the labour that went into making them.

The focus of some anarchists on the importance of different class interests is shown by the activities of Class War, described in Box 5.4.

> **Knowledge check**
>
> 26 What would be the key features of a syndicalist society?

Box 5.4: Anarchism in action – Class War

Founded in 1983 by Ian Bone, Class War became known in the 1980s for their 'Bash the Rich' march which took place in prosperous London neighbourhoods, such as Kensington. From 2010 to 2015 Class War was registered as a political party and seven Class War candidates stood in the 2015 general election. LSE Class War, a group based at the London School of Economics, emerged in 2021. They have called for the abolition of the LSE's Hayek Society, which exists to encourage the spread of libertarian and free-market philosophies. It also wants the university to stop offering places to students from private schools.

Egoism

In Europe, a more violent, radical form of individualism developed during the nineteenth century. This is sometimes described as egoism and is associated with **Max Stirner**. Central to its view of human nature is the idea that the ego dictates what each individual does. The ego is a person's desire for self-realisation.

Key terms

Autonomy This is achieved when a person is not restricted by rules or laws but has complete freedom to think and act as they choose. Individualist anarchists argue that individuals should aim for autoomy.

Nihilism A term used to describe the most extreme examples of individualist anarchism. Nihilists oppose all forms of social organisation, including government, proposing instead a society of free individuals. Most nihilists are also known for their violent methods.

Knowledge check

27 Who developed the ideas of egoism?

28 What reasons do egoists give for prioritising individual rights?

Egoists believe that people are self-interested. They are naturally inclined to put their own wants and needs before those of others. People see themselves as the centre of their own universe. This leads them to believe that any kind of social intercourse is a threat to their freedom and individuality. The state must be abolished because it is a barrier to individual **autonomy**.

Stirner wrote that people are rational creatures without morality who act to satisfy their own wants and needs. Only fear of disapproval from wider society, **Stirner** argued, restrains people's behaviour and prevents them achieving liberation. Another of **Stirner**'s beliefs was that people will only be prepared to co-operate with each other if they will gain some benefit from doing so. This left open the possibility that co-operative individualist anarchist communities would form. If they did, **Stirner** suggested that they be referred to as unions of egoists, but he did not believe in society in the conventional sense. **Stirner**'s concept of a union of egoists was not really a social grouping. It was a collection of individuals held together by a desire to serve their own interests. In *The Ego and His Own* (1844), **Stirner** wrote that other people meant nothing to him on a personal level. He was only interested in how they could be useful to him.

The egoists developed a reputation for extreme violence and opposing any form of organisation imposed from above. The notorious egoist Sergei Nechaev (1847–82) argued that a true revolutionary needed to hate 'everyone and everything' in order to be single minded in their goal of destroying the state. Egoists are intensely pessimistic about both human nature and the possibility of creating an anarchist community. Like all anarchists, they hate the state but they have few positive ideas about what should replace it. Nor have they developed coherent economic ideas, save for the notion that free individuals would find a way to trade with each other in pursuit of their rational self-interest. As this suggests, the egoist conception of economic life is very much associated with the accumulation of property. They believe that all people are driven to obtain possessions and, having obtained them, to retain them.

The more extreme individual anarchists are sometimes called nihilists. This label describes someone who dismisses the idea that humanity has common values or that there is such a thing as objective truth. Supporters of **nihilism** ('nihil' meaning 'nothing'). reject all social and political organisation and think that individual liberty is a more powerful force than either society or morality. The two other main individualist anarchist traditions, anarcho-capitalism and egoism, have more developed ideas about how anarchism should operate.

Anarcho-capitalism

Anarcho-capitalism is a relatively modern philosophy. It emerged in the 1970s and 1980s, partly in reaction to the increasing involvement of western governments in the regulation of capitalism. It is linked to libertarianism, an extreme form of conservatism associated with **Robert Nozick** (see Chapter 3). **Nozick** sought the abolition of most laws. He wanted individuals to have a much greater degree of freedom than any modern society allowed them. He was not an anarchist because he accepted there was an ongoing need for a small state. The two key figures in the anarcho-capitalist movement, Murray Rothbard and David Friedman, were at odds with **Nozick** on this last point. They entirely rejected state control.

Rothbard coined the term 'anarcho-capitalism' to describe his own philosophy. He claimed it drew on three other traditions:

- Nineteenth-century classical liberalism, which proposed a small, minimalist state.
- Nineteenth-century American individualist anarchism, as expressed by Henry Thoreau, Benjamin Tucker and Lysander Spooner. These individualists opposed the state on the grounds of its denial of individual sovereignty.
- The Austrian school of economics of the mid-twentieth century, which proposed completely free markets for goods, labour and finance, with little or no government regulation.

For Rothbard, economic freedom is a fundamental value, but it is threatened by the power of the state. Put another way, he argued that political and economic freedom cannot be separated. The main aspect of the state he attacked was taxation. If we are entitled to everything we earn with our labour, then taxation becomes a form of institutionalised theft.

Friedman, like Rothbard, focuses on free-market economics. For Friedman, people are fundamentally economic, rather than social, animals. He argues that people have a justified sense of entitlement to anything they have worked to gain. In order that people can gain everything they want, they must be free to enter into economic relations with others. Only unregulated capitalism will ensure this freedom and promote mutually beneficial trade.

The state is the enemy to anarcho-capitalists. Its laws undermine individual liberty. Its economic regulations disrupt free trade and prevent people from acting in their own best interests. It is the anarcho-capitalist view of human nature that leads it to prize freedom. Anarcho-capitalists see people's desire to act in a self-interested way as proof that they are rational and enlightened creatures.

An anarcho-capitalist society would be a socially Darwinian place. Only the fittest would prosper. There would be no welfare state to support those who struggled. Anarcho-capitalists would defend their vision of society on the basis that capitalism creates connections which are in everyone's self-interest to preserve. Employees have an incentive to support the system that has provided them with a job. The buyer and seller rely on one another. Competition acts as a spur. It encourages people to work hard and do their best. All this prevents disorder. In a free-market system, all the functions normally provided by the state can be delivered by individuals and private firms. As long as there is demand for a service, the market will supply it. Services including health, education, social care and law enforcement will come about without a state to provide them.

Anarcho-capitalists take a relatively simple view of economics. The world is a competitive place. Scarcity and competition exist in the natural world, where the fittest progress and the weak suffer. It is right to allow capitalism to produce an economic environment based on this model, especially as a free market has clear benefits. Monopolies and trade unions, which are barriers to the creation of a completely open capitalist market, will be dissolved in the face of free competition. Free-market competition is also healthy because it creates incentives and therefore promotes innovation and growth. State interference in the economy cannot be justified as it is a denial of what is natural.

Key distinctions among the different types of anarchism are summarised in Table 5.3.

Debate 3

Do individualist and collectivist anarchists have a shared vision of the future?

Yes
- Both want to maximise individual freedom.
- Both seek the abolition of the state and other oppressive institutions, and believe that neither the state nor laws are necessary to the creation of a peaceful future.
- Both predict that people will co-operate within anarchist societies.

No
- Individualist anarchists support capitalism. Collectivist anarchists want to abolish capitalism.
- Individualists expect people to become more self-interested and self-serving when living in an anarchy. Collectivists expect people to be more caring and empathetic towards wider society.
- Individualists downplay the importance of communities. They think of people first and foremost as individuals. Collectivist anarchists think that people are naturally social and want to form harmonious communities.

Evaluation check: To what extent do anarchists believe that people's bonds with the wider community will be important in an anarchist society?

Table 5.3 Key distinctions within anarchism

	Anarcho-communists	Anarcho-syndicalists	Egoists	Anarcho-capitalists
Human nature	People are social animals who prefer to achieve their goals collectively. With the corrupting influence of the state removed, people's caring, empathetic nature will come to the fore.	People need and benefit from social solidarity. With the removal of the oppressive state, a person's occupation can become truly fulfilling. It will also become an expression of that person's personality.	The ego is a person's desire for self realisation. It drives a person's behaviour and choices. People are naturally inclined to put their own wants and needs first.	People are rational and self-interested. Being selfish is logical and reasonable. No one should expect to rely on anyone else.
The state	The state should be abolished because it suppresses individual liberty and exploits producers and consumers. It is acceptable to use violent means to abolish state power.	The state should be removed, ideally through a revolution.	The state should be abolished. No form of organisation should be imposed on society.	The state should not exist because it is the enemy of free-market capitalism. If individuals withdraw from society and manage their own affairs, the state will become irrelevant and wither away.
Society	People should live in co-operative communities which are free from coercion. Society should not involve any element of force or power.	A new social order would emerge following the removal of the state, based on trade union organisation. The different trade unions would exchange labour and goods freely in such a way as to promote the best interests of everyone in society.	People might choose to form connections with others and be part of 'unions of egoists', but no one should be forced to be part of any social groupings.	People should not be expected or required to be part of a wider society. Nothing should restrict individual sovereignty.
The economy	Capitalism should be abolished and replaced with the common ownership of the means of production, distribution and exchange. The organisation into communes would be voluntary and free from control from above.	Workers are naturally inclined to form groups with those in similar occupations. These groups allow workers collectively to resist capitalism. Once capitalism has been overthrown, these groups will form the basis of economic organisation.	Free individuals will find beneficial ways to trade with one another.	Capitalism must be allowed to flourish free from state interference. Individuals should be free to maximise the benefits and rewards which capitalism can provide for them.

Conclusion: anarchism today

Anarchist ideas continue to inspire political activists across the world. There are many examples of anarchist groups and movements in operation today. Freetown Christiania is a small suburb of Copenhagen. Set up in 1971 in a former military base, it describes itself as a commune. Its founders aimed to create a society that was self-governing and in which all residents recognised that they had a responsibility to the wider community. At first, the residents of Christiania resisted control from the Danish state because they believed that, as anarchists, they should reject state power.

Part of the initial motivation for the creation of Christiania was that there was not enough affordable housing in Copenhagen. Within Christiania people squatted in existing buildings and constructed new ones to serve their needs. They agreed their own rules, banning theft, violence, dangerous weapons and class A drugs, such as heroin and cocaine. They also refused to pay taxes because that would involve recognising the state as legitimate. Since 1994, this has changed. Those living in Christiania now pay tax to the Danish authorities for vital services such as water and electricity. As of July 2012, they have also started making payments to buy the land on which they live. Christiania continues to have its own unique culture, but it is now recognised as part of Denmark and Danish law is upheld in the commune, meaning that the experiment with anarchism in Christiania is over.

Occupy Wall Street protest, NYC, 2011

Occupy Wall Street was founded in 2011 to protest against the power of big corporations and the unequal distribution of resources in society. The principles under which the Occupy movement operates are anarchist ones. The group has no leaders. Decisions are made on a consensus basis. It uses direct action to draw attention to what it believes to be the unfairness in modern society. It refuses to acknowledge that current political and legal systems are lawful. The group views modern states as responsible for political and economic inequality.

Many groups with similar principles to Occupy Wall Street have sprung up in response to the Covid-19 pandemic. In the USA, the DC Mutual Aid Network, based in Washington DC, has encouraged people to volunteer to support their community by, for example, shopping for those who are sick or self-isolating. In the UK, the Mutual Aid UK website helps thousands of small, local groups that were created following the March 2020 lockdown. By putting those in need in touch with those willing to assist them, Mutual Aid UK hopes that it has strengthened the bonds of solidarity in communities across the country and encouraged people to take action themselves, rather than wait for the state to act. This is in keeping with the anarchist idea that people do not need a state to direct or organise them.

It is unlikely that a truly anarchist society will ever exist, but the fact that anarchism is still seen by many as a meaningful response in times of trouble demonstrates that it has ongoing political significance. Not only will anarchist thinkers continue to be read and studied, but their ideas will continue to prompt people to take practical action to achieve their aims.

Summary: key themes and key thinkers

	Human nature	The state	Society	The economy
Max Stirner	People are self-interested egotists.	The state denies people the right to fulfil their egoism and individualism.	Society of any kind restrains people. We must be completely self-reliant.	The accumulation and retention of property is our main economic motivation.
Peter Kropotkin	People are sociable and prefer collective activity.	The capitalist state must be destroyed by revolution and replaced by a voluntary system of independent, self-governing communities.	The commune should be the basis of society. Communes should be small, independent, internally democratic units.	Capitalism was to be replaced by the communist system of small economic units. Each of these should, as far as possible, be self-sufficient.

191

(handwritten) George Sorel

(handwritten, left margin) all forms of government tend to oppression

(handwritten in Bakunin row) somewhat syndicalist

	Human nature	The state	Society	The economy
Mikhail Bakunin	We are fundamentally social animals and productive work characterises our humanity.	The state is the servant of capitalism. Both the state and capitalism must be destroyed by revolution.	There should be a federal system and the abolition of national boundaries. Federations of workers would cooperate, not compete with each other.	The market system of exchange should be abolished and replaced by exchange based on the true value of labour and goods.
Pierre-Joseph Proudhon	We are characterised by our productive abilities and our creativity as producers.	The state is oppressive and must be abolished. This could happen though peaceful, democratic means but might be achieved by force.	Mutualism is the basis of a strong society. This involves people being bound together by mutually beneficial economic and social relations.	People should be divided into independent productive units, trading with each other on a mutually beneficial basis.
Emma Goldman	Individual liberty must be upheld. The desire for freedom is fundamental to mankind.	The state is only one source of oppression and denial of liberty. Religion and property ownership are equally oppressive.	What is needed is a society in which all people are treated as equal. Also essential are economic, gender and racial equality.	Liberty is more important than economic justice, but communism is preferable to other economic systems.

(handwritten in Goldman row) priority is liberty

(handwritten, right) ↑ direct ac[tion] Wall Street banks

Further reading

Politics Review articles

Garner, R. (2009) 'Anarchism, socialism and utopia', *Politics Review*, vol. 18, no. 2.
Graham, P. (2011) 'Anarchism: a utopian creed?', *Politics Review*, vol. 20, no. 2.
Limieux, S. (2019) 'Anarchism: unity within diversity?', *Politics Review*, vol. 28, no. 4.
Walker, M. (2020) 'Focus on anarchism', *Politics Review*, vol. 30, no. 1.
Walker, M. (2021) 'Focus on Peter Kropotkin: anarchist key thinker', *Politics Review*, vol. 31, no. 1.

Books

Chomsky, N. (2014) *On Anarchism*, Penguin.
Ervin, L.K. (2021) *Anarchism and the Black Revolution: The Definitive Edition*, Pluto Press.
Honeywell, C. (2021) *Anarchism*, Polity Press.
Kinna, R. (2019) *The Government of No One: The Theory and Practice of Anarchism*, Pelican.
Marshall, P. (2010) *Demanding the Impossible: A History of Anarchism*, PM Press.
Ward, C. (2004) *Anarchism: A Very Short Introduction*, Oxford University Press.

(handwritten, bottom) anarcho capitalism: capitalism without the state
capitalism pays for public health 800...

Exam-style questions

AQA

Essay questions

1 'All anarchists make the same criticisms of the state.' Analyse and evaluate this statement with reference to the anarchist thinkers you have studied. (25 marks)

2 'Anarchists oppose capitalism.' Analyse and evaluate this statement with reference to the anarchist thinkers you have studied. (25 marks)

3 'Anarchists are united in their view of society.' Analyse and evaluate this statement with reference to the anarchist thinkers you have studied. (25 marks)

In your answers you should draw on material from across the whole range of your course of study in Politics.

Edexcel

Essay questions

4 To what extent do anarchists put the individual above society? You must use appropriate thinkers you have studied to support your answer and consider differing views in a balanced way. (24 marks)

5 To what extent do anarchists have a coherent view of human nature? You must use appropriate thinkers you have studied to support your answer and consider differing views in a balanced way. (24 marks)

6 To what extent are anarchist ideas utopian? You must use appropriate thinkers you have studied to support your answer and consider differing views in a balanced way. (24 marks)

Index